R.A.FLEMING & K.BURKOWSKI

# WHY MEN MADE GOD

*To Anita,
Enjoy the Journey!
Burkowski
(Karis)*

## REDEFINING THE SACRED

Published in 2015 by
Redefining The Sacred (International)

First Edition

ISBN: 978-0-9572612-2-8

Redefining The Sacred (International) is an imprint of:
PlashMill Press
Scotland.

www.redefiningthesacred.com
www.rodfleming.com
www.plashmillpress.com

Printed by Lightning Source

# Dedications

This book is dedicated to mothers everywhere. Without their love, nurture and wisdom, we would not be here. They are the future of humanity.

The authors would like to specifically dedicate this book to Gladys Rollo Fleming and Pearl Ruth Heimpel. There is no love like that of a mother and we deeply appreciate it.

# CONTENTS

# FOREWORD

Between 69,000 and 75,000 years ago, in Indonesia, a gigantic super-volcano called Toba erupted. This spectacular explosion was an evolutionary forcing event that would change our human species dramatically.

When a volcano erupts, it sends a column of super-heated gas miles up into the atmosphere, carrying huge amounts of ash and pumice with it. As the column rises, the energy in it dissipates, and the column collapses in a searing torrent of ash called a pyroclastic flow. Everything it touches is incinerated.

For hundreds of miles around, nothing survived the initial stages of the eruption. Toba's flows blasted outwards, consuming everything in their path. At first, the energy in the flow made it hurtle across the surface of the oceans, supported like a terrible hovercraft on a cushion of superheated steam. Then it plunged down under the surface, creating tsunamis that rose tens of metres into the air, radiating outwards at terrific speed and utterly devastating the coastal areas they struck. Sulphur dioxide caused highly acidic rain that withered and killed all but the most resistant plants. Thick layers of volcanic ash covered the ground, choking new growth, and the effects lasted for many human lifetimes.

Toba was one of the biggest eruptions ever and certainly the greatest in human times. Mount St. Helens, which exploded in 1980, erupted about half a cubic kilometre of material. Krakatoa, in East Asia, erupted about 18 cubic kilometres in 1883. Thera, or Santorini, which devastated the Minoans about 3500 years ago, was, by comparison, huge and erupted at least 60 cubic kilometres of material, with global consequences and volcanic effects that went on for years. Toba was of a completely different scale. It erupted as much as 3,000 cubic kilometres of ash and other material, making it fifty times greater even than Thera. The Earth was plunged into a six-year volcanic winter followed by a 1000-year ice age.

*Homo sapiens* first appeared in Africa around 150,000 years ago; one of a closely-related group of hominids that had populated the savannah over the preceding three million years. During that time, our ancestors learned how to talk, how to make fire and cook, and how to cooperate in groups. The first modern humans probably lived in a very similar way to earlier hominids.

When Toba erupted, thousands of kilometres away, the skies over Africa darkened – not for weeks or months, but for years. The weather grew cold. Strange dust fell, followed by acid rain. Vegetation died. Herbivores died in huge numbers. Carnivores died. And people died. Those who remained had to adapt or disappear.

The consensus amongst geneticists is that our numbers dropped to 2000 – 10,000 individuals. We were an endangered species.[1] Somehow, we survived and slowly began not only to recover numbers but also to expand and develop our geographical range. We now recognise that the defining characteristics of modern humans, such as our sophisticated language, love of art, creativity and the beginnings of our culture appeared only after Toba. All the evidence that we have for the evolution of faith and belief also comes from after the Toba event. We do not know if the people before it believed in deities, spirits or the supernatural. We have evidence that by 35,000 years ago, these cultural traditions were well established.

Cults and religions have several functions. In their simplest form, they represent an attempt to understand the Universe, to answer the questions 'What am I?' and 'How did I get here?' These questions are a constant in human history. They form the basis of religion, philosophy and science, each attempting to answer them in a different way. They have prompted humanity to scale the peaks of intellectual achievement. Without them, our culture would be very different and might not exist at all. We are what we are because we wonder, and our previous attempts to answer these fundamental questions have shaped us. They have informed our culture for tens of millennia and the consequences – for better or worse – cannot easily be escaped.

---

1 Other species show similar bottlenecks at around the same time, including Lowland Gorillas. (Scally *et al. Insights into hominid evolution from the gorilla genome sequence.* Nature 483. March 2012.)

This book tells the story of how the first recognisably modern human culture evolved and came to dominate the Earth. Using the most recent and solid research, we tell the story in a way that provides new insights and allows a deeper understanding of how we came to be as we are; the story of what went wrong, and how.

The evidence, from contemporary archaeology, anthropology, biology, mythology and other disciplines tells us that our ancestors lived in a form of social organisation very different from that which we have long considered the human norm. This evidence suggests that in spite of our centuries of bloody history, we humans could still find a way to live together without violence; without domination of one another; in cooperation; and in respect both of each other and the planet we live on.

After all, this is how we lived for tens of thousands of years – before men made God.

# SECTION ONE:

## The Foragers

Fifty thousand years ago, the climate was much colder and drier and because so much water was retained in the polar ice, sea levels were perhaps seventy metres lower than today. A small bridge of islands emerged, separated by swamp, marshland and narrow stretches of open sea, between the Horn of Africa and Sudan, at the south-east end of the Red Sea. This area is known today as the Gates of Grief. One group of *Homo sapiens* came out of the continent via this route. These were the ancestors of all non-African modern humans.[2]

## The First Goddess: The Sea

To the people wandering along the shore, the sea must have seemed to be the source of life itself. Everywhere they looked, in the rock pools, in the mud, in the shallows, in the inter-tidal zone, the waters teemed with living things. They had simply to gather up the food that nature provided for them. There would have been driftwood to build fires and shelters, and from the land near the coast they would have gleaned vegetables and other useful things, like grass to weave into baskets. The food supply would have been adequate and as they depleted each local resource, the group moved on.

When fresh water is scarce, one is certain to find it where rivers enter the sea, and many littoral plants, for example, coconuts, are a source of potable liquids. Palms and other shoreline plants would have provided shade and shelter. Our ancient foremothers wandered, moving along the shore from river mouth to river mouth.

The people who came across the Red Sea were modern, thinking,

2 Oppenheimer, Stephen. *Out of Eden: The Peopling of the World*. Robinson. 2004.

*1*

articulate humans like us. They would have tried to understand who they were and where they came from, just as we do.

Humans seek design and agency in everything.[3] When we see random patterns, we interpret them in anthropomorphic terms. We see faces in rock formations, in the branches of trees and in clouds. Whenever we encounter something we do not understand our first reaction is to personalise it, to make it like us so that we can conceptualise it. We see causality in random events and constantly ascribe a sense of agency to the world around us. This is the root of the earliest belief system we know of, animism, which holds that everything – and depending on the culture this may include completely inanimate objects like rocks and mountains – contains a spirit force that is a form of will that can be helpful or malign, benevolent or dangerous, depending on how we behave towards it. Animism remains an important world faith even today.

Women living by the sea would have noticed that their menstruation coincided with the same phase of the moon and pattern of tides. They knew that when they gave birth, first came their waters, and it was within these that their babies had grown. Everywhere they looked, the sea's water teemed with living things. What created this life? Having experienced the pain, delirium and delight of bringing forth life themselves, women must have wondered at the sea, always at the moment of parturition, constantly creating life on an immeasurable scale.

The natural reaction of a human mother pondering the mysteries of life beside the mighty ocean would be to conceptualise it as a living being, but on a scale so great as to be beyond comprehension. She would create, in her mind, a being with attributes like hers, yet multiplied immeasurably in power. This being would be the animating force that guided the mighty ocean and controlled not only its destructive force but also its power of creation. The woman would create a deity: a Great Mother.

At that moment, the Goddess opened her eyes and smiled on the children who so fondly invented her. She answered their deep psychological need to know about themselves, and to find a reason for

---

3 Shermer, Michael. *Patternicity: Finding Meaningful Patterns in Meaningless Noise.* Scientific American. Nov. 2008. (http://www.scientificamerican.com/article/patternicity-finding-meaningful-patterns/) retrieved 25/5/2015

their lives: the Goddess-Sea provided for the people and in return, the people praised the sea, came to worship her as their mother. They found spiritual purpose in devotion to her.

The Sea features in the original creation myth in many ancient cultures. We shall look in detail at the Sumerian mythology, the earliest for which we have a written record, because it directly informs so many other, later cultures. Here, the first Goddess was Nammu, the Eternal Sea, who created, alone, the Earth and the Sky in her womb. This element in the creation-myth of a people who lived so far inland may be a lingering folk-memory of a time when their ancestors lived by and from the sea, which was their first mother, their protector, their Goddess.

Life was probably good for the people wandering naked along the shore. A tropical littoral forest is a paradise, a genuine nature's larder. One can pick the food from the trees or scoop it from the rivers or the shoreline, and this largesse is available all year round. During the day, women would gather fuel and forage for food and prepare it, and as the sun set the people would group around the fire to eat and talk. This is how we are, we humans: at the end of the day of toil we come together to cook our food, eat and chat, and tell stories. So there would have been story-tellers. Sitting in the dancing firelight in the balmy tropical evening, for night falls early there, people would tell stories to amuse and teach each other. Those who clustered together in the evening were less likely to become prey, get lost or have an accident in the dark, so entertaining the group, making it stay together, would have had an evolutionary benefit. Storytelling, the basis of all art, became innate to humans.

The stories they told were handed down from generation to generation. But there are many nights and much need of stories, so new ones would have been invented all the time. These may have told of the old days, perhaps recalling a dim memory of life in the interior of the great continent. Perhaps the ancestors themselves were remembered in tales that grew in the retelling, until their strength or wisdom or beauty was more than merely human; that is a tradition that has carried forward to this day.

Some tales might have explained distant features that they could see, such as mountains and forests, and strange beings that might live there. They might explain the animals that they hunted, or that hunted them. And what of the sea itself? Did it extend only as far as the eye could see and then come to an end, or did it go on forever? Sometimes, the stories would have been funny. There would have been jokes and laughter. Sometimes the stories were sad and told of lost loves or the parting of the ways. Often they taught lessons or provided warnings, and served to teach the young or to establish the moral rules for the group.

This telling of stories was the beginning of the oral tradition, the origin of myth, and germs of these myths were retained and handed down for hundreds of generations. Humans then were just like humans now and story-telling is an ancient craft indeed.

In this society the women and children formed the hub around which the group of male hunters orbited. Women, sharing the power of creation with the Sea Goddess, appeared to be part of her. Their bodies cycled with the moon and the tides. And they were able to bring forth life and sustain it by the magical power to make milk until the child was old enough to eat solid food.

# What Makes Us Human

## Cooking

Cooking is now seen by many as the definitive characteristic of modern humans, from which all others followed. It seems to have directly influenced the development of tools, especially blade design, but it had many other consequences.[4]

Cooking, particularly of meats and fats but also starches, partially pre-digests the food, making more energy available to us and allowing us to use less to digest it. We put this extra energy into growing brains. Growing big brains burns many calories and just running them consumes a significant part of our daily food intake. We know that the physical structures that allow us to speak were evolving at the same time as our brains were growing larger. Speech allowed more complex and efficient communication and cooperation. This encouraged conceptual thinking and other intellectual skills, again leading to the development of bigger brains.

## Chattering

The complex anatomy required for sophisticated language, as opposed to grunts and shrieks, developed over a million years ago in hominids. These physical structures did not evolve before we decided to speak; they evolved because we *were* speaking. Language gave us an evolutionary advantage. Human culture, the product of all that chattering and storytelling and the incessant posing and answering of questions, is not only innate to us, but essential to our survival.

---

4 Wrangham, Richard. *Catching Fire: How Cooking Made Us Human.* Profile Books, 2009.

*Homo sapiens'* vocalising structures are markedly more sophisticated than those of earlier hominids, such as *Homo erectus*. We have a hyoid bone, which is what allows us to modulate the pitch of our voices by stretching vocal cords anchored to it. *H. erectus* and modern chimps and other primates have hyoid bones, but we go further and add a space behind the hyoid called a 'dropped larynx'. This development, like other human evolutionary adaptations, is fascinating because it is dangerous. It is possible for a human to choke to death on her tongue; other hominids have no space into which it could fall. So the advantage of speech – and its consequence, culture – must be much greater than the risk of accidental death. The adaptation is like our upright postures, which allowed us to use our hands while moving but at the same time forced skeletal changes that made childbirth difficult and dangerous.

It is likely that the anatomical ability to speak, the neurological ability to form complex languages, and the more complicated and successful techniques of cooperation that these afforded, progressed hand in hand.

Dr Michael Tomasello has collated peer-reviewed research that shows how cooperation is not only innate to humans, but an intrinsic part of our character, and essential to our success.[5] His studies suggest that when the first *Homo habilis* left the African jungles and began to populate the savannahs, they were at a disadvantage to the large carnivores that were already present. However, rather than competing directly with these predators, they developed a strategy of scavenging from their kills. He concludes:

> 'The result was a new kind of interdependence and group-mindedness...at the level of the entire society.'[6]

Being able to talk to each other made us more successful. Once we could express complicated plans clearly and give quick commands and instructions, we could progress from scavenging to hunting.

5 Tomasello is co-director of the Max Planck Institute for Evolutionary Anthropology in Leipzig in Germany.
6 Johnson, Eric Michael. *Survival of the ... Nicest? Check Out the Other Theory of Evolution.* http://www.yesmagazine.org/issues/how-cooperatives-are-driving-the-new-economy/survival-of-the-nicest-the-other-theory-of-evolution Retrieved 26/06/14.

This increased dependence on sophisticated levels of cooperation would have been facilitated by verbal communication and this in turn would have led to an evolutionary impetus towards increasingly complex cooperation and language.

This combination of factors makes an early date for the development of sophisticated language more probable. The first *Homo sapiens* communicated in ways that we could understand although we might not know their language. Not only were the people in the single group that left Africa to populate the world talking, they also would have spoken the same language and shared the same culture.[7]

## Telling Time

In the tropics, the sun always comes up at around the same time and rises to the same height in the sky. Some parts of the year may be wetter than others, but that matters little if the sea, which remains a constant temperature all year round, continually brings forth food. Days are easily measured by the rising and setting of the sun, which varies little throughout the year. Lacking the obvious measure of longer intervals that the annual changes in declination of the sun afford to temperate-zone dwellers, the most obvious indicator of the passage of time would have been the monthly phases of the moon.

As ever, our natural reaction was to explain the moon's phases in human terms, albeit on a supra-natural scale. We had already invented the Goddess, and the moon's phases became the ages of her life. The new, waxing moon became the Maiden, a young girl. She was full of charm and beauty, the fount of burgeoning fertility, but not yet a mother. The full moon was the Mother, the Goddess at her most resplendent, representing the prime of a woman's life, fully integrated into the sacred sisterhood of mothers. The waning, dying moon became the Crone, the older woman, perhaps no longer fertile,

---

7 It has been established that only one small group of related humans, numbering under 200, left Africa to colonise the rest of the world. (University Of Cambridge. *New Research Confirms 'Out Of Africa' Theory Of Human Evolution. Science Daily.* 10 May 2007. www.sciencedaily.com/releases/2007/05/070509161829.html)

yet full of knowledge and wisdom. There is a three-night period of darkness in each lunar cycle, and this apparent absence of the moon would be associated with death.

The lunar cycle is regenerative. Metaphorically the moon is born, grows to its full splendour, reduces and then disappears. Three days later it regenerates, and the cycle begins again. This would lead to the notions of reincarnation and resurrection that are at the heart of modern religious beliefs. It would become one of the most important concepts in human culture.

Tides also follow a cycle, with the tidal range growing and diminishing. At 'spring' and 'neap' tides the range is greatest and smallest respectively. This cycle is caused by the moon's gravity, and spring tides occur at the full and no moon, with neap tides at the half-moon phases. Our ancestors would have noticed this difference in tidal range, since it affected their access to food; far more of the intertidal zone is accessible at the springs than the neaps. Ancient people may have had no idea of gravity but it would have been clear that, in some profoundly mysterious way, the waxing and waning of the tides were related to the phases of the moon. For the pattern-seeking humans the tides came to represent the cycles of the deity they had identified with the sea. This correlation would develop into the idea that the Goddess controlled time which, along with that of the regeneration of life, was to become another foundation stone of religion.

The sea was a supra-natural Mother, and her cycle of twenty-eight days showed in the tides and the phases of the moon. The moon and the tides must, therefore, be very special, sacred things. Women also had a cycle in which their fluids came and went, and it too repeated every twenty-eight days.

The first outward sign that a woman has conceived is in the cessation of the menstrual cycle. Without any understanding of biology, ancient women would still have connected these events. This association made menstruation very important; menstrual blood was sacred and more than that, magical: it had the power to make life. Thousands of years later the Greeks still believed that women retained their menstrual blood within their bodies and made life from it. Perhaps the fluid was even used as a medicine, the original 'magic potion'. Women were the first midwives, and they were probably the first healers too, since it is a practice that is still observable in modern shamanistic cultures.

Survival, and in particular, survival of the women and children, was the primary aim of the culture. Since mating does not always lead to procreation, and the first months of a pregnancy are not visible, perhaps people did not fully understand the process of reproduction. Alternatively, since the first small signs of pregnancy are noticeable almost immediately to the mother, it is possible that the mothers amongst the close group of women knew, and guarded, this 'women's wisdom'.

For those who were not privy, the ability of women to create life would have seemed mysterious and, apparently, supernatural. Tantalising tales linger in the myth-cycles of many cultures which suggest a belief that conception was due to the north wind, the bite of certain insects, eating particular foods or walking under a full moon. These echoes support the idea that the precise mechanism of conception was knowledge that women kept to themselves.

The passage of time was reckoned in terms of the phases of the moon and the ebb and flow of the tides, the creative cycles of the Goddess. Since women shared these cycles as well as the gift of creating life, motherhood was sacred, menstruation was sacred, and ultimately, to be a woman was sacred. Women were one with the Goddess, the most powerful being the people could conceptualise.

## The Menopause and Longevity

Fertile women cycle until they are around fifty years old, at which point a phenomenon called menopause occurs, when a woman ceases to release eggs for fertilisation. Millions of ova develop within the female foetus, far more than the 450 or so that are ever used, so why has this cut-off point evolved?

There are a number of possible explanations. One is that it prevents older ova, which may lead to birth problems, defects or stillbirth, from being fertilised. Since the ova are formed in the early stages of foetal development, they might be fifty or more years old in an older woman. Very few cells in the body survive that long without replacement. DNA degrades through time and is constantly being repaired in living cells, so cells of this age may have more defects. The cessation of ovulation might be a mechanism evolved to reduce the number of unviable offspring due to defective ova.

Another possibility is that because pregnancy later in life places greater demands on the mother's bodily reserves, the menopause evolved to ensure that women survived long enough to raise their children.[8] Also, menopause may allow the energy otherwise used to ovulate to be conserved and directed towards the support of existing children.[9]

Probably all of these factors played a role in the evolution of this human adaptation. Whatever the cause, the existence of the menopause completely refutes the suggestion that our ancestors had short lifespans, since it could *only* have evolved in women living longer than the age of menopause and into their 60s and 70s.

So ancient women lived similar lifespans to those lived today. In extant hunter-gatherer societies, women live into their 80s. There is very little difference between their lifestyle and that of Palaeolithic women. Our foremothers did not die young, excepting death by hazard or in childbirth. Once one allows for such deaths, a more accurate estimate suggests that women, and probably men, lived till they were between sixty and ninety years old.[10]

The wanderers had a healthy diet of fresh fish, meat and plants with little starch or fats. They exercised well and had none of the diseases that would so scourge city-based societies, like cholera or typhus. These people would have had relatively high infant mortality as well as

---

8 Sievert, Lynnette Leidy. *Menopause A Biocultural Perspective*. Rutgers University Press, 2006.

9 *Ibid.*

10 There is strong evidence for shorter lifespans after settled agrarian living develops. This was due to a number of factors, including: increased child mortality; increased death in childbirth, since women were having more babies; poor and unvaried diet; poor dental health; inadequate sanitation and a major increase in socially-transmitted diseases; work-related trauma and increased violence. (Jetha, C & Ryan, C. *Sex at Dawn: The Prehistoric Origins of Modern Sexuality*. HarperTorch. 2010.) None of these apply to the hunter-gatherers.

death in childbirth and unhappy accidents, but the idea that they had lives only into their twenties or thirties is unsustainable.

Could it be that long life, especially amongst women, is an evolutionary advantage? If so how would this work? Clearly, women in their eighties are less able than they once were, and contribute less to the daily tasks of the group; the cost of maintaining them is high. What benefit could offset that? Could it have been knowledge?

The longer a successful mother can continue to reproduce and care for children, the more useful she is in maintaining and increasing the numbers of her group. The grandmothers would have assisted with care of the children. They may even have been wet-nurses.[11] Equally important, perhaps, was that older women were repositories of the group's learning, and probably were shamans who communicated with the spirit-world. All of this amounts to real cultural power. Motherhood was central to survival, and so the Goddess, who is the Great Mother, was revered in all her ages.

A young girl at the point of her sexual maturity is the symbol of fertility, for she is potential lover and mother, yet still a girl, with all the frivolity and capriciousness of any teenager. Once she becomes pregnant, carries to term and passes through the ordeal of parturition, she will become a fully-fledged mother, a sister to the Goddess. And in later life she remains the Goddess, older, with the collected wisdom of the decades of her life, passing this on to the younger women around her.

This culture was centred on the survival of children through the empowerment of women and depended on their knowledge, passed orally from generation to generation, for survival. Culture itself – the totality of ideas and beliefs that a population holds – is a tool that helps us to survive.

## Division of Tasks

Early human society was fluid, with survival always the goal. It was,

---

11 Sloan, Cecil. *Nonpuerperal lactation in grandmothers.* The Journal of Pediatrics, 1956.

in general, divided by gender. Women and children formed a home group, which focussed on protection of the children and nursing mothers, foraging, perhaps trapping small game and birds, and the preparation and cooking of food. This group would have been a sisterhood of equals, but led, in all probability, by the elder women, the grandmothers, who were also the teachers, the midwives and shamans.[12]

The other group was of men and older boys, based on the hunt. This group had to be able to respond quickly to the changing circumstances of the hunt, which could, especially when hunting large game, be lethal. A command system developed, probably around the best and most experienced hunters.

These two social models give us the archetypes of the two earliest deities we know of: the Mother Goddess and the God of the Hunt. The former represents the idealisation of the women at the centre of the home group and the latter the idealisation of the hunters.

This 'two-group' arrangement minimised the risk to fertile women and young children, and meant that hunters could move quickly and silently, an impossible thing to do with babies or toddlers. Neither group was superior. Each had its area of life, which did not interfere with the other. The hunters could provide meat, animal fat, skin and bone, and the gatherers would catch small game and collect vegetables and grains, nuts, berries, roots and fungi, as well as firewood.[13] The division of roles by gender was the beginning of task specialisation, which leads to improvements in performance.[14] It is likely that without such a social structure, *Homo sapiens* would not have been nearly as successful as a species.

Discussing this separation of tasks by gender, Steven Kuhn, from

---

12 A woman in this culture could easily be a grandmother by the time she reached thirty. The term should not be taken here to suggest great age, but greater experience and knowledge.

13 Possibly, these were not just women, but the older males who could no longer hunt, and the young boys. Alternatively, the older males may have taken the juvenile boys to hunt small game and introduce them to the skills needed by a hunter. It is likely that both models existed, at least initially.

14 Note: NOT genetic specialisation, which is the tendency for organisms to evolve such that they can better exploit specific environmental niches. This tends to make them less able to cope with changes in environment. Human task specialisation made the entire species more adaptable.

the University of Arizona, says:

> 'The competitive advantage enjoyed by modern humans came not just from new weapons and devices but from the ways in which their economic lives were organized around…roles for men, women, and children.'[15]

Kuhn and co-author Mary Stiner suggest that this division took place in Eurasia between 45,000 and 10,000 years ago.[16] But the weight of evidence, in archaeology and mythology, suggests that the division of tasks evolved no later than the early part of the Upper Palaeolithic, between 45,000 and 35,000 years ago. It is likely to be one of the adaptations peculiar to the survivors of Toba, which ensured the success of our species.

These divisions between groups were not rigid. When game was scarce or the weather too bad to hunt, the men would join in to help the women to forage, set snares for small game and catch fish in the rivers. When a herd of big game that could feed and clothe the tribe for months was spotted, everyone, men, women, and children, might have joined in to drive them towards the spears or over the edge of a cliff.[17] In some modern hunter-gatherer cultures, women and children even follow the hunting men, as spectators.

The divisions, which we still find in extant hunter-gatherer societies, may have had a consequence that remains important. When men hunted for bigger game they would travel far from their bases, and inevitably would have come into contact with other people. Should the two tribes come together and cooperate? If they do, who will lead them? There is game nearby – should we cooperate just on this occasion, to improve the chance of success? Suppose the other group is hostile – should we stand our ground and fight for this

---

15 Cited at: Lovgren, S. *Sex-Based Roles Gave Modern Humans an Edge, Study Says. National Geographic News,* 07/12/06, retrieved from http://news.nationalgeographic.com/news/2006/12/061207-sex-humans.html accessed 12/02/12.

16 Kuhn S. and Stiner, M. *What's a Mother to Do? Current Anthropology,* Volume 47 No 6, December 2006, pp 953-962.

17 In good weather, a drive like this would have been a pleasure for the people, not least because of the anticipation for the feast they looked forward to after its success. At the same time, a large party making as much noise as possible would be likely to drive off any other predators. So this was a relatively safe form of hunting.

territory, move on, or just agree on a boundary? These difficult and important decisions, which impacted the whole tribe, would necessarily have been made there and then by men. Perhaps here we see the beginning of political activity between societies, and already the separation of tasks tended to ensure that it would be the domain of men.[18]

Human males and females have morphological, skeletal and physiological differences. Women are on average 20% smaller and lighter than men. Women's pelvises are different from men's, in order for them to pass the large head of a human baby. Instead of the strong, boxy male pelvis, women have a wide, shallow one, which forces their hips out. The legs have to turn in toward the midline, causing the classic reverse angle at the knee so that their tibias can be more vertical. Women's upper bodies are very much less massive than men's, and their shoulders tend to be narrow.[19]

The differences are not just skeletal. There are two types of muscle fibre, one adapted for the explosive release of large amounts of energy and one for repetitive but long-lasting release. Men mostly have the first type, women the second. Normal, healthy women of appropriate weight carry a greater percentage of body fat than any other land animal except polar bears. Far more of their body mass is fat than in men, enabling them to build up reserves to sustain them through childbirth and breastfeeding. Women's weight is lower down, to help them balance when heavily pregnant and carrying children. Men's weight is higher up, in powerful muscular torsos perfect for running and throwing, and their high centre of balance lets them knock down a prey animal. There are differences in the brain, in areas such as the amygdala. These are all species characteristics: all humans, everywhere, on average, hold true to this model. In other words, women are morphologically suited to one set of tasks, and men to another; women are indeed, on average, better adapted to gathering and raising children, and men to hunting.

The division of tasks by gender and the consequent establish-

---

18 Ortner, Sherry. *Making gender: the politics and erotics of gender.* Beacon Press. 1996.

19 We hasten to add that this is on average. Successful women runners tend to have narrower than average hips, straighter than average legs and are taller than average – in other words, their morphology more closely resembles an average male's. All living things exhibit variation and this is just an example of it.

ment of two complementary groups with differing roles and responsibilities was an essential part of human development. Since the underlying function of human society is to continue through reproduction and the survival of the young, which was dependent on women,
in matters concerning the home and children they had authority.[20]
There was a balance, an equilibrium that allowed the two groups
to function independently yet in a co-operative manner. However,
the division of tasks exposed men to higher risk of violent death or
life-shortening injury. Since age and experience were regarded as important and the elder mothers were probably the oldest and wisest
people in the tribe, they were natural candidates for leadership.

Here we see a birth-oriented culture in which the leader, certainly of the home group and possibly of the entire tribe, would have
been the most trusted mother. She was sacred in her motherhood, respected for her wisdom, knowledge and shamanistic power, loved by
and loving the people around her, many of whom would have been
her children.

# Choosing to Create Life

Imagine: a woman decided, possibly after consultation with her elders or the shaman, that it was time to create a new life. This was a
decision of huge significance that would lead her to pass through
the dangerous and painful act of childbirth. She might not survive:
death in childbirth, up to the advent of modern medicine, was a risk
every mother took whenever she became pregnant. It was not something to be undertaken lightly.

Perhaps she adorned herself a little more than usual with beads
and trinkets, dressed her hair and coloured her skin and eyes, perhaps with henna or another root, or with coloured earth.[21] Perhaps
she did this before a pool of water or perhaps the women joined to-

---

20 The reproductive potential of any mammal is a function of the numbers of females, not
males. We will encounter this again.

21 In surviving hunter-gatherer cultures, women do this. Ornamenting oneself is an ancient human trait.

gether to help make each other beautiful. These extra preparations would send a signal to the men of the tribe. Her confident beauty and her enhanced charms would attract them to her.

When she chose her partner, the couple may have retired somewhere to consummate their love. Perhaps they would have remained together as long as it took for the woman to become pregnant, or perhaps she would have taken many lovers, taking pleasure in the power that her sexuality gave her. When she realised that her menstrual flow had stopped, she would return to the sisterhood of mothers, who might in the meantime have been caring for her other children.

As the woman aged, her knowledge and wisdom increased. Almost certainly, she knew the sadness of the death of a child. She had seen the elderly in the tribe pass into the dark and die. She knew the pleasure of suckling a child at her breast, as well as the pain of birth, and the relief and joy at passing through the ordeal of parturition. She knew what it was to have authority, to discipline her children when they disobeyed her or did something dangerous. And she knew and enjoyed her sexuality, aware that she was desired because of the way the men's eyes hotly followed her, the flickering firelight making her skin glow and her eyes sparkle. She knew she had that power and could amuse herself teasing the men, playing the coquette. And she knew the power of choice, when she had taken the hand of the man with whom she would make life.

She was the Goddess, at once Maiden, Mother and Crone. She was beautiful and desirable, loving and nurturing, stern and strict, capable of jealousy and anger, yet also of compassion and forgiveness. She was clever: clever in her mind and with her hands. She could weave and make baskets and clothes. She could stitch and sew, and she could draw and paint. She could make fire, and she could cook. She could make herself and the world about her beautiful. She had knowledge: knowledge of plants and herbs, infusions and potions, medicine and healing, and knowledge of pain, too. She knew that her sex was a sacred, magical thing that gave her both pleasure and power.

# Shamanism and Revelation.

Shamans are believed to be able to travel into the world of the spirits. There they receive knowledge and enlightenment as well as visions of the future, and, sometimes, the power to influence it. They are still found across the modern world. The earliest archaeological evidence we have of them is from the Upper Palaeolithic and it suggests that the first shamans were women;[22] yet their presence within our culture may be much older.

A shaman is not part of a formal religious hierarchy. She learns a mythology and a set of rituals and then combines and enhances this learned knowledge with personal voyages into the spirit world, where 'real' knowledge is revealed to her. Shamans may learn from a more experienced mentor, who will guide the novice in her first journeys in the spirit world.[23] Typically, shamans will use mental focussing techniques such as meditation, repetitive movement like dancing, drumming, or chanting a repeated phrase. Often they use hallucinogenic drugs, for example, peyote, marijuana or even alcohol. Most of all, however, the shaman will use ritual, a series of acts that will lead her to the doorway into the spirit world – and also protect her and allow her to return.

Shamans are intermediaries between the supernatural world and the human, and can use the powers of this interaction in a variety of ways. These include the ability to predict weather, to see where prey animals will be, to heal the sick, to cure infertility and, most importantly, to communicate with beings in the spirit world. Shamanism has existed across human culture and while each form differs from the others, they all focus on revelation that can only be obtained in a mind-altered state, by personally entering the supernatural realm.

What shamanism gives to successor religions is the belief that

---

22 Barbara Tedlock has suggested that the earliest known shamans, found in what is now the Czech Republic, were women. (Tedlock, Barbara. *The Woman in the Shaman's Body: Reclaiming the Feminine in Religion and Medicine.* Bantam. 2005.)

23 Anthropologist Carlos Castaneda describes his own relationship to a shaman in the book Don Juan. (Castaneda, C. *The Teachings of Don Juan: A Yaqui Way of Knowledge.* Penguin. 1990.)

through certain practices, truth might be revealed. Using ritual, fasting, narcotic drugs, meditation, by passing through a portal or entering a sacred place, or by some other means, the shaman arrives at a mental state that is not normal, typically some sort of trance, during which her critical faculties are suspended and her innate desire to see pattern and agency is most profound. In this state, she experiences something which she believes has been revealed to her by the supernatural world. She then has to interpret this; its meaning may not be clear, and her skill and experience come into play in the reading of the signs that she has seen. In this sense, shamanistic practice is like reading auguries, tea-leaves, patterns in the clouds, Ouija boards or many other practices to explain the world, communicate with the dead or the gods, visit the spirit world or foretell the future.[24]

*Revelation* is the idea that we can know something because it has been shown to us, without any other explanation, usually by an agency that cannot be explained in material terms. People who accept such answers and guidance believe that revealed truth is not only true but the most profound truth; that it provides the best possible answers to important questions. This is the foundation of faith, which is belief in something that has not been or cannot be proved. In turn, this leads to harsh criticism and even punishment of anyone who does question the answers provided by revelation.

It follows that she to whom the knowledge is revealed, who furthermore interprets that message and relays it to others, becomes powerful, not only in a spiritual sense but also in a temporal one.

Imagine an ancient shaman, deep within the cave that for her is the womb of the Goddess, flickering firelight illuminating the intense darkness. She may be painting or carrying out some ritual, perhaps having consumed some herb or drug such as cannabis, nutmeg, psilocybin or fly agaric mushrooms, or having fasted, or chanted or danced until she passed out of her body. In this journey she may or may not be alone. In Mexico, where there is still a strong tradition of female shamans, women group together either to travel into the spir-

---

24 The techniques of fasting, incense, chanting, dancing, meditation, trance and so on, used by people seeking religious enlightenment are similar to those used by shamans because they were inherited by more recent, organised religions from the older culture.

it world or to support the one who does. For these women, the ritual is a uniquely bonding part of their lives, reinforcing their group identity, as well as a venture into the supernatural. Palaeolithic shamans would have been no different.

If the first shamans were women and the state of motherhood venerated, and the social group of women was the hub of the culture, then it is likely that women, not men, were the governing voice within the society. Indeed the early groups were almost certainly focussed on the core of fertile breeding mothers and their children, and in turn were quite possibly governed by those women.

## Sex, Sexuality and Social Structure

Success in evolutionary terms is blunt and focussed; the more a gene replicates itself, the more successful it is. Genes do not care about the organisms that carry them around or how they live; their only function is to reproduce themselves. For the organisms they animate, this translates to numbers; the more there are the better.

Human children take a long time to develop because of their big brains. We could grow to adult size and strength much more quickly than we do. Young horses or cattle make the journey from a single cell to fully reproductive organism in two years or less, and have far greater body mass than ours. A Friesian calf reaches the body weight of an adult human in a matter of months. Our rate of body growth is genetically slowed in order to give our complex brains the energy they require while developing.[25]

The number of children a woman can raise is limited, not simply by the length of her gestation, but by the number of dependent children she already has. The success of a gene depends on the organism carrying it reaching sexual maturity and passing the gene on to its own young. Humans do not become sexually mature until their early teens, and be-

---

25 Kuzawa, C. *et al*. *Metabolic costs and evolutionary implications of human brain development PNAS 2014* ; published ahead of print August 25, 2014. (http://www.pnas.org/content/early/2014/08/21/1323099111.full.pdf+html)

low that age are dependent on adults, who must protect and feed them.

In a hunter-gatherer society, the number of children that a group can support depends on the amount of nourishment that can be found by the adults. Separating tasks made us more efficient at exploiting the available food reserves, but this was not sufficient for women to realise their full genetic potential to make babies. Instead, women traded off sheer numbers against survival. Their strategy, rather than simply producing as many children as they could, was to concentrate on ensuring the survival to reproductive age of the children they conceived and brought to term.

Fertile women may conceive within weeks of giving birth, leading to their potentially having twenty-five or more babies each; an explosive birth rate. The very slow expansion of human numbers, from a few thousand after Toba to five million 50,000 years later, means that women could not have been raising all the children they might have. Most likely this was because to have done so would have caused the wandering tribe to have become too big, outstripping both the food supply and the social structure. At any given time, some of the women would have been in their third trimesters and much less mobile. If too many women were pregnant, or there were too many very small infants, the group would have become an easy target for predators. So women controlled their reproduction, which was a successful strategy in evolutionary terms.

It has been suggested that our ancestors practised infanticide to regulate their reproduction and that this contributed to an elevated rate of infant mortality. Infanticide, however, is an extremely wasteful policy. A pregnant woman uses a great deal of energy developing a foetus and, especially while she is in her third trimester, is limited in the assistance she can give to the group and to her existing children. There are modern hunter-gatherer cultures where the women use abortion-inducing herbs, and the ancient mothers probably understood this too. However, these herbs are essentially poisons and their use is risky. More likely, the women were regulating their reproduction by other means, and the simplest of these is control over access to sex.

Women are not less enthusiastic about sex than men, but they may be more cautious because they know that a night of pleasure may have long-lasting consequences. Denying sexual access to their male partners is the most effective and least costly method by which women may control their reproduction.

Perhaps women understood the times of their cycles when they were least or most likely to conceive. Those most at risk of falling pregnant could refrain from sex while their sisters, at a different point in their cycle, could enjoy it. Or, perhaps, they simply did not have sex with men until they desired to conceive, and instead maintained same-sex bonds within the group.

Dr Diana Fleischman, of the University of Portsmouth, published findings in November 2014 that strongly suggest that both women and men naturally indulge in same-sex activities far more frequently than is often thought.[26] Dr Fleischman, an expert in the influences of hormones on the psychology of women, was studying the effect of progesterone on attitudes towards homosexuality. She questioned whether progesterone, a hormone that has been shown to increase motivation to form close bonds, might also underlie the motivation to affiliate with those of the same sex, sexually. She studied groups of both men and women who did not identify as homosexual and found that women are more likely to be positively responsive to the idea of sex with other women when their progesterone is highest, and the same is true of men with other men. This fundamentally challenges the notion that sexual interest in humans is only related to procreation, and Dr Fleischman said,

> 'Humans are among a group of animals who have sex for many reasons, not just to reproduce. Reasons can include pleasure, a reward, a way of saying "please be nice to me" or exerting dominance.'[27]

Such behaviour may also strengthen social bonding between individuals and into the group hierarchies.[28] In Spartan society, for example, same-sex bonds were formalised, and amongst the 'Sambia' people

---

26 Fleischman, D.S *et al*. *Testing the Affiliation Hypothesis of Homoerotic Motivation in Humans: The Effects of Progesterone and Priming.* Archive of Sexual Behaviour. 2014.

27 http://www.port.ac.uk/uopnews/2014/11/25/homosexuality-may-help-us-bond/ retrieved 27/11/2014.

28 In Spartan society, same-sex bonds were formalised. While this is usually taken to mean those between males, it is clear that Spartan women also maintained such bonds, although patriarchal historians have tended to overlook this.

of Papua New Guinea, a similar phenomenon occurs.[29],[30] This is a jungle-dwelling, horticulturalist and hunter-gatherer society. All Sambian boys ingest a large amount of semen from older males, which the Sambians believe is what turns them into men. Yet the prevalence of adult Sambian men who identify as homosexual is around 5%, in line with other populations.[31] So in these cultures, same-sex bonding is not seen in a negative light, but in a socially-approved one that contributes to the overall integrity of the culture.[32]

Another reason for same-sex bonding, as supported by Dr Fleischman's study, would be the control of reproduction. This might work in two ways. In the first, adult males are bonded with adolescent boys, and this satisfies the sexual urges of both groups. The idea that young males are constantly seeking sex with women is diluted when they are already in bonds with other men, especially when the culture approves those bonds. Men might only pair with women who desire to conceive and indeed, Spartan men became so attached to their boy lovers that it was said that they often had difficulty in sex with women. At the same time, same-sex bonding between women would not only bind the group of women together through the pleasurable social and physical contact, but also satisfy the urge for sexual release that might otherwise result in unwanted pregnancy. Same-sex contact in such cultures is not condemned, nor is it detrimental. It is helpful to the society as a whole and to women in particular, by allowing them the freedom to choose when to become pregnant.

Control over their reproduction is the primary means by which women may be empowered, and socially-approved, same-sex bonds are one way to achieve this. The empowerment goes far beyond sex.

29 Herdt, Gilbert, ed. *Ritualized Homosexuality in Melanesia*. University of California Press, 1984.

30 'Sambian' is a pseudonym invented by Gilbert Herdt in order to protect the tribe's privacy.

31 Ogas, O. and Gaddam, S. *A Billion Wicked Thoughts*. Penguin Group US. E-book 2011.

32 Contemporary Western notions of sexual orientations and gender identities may simply be a function of the patriarchal prejudices surrounding sex. See: Caramagno, Thomas. *Irreconcilable Differences? Intellectual Stalemate in the Gay Rights Debate*. Praeger, 2002.

## Contemporary Examples

It is one thing to make conjectures about how this sort of society might have worked for our ancient ancestors, but quite another to have living proof. Fortunately, there are still hunter-gatherer groups in remote regions, with extant cultures that function in just this way.

Anthropologist Richard B Lee, known for his work with the !Kung San, a people living in the Kalahari today, notes that most of the food eaten by the whole tribe is provided by the foraging women.[33] !Kung San women only spend fifteen hours per week foraging. They spend about three hours a day sewing, collecting firewood and water, preparing food and other domestic activities, and the rest of their time is spent in relaxing and in social activities. The inference is clear: in their culture, women are the main providers of food, not men. This fact challenges the proposition that women are dependent on male partners to provide food and surrender their sexual freedom to one man in return. In fact, in hunter-gatherer cultures all over the world and throughout history, the male hunt is incidental to the provision of food. It almost appears to be a social activity for the men, since the women's efforts provide enough food to sustain their families.

There is no natural requirement that says that a woman's partner must always be the same man. We have grown used to the idea of men and women pairing for life, but this is a recent cultural invention. Within a society where mothers group together to forage and men travel to hunt, it is not mothers and fathers who bring up children, but the community of mothers.[34] Within this culture, the need for men and women to pair-bond even for the time it takes to raise a child to maturity is much reduced.

A child will always know who her mother is, but she may not know her father, for a woman may have sex with several men at the time she desires to conceive. Without the artificial morality of pa-

---

33 Lee, Richard B. *The !Kung San: Men, Women and Work in a Foraging Society*. Cambridge University Press. 1979.

34 This still happens, today, in many modern cultures: the women stay together to raise children communally while the men go out to work, our equivalent of hunting.

triarchal religion, the imperative for her is that she conceives, and having sex with multiple partners may increase the chances of this. At the same time, in such a culture, men never know which sons are their own and this strengthens the bonds of loyalty within the group of men. The male 'investment in paternity' is via the brothers of the mothers; uncles, not fathers.

Women had status, not through force of arms or feats of physical prowess, but through the power of their bodies to make life. This arrangement ensured the survival not only of their own genes but also those of the men.

## Polyamory

Polyandry describes the practice of a woman having several male sexual partners. She has no husband in the sense that her sexuality and fertility is bound to one man. Instead, in polyandrous cultures, women have a group of occasional, semi-permanent or permanent partners. The term is the inverse of polygyny, where one man has several female sexual partners. As a general rule, polygyny is associated with extremely patriarchal cultures, for example, Islam and Mormonism. When polyandry and polygyny are operating in tandem, the culture is sometimes called 'polyamorous'.

In a patriarchy, men are rewarded with raised status in terms of the number of high-ranking 'target' women they have sex with, while women who do the inverse are derided and insulted. The fact that most people assume 'polygamy' means 'multiple wives' is evidence of this prejudice, since the word means 'many spouses'. It is a central tenet of the patriarchy that each woman's sexuality is the property of a specific man, and this is what drives the cultural opprobrium faced by promiscuous men – they are having sex with someone else's property.[35] Polyandry, on the other hand, is universally condemned

35 In all patriarchal cultures a woman is either the property of her father or her husband, or failing those, her brothers or nearest male relative. The Bible condemns an unmarried woman having sex for the same reason as it does a wife having sex outside the marriage: the transgression of absolute male property right over her sexuality and reproduction.

in the patriarchy, where women are legally and socially constrained from having multiple partners.

As a result, polyandry is almost non-existent in the patriarchy. Its socially-accepted presence indicates another social order, one where women have control over their sexuality and fertility. There is a great deal of evidence to support the claim that it was once widespread, and it persists in many cultures today.

Lewis Henry Morgan (1818–1881) is considered by many to be the founder of modern American anthropology and influenced Darwin, Freud and Marx. In his view, early human society was based on both polygyny and polyandry, a sort of collective sexual partnership. He thought that this arrangement was

> 'as ancient as human society. Such a family was neither unnatural nor remarkable...It would be difficult to show any other possible beginning of the family in the primitive period.'

Many other scholars and thinkers have subscribed to this view, including Darwin, who called it 'communal marriage'.

Hunter-gatherer groups, either in the past or now, rarely exceed 150-200 people. The individuals within the groups are closely related, and all know each other well; indeed the size limit of the group is governed by the approximate maximum number of people who can maintain intimate bonds. These are sexualised bonds and are a fundamental part of the structure of the society. When the group gets too big, it will split in two.

In many polyamorous cultures, children are raised by the women and the maternal uncles. However, fathers do form filial bonds, and the solution to the obvious question, 'which of a woman's partners is the father of a specific child?' is often 'they all are'. The notion that several fathers can contribute genetic material to the conception of a child and so share fatherhood is called 'partible paternity'.

For a closely related group of individuals living and moving together, this arrangement has so many advantages that it is almost

---

A woman's vagina, in the patriarchy, is not hers, but the property of whichever man she 'belongs' to, and her life itself is of less value than his 'legal right'.

illogical to assume any other model. Each male has more chances of his genes being carried forward if he has multiple receptive partners. Having many mates is also beneficial to a woman, because it means that she has multiple males associated with her and able to assist and protect her and, crucially, her children. If one of the males dies, there are others, and since no one male knows which children were fathered by him, they will tend to bond with and protect them all.

We share over 98% of our DNA with our closest primate relatives, bonobos or Dwarf Chimpanzees (*Pan paniscus*). Sex with multiple partners is normal amongst bonobos. It has been shown to increase bonding and mutual trust within the group, food-sharing, mutual co-operation and sharing of responsibilities. It reduces stress and male aggression significantly. Since all the males have multiple receptive females willing to have sex with them, there is no dominance rivalry, and rape – common in other ape species – has never been observed in bonobos, either in the wild or in captivity.[36]

Are there modern human cultures in which these behaviours may be observed? Are there cultures in which people live peaceful lives, where women are equal to men and violence and warfare are rare if not unknown? Societies based on non-exclusive, non-proprietorial sexual bonds? If there were, that would make suggestions that the Western model is the only viable one untenable.

The answer is that there are many. In South America alone partible paternity is practised by the Aché, the Araweté, the Barí, the Canela, the Cashinahua, the Curripaco, the Ese Eja, the Kayapó, the Kulina, the Matis, the Mehinaku, the Piaroa, the Pirahã, the Secoya, the Siona, the Warao, the Yanomami, and the Ye'kwana, amongst others.[37] It occurs throughout the world on all the inhabited continents.

One example is the Zo'é. Their name just means 'people'.[38] They are also known, to some outsiders, as 'The Marrying People' because

---

36 Unfortunately, many researchers have tried to relate human behaviour to more distant relatives, such as the Common Chimpanzee, *Pan troglodytes*, or even use data from baboons, which are not closely related to us. They suggest that aggression, competition, rape etc., are 'natural' to humans, while ignoring the evidence from bonobos. We are sceptical of their motivation.

37 Jetha & Ryan 2010.

38 The Zo'é themselves only use the term to differentiate from white people.

of their sexual customs. They live in the province of Pará, in the northern Brazilian rainforest, which for millennia succoured and hid them. The Zo'é are polyamorous. Both men and women have multiple partners, and women are equal in status to men.

Zo'é women are familiar with abortion-inducing herbs and use them to regulate their fertility. Babies born with defects are killed before they first cry in order to avoid 'bad luck'.[39] On the other hand, this is not a cruel society, but one based on love and respect. The Zo'é are semi-nomadic hunter-gatherers and monkeys are the favourite game of the hunters. If one is killed and found to have had young, these are brought back to the camp and raised alongside the human children. They are given their own hammocks and are never eaten. The Zo'é appear to regard them less as pets than as another kind of people, an expression of the closeness they feel to nature.

From the age of six, women and men wear the poturu, a wooden plug piercing the lower lip. Women keep their hair long and well coiffed, and wear decorative headdresses made of vulture-down. Apart from these, they go completely naked, but take care to conceal their vulvas when sitting. The men all wear a restraint on their penises, which they only remove in order to relieve themselves or to have sex. This is noteworthy since the phallus is regarded across human culture as the seat of male power. Men being obliged to wear a restraint on it indicates that male power is being restrained. At the same time, Zo'é women wear no such restraint and go naked; a clear indicator of the relative statures of the genders.

The life of the tribe revolves around the women and children, and older mothers are highly revered. Long after their ability to contribute to the provision of food is over, the grandmothers continue to be provided for and respected, and they enjoy a long evening of life surrounded by their families. The eldest among them are often given baby monkeys to raise when they become too old to look after a human child, indicating the reverence for motherhood within the culture.

The Zo'é are partial horticulturalists. They have areas near their settlements where they cultivate manioc, bananas, sweet potatoes

---

39 This may shed light on the infanticide believed to have occurred in Palaeolithic human groups.

and urucum, which provides a red dye that the Zo'é women use to cover their bodies.[40] They cultivate a species of bamboo, to make arrows. They also keep and breed animals and birds for eating. Pigs are regarded as having special powers and sometimes accompany the hunters to protect them from jaguars.

They have simple technologies, such as spinning wild cotton into thread. Fire is central to the society and is never allowed to go out. The people believe that their fires were lit in the dawn of time.

The hunters do not hunt their prey animals during their breeding seasons and take care not to deplete the resources that sustain them. As well as knowing plants that cause abortion, Zo'é women have an encyclopaedic knowledge of forest plants for eating and making medicines. They are comfortable, well fed and have good lives, loved by the people around them.

The Zo'é consider that they belong to the land and are part of it. They do not possess it, nor do they distinguish between themselves and their environment. Their only personal possessions are those they make themselves and are limited; women wear hair bands and bangles on their wrists and men paint intricate designs on their hunting arrows to identify them. There is no concept of wealth other than love.

Despite the fact that both women and men share sexual partners, no sign of jealousy has been observed in their culture. The people are peaceful and non-violent. Zo'é children are rarely punished except in severe cases, when they are lightly scratched with a fish bone 'to let out the bad blood'. Since, in Western cultures, violent behaviour tends to run down the generations, this must make us ask whether the violence that is endemic to modern Western society is actually a product of the culture that informs it.[41]

The Zo'é are just one of a great many examples of cultures that practise polyamory or partible paternity. These cultures are not a new

---

40 In many ancient cultures, ochre or 'ruddle' was used in this way. It represented the blood of parturition as well as the menstrual blood of the Goddess. While we do not know the precise meaning of the Zo'é equivalent, the parallel is striking.

41 Consider, in this light, the well-known patriarchal aphorism 'spare the rod and spoil the child'. Patriarchal attitudes are imprinted on children through violence and this is then passed on down the generations.

development. Two thousand years ago, Julius Caesar observed of the Celtic people of Britain that: 'Ten and even twelve have wives common to them, and particularly brothers among brothers'. One woman would have several brothers as regular sexual partners. Furthermore, the Picts, who were a Brittonic Celtic people living in what is now Scotland, were matrilineal. Sons were known in reference to their mothers and property was descended through the mother's line, which almost certainly indicates the practice of polyandry.

Nor is there anything secretive about sex in polyamorous cultures. Captain James Cook spent three months in Tahiti in 1769 while exploring the Pacific. He noted that the Tahitians 'gratified every appetite and passion before witnesses.' John Hawkesworth's official record of the journey explains:

'(a) young man perform(ed) the rites of Venus with a ... girl about 11 or 12 years of age, before several of our people and a great number of natives, without the least sense of its being indecent or improper, but, as appeared, in perfect conformity to the custom of the place.'[42]

Cook corroborates this and notes that there were many women in the watching crowd who called advice to the girl in a good-humoured and encouraging way, but

'Young as she was, she did not seem to (need) it.'[43]

Sex in this community was nothing to be ashamed of or hidden away, but an everyday part of life, indulged in by women as eagerly as men, with multiple partners. Similar behaviours were found all over the Pacific and Africa. Indeed the principal role of Christian missionaries to these places was to destroy their natural culture, which the people had been enjoying for thousands of years with no ill-effects, and replace it with the hidebound, patriarchal one of Europe. The notions that women are sexually reluctant, and that the exclusive

---

42 Hawkesworth, John. *An account of the voyages undertaken by the order of His present Majesty*. London 1773.

43 Captain Cook's Log Entry for 14 May 1769 (http://southseas.nla.gov.au/journals/cook/17690514.html).

pattern for human society is monogamous pair-bonding, turn out to be anything but natural.

Cook also noted the 'two-group' structure of the local communities and other details typical of polyamorous cultures.[44],[45] These included, to Cook's evident dismay, a complete lack of comprehension of the notion of personal property, which resulted in the islanders helping themselves to anything that took their fancy. He appears to have become inured to this, as this note from his log of 20 June suggests: 'I now gave over all thought of recovering any of the things the natives had stolen from us.'[46]

Another current example of a polyamorous culture exists in the Mosuo or Na people of China. These people were first reported by Marco Polo in 1265. They still live where they lived then, on the shore of a lake called Lugu. The Mosuo worship Lugu as the Mother Goddess. The mountain that rises above it, Ganmo, is also revered, as the goddess of love. The Mosuo are a famously tranquil and relaxed people. Their pictographic language, called Dongba, the only such still being used today, tellingly contains no words for 'murder', 'war' or 'rape'!

The Mosuo are matrilineal. The family name and property pass through the female side and the family revolves around the group of mothers. Traditionally, they do not marry or 'pair-bond' at all. Instead, Mosuo girls, when they become sexually mature, are given bedrooms with two doors, one into a common courtyard shared by the family and the other into the street. This door is to allow men to enter her bedroom, which the Mosuo call her 'Flower Room' or 'babahuago'. The girl has full control over who may enter her bedroom from the street and needs no permission from anyone.[47] She can have as many different sexual partners in a night as she wishes, and while she may see the same one again and again, they all must be gone by daybreak.

---

44 http://southseas.nla.gov.au/journals/cook/17690505.html

45 Captain Cook was a professional mariner and his log entries are typical of the type: mainly dry, informative and factual. Nevertheless his sense of amazement and culture shock comes through clearly, especially in gems such as this, 'the Women were so very liberal with their favours'. (6 June 1769.)

46 http://southseas.nla.gov.au/journals/cook/17690620.html

47 Least of all her father, whose identity is impossible for her to know.

If she becomes pregnant, the baby is raised in the matriarchal household where she lives, with the aid of her brothers. There is no paternal role in Mosuo culture for the biological father; this role is played by the uncles, who, of course, are out every night visiting other Mosuo women. They have to do this because they are not allowed to sleep in the matriarchal household!

There is no 'parental investment' for biological fathers in this culture whatsoever. The people worship the Mother Goddess, and the society consists of collective groups centred on mothers and their children.

Sadly, the Mosuo have had to suffer much abuse from both missionaries and government officials trying to eradicate their culture. As a result of this, the 'walking marriage' as described above now exists alongside patriarchally-derived models. Nevertheless, the fact that such a society should survive at all after so much pressure attests to its resilience.

Yet another example can be found in the four million or so Minangkabau people who live in Western Sumatra, part of Indonesia. Fascinatingly, they are Muslim, having converted in the 16th century. Though clearly this is in conflict with the patriarchal code of Sharia Law, the Minangkabau are matrilineal, with property and family names passing through the mother. According to the anthropologist Peggy Reeves Sanday, who has spent over twenty years studying them, they consider themselves to be a matriarchal society. They resolve this through their *adat* or ethnic tradition, which for them exists in parallel with their faith. In common with the practices in other parts of Asia such as the Philippines and Thailand, animist belief is a part of Minang society, and animism is often associated with matriarchal, Goddess-worshipping cultures. According to Sanday, Minangs revere a mythical Queen Mother, and women's prestige increases with age. They favour cooperation over competition, which is also typical of matriarchal cultures.[48]

---

48 Sanday, Peggy Reeves. *Matriarchal Values and World Peace: The Case of the Minangkabau*. Paper delivered to the 2nd World Congress on Matriarchal Studies, University of San Marcos, Texas 2005. (see http://www.second-congress-matriarchal-studies.com/).

The preceding are only a few examples from what remains, despite millennia of attempts to crush them, a significant number of polyamorous cultures across the globe. In all we see a similar set of characteristics: the people are non-violent and peaceful; rape is unknown; children are treated kindly and never punished severely and sexual jealousy, a cause of discord and violence, does not appear. In addition, in many such cultures, the notion of possession of property either does not exist or is restricted to items like personal jewellery or hunting weapons.

# SECTION TWO:

## Moving Inland

## Seasonal Cycles

For tropical beachcombers, the seasons were of little importance. The temperature of the sea remains more-or-less the same all year round, and the flora and fauna are just as abundant at all times. But life in a temperate zone is based on an annual, not a monthly cycle, and the further away from the tropics the more marked this becomes. The cyclical pattern of life, which had been associated with the waxing and waning of the moon, the ebb and flow of the tides and the cycles of menstruation, began to be adapted to an annual cycle measured by the seasonal changes.

After crossing the Red Sea at the Gates of Grief, our wandering ancestors at first followed the shore of what is now called the Gulf of Aden. They began to move inland, where new landscapes brought new experiences and new phenomena to explain. As the people moved further away from the sea, many would live all their lives without ever seeing it. They still had their primary reverence for the Mother, the bringer-forth of life, but they needed another manifestation of the eternal life-giving force that had brought them into being and protected them.

From the Goddess being an unlimited, eternal Sea, to becoming an unlimited, eternal Earth, was an easy step. Here, away from the sea, life sprang forth from the Earth, from the land, from the ground. Therefore, the Mother must be within the ground: she was the Earth. Rivers, themselves bearers of life, rose from springs that came out of Mother Earth, so they were sacred too.

The seasons of the Earth came to be associated with the Ages of the Goddess, as the phases of the moon had been. Spring became the

Maid, the youthful goddess, summer the Mother, her maturity, autumn the Crone, and her passage into old age and winter, death. The seasons became metaphors for birth, life and death, but also a cycle of life, death and rebirth.

Triplism refers to the recurrent symbolism of the number three, and we shall encounter this frequently. It manifests in many ways, from triple deities to three-day solstices and many other cultural motifs, especially the three-day interval between the death of a deity and her resurrection.[49]

The three aspects of a triple-goddess, the Maiden, the Mother and the Crone, are at once the whole Goddess and part of her. Even if they happen to be manifesting individually, they can never be separated; they remain one entity. Deities, after all, are not governed by natural rules.

Triple deities do not always conform exactly to this model, as in the pre-Islamic Arab triple-goddess al-Lat, al-Uzza and Manat. Not all three representations need be visibly present. In the Christian triple-deity expressed as Father, Son and Holy Spirit, the last is completely incomprehensible in terms of human morphology but is perhaps best explained as equivalent to the Judaic shekinah or divine breath.[50] Nevertheless, they are three and one at the same time.

An awareness of the annual seasonal cycle soon became essential to hunter-gatherers living outside the tropics. They closely observed when and where game animals or food plants were available, allowing them to predict the availability of supplies. With the advantage of big, thinking brains and highly developed, articulate speech, they assimilated this knowledge into stories and passed it from one generation to the next. People living in the temperate zones became avid observers of the sun, the planets and the stars because of the clues they could give that might help in the search for food and shelter, and these celestial objects were included in the stories.

---

49 Although in later versions those who reappear after three days became male, e.g., Jesus from the tomb and Zarathustra from the river, in the beginning, the deity who died and resurrected herself was the Goddess.

50 The word 'shekinah' is feminine grammatically but this has been extended to mean 'the feminine creative power of God', especially by the Kabbalists.

For hunters, winter can be good. There is far less cover to conceal game, and herbivorous animals may be weaker due to hunger, and easier to chase and kill. On the other hand, for the home group of women and children, winter is challenging. There are few plants to gather and the imperative to keep warm and sheltered is even more compelling. In summer and autumn the group of women could, as they always had, easily provide for the whole tribe. In winter and spring, they may have been far more reliant on the hunting men to supply food and the animal skins they used to keep warm.

## Life After Death

Although humans may have arrived at these concepts even earlier, the mythological record shows that, in the temperate zone, we established human life as a cycle. Like the seasons of the solar year, death would be followed by rebirth. But bodies visibly decayed after death and did not come back to life. For a cyclical conception of human life to have any meaning, there would have to be a part of us that did not corrupt.

We already had a model for this. We had given, first to the sea and then to the Earth, an immortal, all-powerful animating spirit, the Great Mother Goddess, who could survive death and be born anew. This rebirth could be observed whenever the new moon appeared, or when the sun began to rise after the winter solstice. If the Goddess had both physical and metaphysical forms, then would not humans? And if the Goddess could survive death, could not we? Very early on, we developed the idea of the human consciousness being separate from the physical body, the idea of a soul or spirit, and related this to the notion of a return to life.

At the same time, we began to identify the place of death as being under the ground, which would lead to the concept of the Underworld. Burials, probably initially performed to avoid the spread of odour and disease and to keep animals from disturbing the bodies, became commonplace and were ceremonialised.

In the earliest mythological conceptions of the Underworld, it is ruled by the Goddess. Her control of death is as important an aspect as that of Mother. The Goddess gives life but, crucially, she takes it back. Just as the corruptible part of us is placed inside the Earth, which is the physical manifestation of the Goddess, so our souls are taken back inside her metaphysical manifestation to await the time when we may be reborn. Our souls, in this concept, become part of the Goddess' soul, just as our bodies become part of the Earth.

Burial symbolised a return to the Mother's womb. All over the world we have evidence of tomb burials which are clear metaphors for this. In prehistoric Scotland, for example, lived the Beaker People, who buried their dead almost in the foetal position, in pots or pot-like tombs.[51] The motif of the pot signifies the womb, and so these people placed their dead into the womb of the Goddess, the Earth, to await rebirth.

Today, this cyclical conception of life-death-rebirth remains the core belief of billions of people. It is widespread across Africa, Asia, the Americas and elsewhere. It is only where the Abrahamic death-cults, Judaism, Christianity and Islam, along with their splinter groups like the Mormons and Baha'i, have been implanted, that a linear understanding is accepted.[52] Even there, a little investigation shows that the linear beliefs are overlaid on deeper, older, cyclical conceptions. In the Philippines, for example, which is a strongly Christian nation, the belief that the spirits of the dead are close by and watching over the living is widespread and profound. Since it is not at all the Christian understanding, this belief must come from the earlier religion.

Some people, especially those brought up within cultures influenced by the death-cults, believe that the Goddess was only concerned with motherhood, nurture and childbirth, but this is a mistake. These are only a part of her role. The other side of the Goddess is death, darkness, and decay. She is the Underworld, the dark void before and after life. We come from this when we are born and return to it when we die. Unfortunately, the failure to understand that the

---

51 The witches' cauldron, a large, bowl-shaped cooking pot is a practical tool for the (transformative) processing of herbs and other ingredients, but it is also a metaphor for a woman's womb. In Egypt, the hieroglyphs for 'pot' and 'womb' were the same.

52 The concept of death-cults will be described in detail in later chapters.

Goddess is both Light and Dark has led many to false conclusions about the nature of the Goddess and goddess thealogy.[53]

The Goddess is primal, because it is from her that all life proceeds, including that of the other deities. She alone has the gift of life – and of death. Most pre-Abrahamic cultures saw death, as well as birth, as a woman: she was Ereshkigal in Sumer, Kali in India, the Morrigan in her crone aspect to the Celts and Hel to the Scandinavians.

The Goddess can become angry and then she can be terrible, as when an earthquake thunders, bringing boulders crashing down or a volcano erupts, spewing fire and destruction. The Goddess is all that women ever have been, and these are not all sweet and pretty things. Women, like men, have tempers. They can be jealous, they can be judgemental, they can tease and torment mercilessly and they can even be violent. Why would a deity made in their image not have these qualities too?

# Folk Memory: the beginning of mythology

Stories are hugely powerful, and this was just as true before the written or pictorial record began. Factual oral narratives can preserve histories and genealogies accurately, and mythical narratives can develop organically to serve changing social purposes.

Recent research shows that an oral tradition concerning a huge earthquake caused by the Cascades Fault off the north-west coast of America existed for three hundred years without being written down. The details described in it have been confirmed by geologists.[54] That means that no-one who experienced the event was still alive, nor their children, nor their grandchildren, when the tradition was written down. In fact, twelve generations separate the event and

---

53 Thealogy is a neologism generally understood as a discourse that reflects on Goddess (thea) in contrast to God (theo).
54 http://walrus.wr.usgs.gov/tsunami/NAlegends.html retrieved 26/07/2014.

the record.[55] Our reliance on the written word should not prevent us recognising the power and durability of oral traditions.

As a performance artist, a story-teller must captivate her listeners and respond to their mood. That requires improvisation, changes in emphasis, asides and appeals to the audience, and so on. When these tales are re-told, the improvisations that best pleased the audience will be retained. In story-telling there is an evolutionary process, driven by on-the-fly improvisation and by the performer's selection and retention of the most effective elements. As stories passed through generations of story-tellers these improvisations accumulated and when wandering groups encountered one another their collections of stories would have merged. As groups separated and travelled apart, the contact between them became less and less until they became isolated from each other. Within each group the oral traditions continued to evolve, but diverged, each reflecting the different accumulated experiences of the tellers.[56]

Later, in the settled period, many stories from different original sources would exist in parallel. Stories would sometimes blend so that each had many contributing sources. This process is called syncretism, and it is one of the most important concepts to grasp in mythology.

In effect, every myth is syncretised from many sources and two stories that sound as if they are different may contain the same, distant germ of an original truth.

No one version is wrong nor is any one right: they are just different. Once, somewhere, someone told a story and ever since it has been evolving like a living thing. There is no definitive version of the story until it is recorded in some permanent way. The recording has to wait until the means to do it is invented, by which time the story might have been circulating and syncretising for tens of thousands of years.

Modern anthropologists go to great lengths to avoid introducing

---

55 Similar links between oral traditions and datable seismic events have been found and documented elsewhere: see King, D.N and Goff, J.R. *Benefiting from differences in knowledge, practice and belief: Maori oral traditions and natural hazards science.* 2010. (http://www.nat-hazards-earth-syst-sci.net/10/1927/2010/nhess-10-1927-2010.pdf retrieved 26/07/2014.)

56 This is a parallel to the biological process of speciation, and points to the evolutionary nature of human culture.

their own voices when transcribing oral traditions, but in ancient times this level of accuracy was of no concern whatsoever. The stories were seen as allegories and their importance was in how well they supported the principles of the dominant culture. Transcribers from different cultures wrote down the same oral tradition in different ways, each emphasising the aspects they felt were important. Myths reflect and promote the views and opinions of the story-tellers and, very importantly, of the scribes who eventually, possibly thousands of years later, wrote them down.

Myths are important; they are useful because they help us to understand the issues that most concerned the people who invented them. As well as this, though they may never be relied upon as literally true, they are a form of collective cultural memory which may contain allegorical or metaphorical truths and references to real events. The study of myths helps us to contextualise archaeological evidence and better understand the cultures that preceded ours.

# Caves and Wombs

Caves are excellent habitations, and our species made great use of them. They provided shelter from weather, protection from predators and a dry place where the essentials of life such as food, skins, and firewood, could be preserved. The snow of winter could be kept outside while the cave within was warm and cosy. Conversely, as the many cave-dwellings that still exist in arid climes attest, they were cool in the summer heat.

The best caves had a narrow entrance and the people would have improved the natural defences by putting up palisades of timber or piling stone to reduce it even more. Behind this was a common fireplace, which was probably kept lit all the time, providing light and heat for comfort and cooking, keeping at bay darkness, cold and predators. Perhaps strips of meat and fish were hung above the fire, to preserve them so that they could be eaten when the hunting was slim.

Within the protection of the cave, young children could play safely while older girls helped their mothers in their daily routine, and learned the responsibilities of women in the tribe: how to forage, which plants were good to eat and which not; how to get honey from a bee-hive; how to snare small game; which plants would make a sick person better, which moulds would help a festering wound. As they were learning all these things, they were taught the stories of the tribe by their mothers and grandmothers. Boys too young to hunt would probably have helped their mothers, or possibly they were put in the care of an older man who had been injured and could no longer hunt. He would teach them how to shape flint, how to make spears and traps, and the lore of the hunter.

The caves were a kind of base-camp, from which the people went out to hunt and forage. A tribe may have had several such shelters, each used at a different time of year as they followed the game and seasonal plants. Caves were more than homes, however. Some were meeting areas, where people would gather together; the purpose being, at least in part, trade. These were the Palaeolithic market-places, where skins, ivory and bone artefacts, as well as, perhaps, jewellery and plant products could be bartered.

Caves have preserved the evidence of life for tens of thousands of years. Where they were few and far between, people built simple shelters of wood, thatch and hide that have long since mouldered to nothing, and the evidence they may have contained has been lost. However, it is likely that those who did not use caves lived similar lives to those who did.

## The Red Lady of Paviland

The first Mother-Goddess, the Sea, had become the Mother-Goddess Earth as the people moved away from the tropical seas into the interiors of the continents. *Homo sapiens* began colonising Europe 43,000 years ago, and soon after this we find the first physical evidence of Mother-Goddess worship, in carved Goddess figurines. The people who made these objects were sophisticated, cultured and they revered the Mother.[57]

A fascinating confirmation of this came when a human fossil was found in 1823 by William Buckland, in a cave in Gower, in Wales. It is known as 'The Red Lady of Paviland'. Although it was originally thought to be much more recent, in 2009 this skeleton was re-dated at 33,000 years old.[58]

The area around the skeleton and the walls of the cave where it was found were thickly coated with ruddle, a red pigment formed from iron oxide. Ruddle is still used today, but it had special significance in the past: it represented the menstrual blood of the Goddess. We find it used in caves all over Europe; it reaffirms that caves were the womb of the mother.

The Red Lady is even more tantalising. Despite the name, this is a male skeleton and the misidentification occurred because it was found with jewellery made of shells and mammoth-bone. It is unusual to find male human remains with jewellery of this type, and this provokes questions about the culture in which the Red Lady lived. Did men wear such jewellery, or was something else going on?

Alternative expressions of gender are not unusual; the rigid division of society into two strictly observed gender expressions appears to have evolved later, as a function of the patriarchy. In Sumer, in later Middle-Eastern cultures, and today across India, South America and South-East Asia, male-to-female transvestites and transsexuals are very common and frequently have significant religious roles.

For example, in the temples of the Sumerian Inanna, the Phrygian Cybele and other goddesses, young men, scarcely more than boys, worked into a religious passion, castrated themselves in order to serve the Goddess as priestesses. This tradition is maintained today in the Indian subcontinent by transwomen known as hijra. As a result of the influence of Western notions implanted by the British, they are today seen as very low in the prevalent caste system but are nevertheless accepted, because they are believed to have been

---

57 In the 19th century these were collectively referred to as Venus figurines but now they are simply called prehistoric figurines.

58 *Out of Africa: modern human origins special feature: isotopic evidence for the diets of European Neanderthals and early modern humans.* Proc. Natl. Acad. Sci. U.S.A. 106 (38): 16034–9. September 2009.

'touched by the Goddess'.[59] Once, however, they were a powerful caste of priestesses. They still perform an important role at weddings and other formal ceremonies, and frequently sell blessings from the Goddess to make a living.

In Thailand, where their presence has been noted by Western observers for centuries, transwomen are often known as sao (or phuying) praphet song, 'second type woman'. Other similar expressions are widely found across Asia, especially where Goddess culture or traditions of domestic matriarchy are strongest, for example in the Philippines. In the Native American nations, there are what Europeans coming into contact with them called *berdache*, but who called themselves 'two-spirited', suggesting that they had both male and female consciousness.[60] These also often had shamanistic or healing roles within their tribe. Amongst the Zo'é and other hunter-gatherers there are traditions of ritual transvestism, where men dress as and behave like women for periods of time.[61]

Elsewhere in pre-Columbian America, transgender was widespread and was described by the conquistadors. In Peru, Pisarro's troops encountered transgender priestesses and described how they were present in each of the temples. Other writers noted the phenomenon in Mexico, Florida, the West Indies and across South America.[62]

This phenomenon is both widespread and has very ancient and deep roots; it would be surprising if it did not appear in the Palaeolithic. Was the Red Lady, perhaps, a transsexual shaman who died as a result of taking powerful drugs that would allow her to go into the spirit-world? Even, possibly, from her ritual castration? We have

---

59 Or by God.

60 *Berdache* is pejorative. According to Merriam-Webster, 'American French, alteration of French *bardache* catamite, from Italian dialect (southern Italy) *bardascio*, from Arabic *bardaj* slave, from Persian *bardag* prisoner, from Middle Persian *vartak*'. It was not used by the Indians.

61 Transsexual refers to an individual whose understanding of their own gender is not the same as the one that would be assumed as a result of their birth genitalia; they live their whole lives in the gender they believe themselves to be. Transvestites dress in the clothes of the opposite gender for periods of time for a variety of reasons, cultural, personal, social and sexual, but always retain an understanding that their own gender conforms to their birth sex.

62 Das Wilhelm, Amara. *Tritiya-Prakriti: People of the Third Sex: Understanding Homosexuality, Transgender Identity, And Intersex Conditions Through Hinduism*. Xlibris Corp. 2010.

other examples from Europe of natal women, identified as shamans, being buried in similar manners, which tends to support this.

## The Goddess of the Cave

A man projects into the world, as he hurls his spear and also his semen. His natural affinity is with the sun, by which he sees his prey, and to see the sun, you have to go outside. A woman takes all within her. Her sex is internal, darkness and mystery, Camille Paglia's 'fecund and fertile swamp of creation', while a man's is external, obvious and exposed.[63]

The limestone caves of France go deep into the ground, a kilometre or more into the dark; and what marvels are found there! Stalactites and stalagmites, the fascination of speleologists, sparkle like heavenly pillars. For the first woman exploring deep into these places in the dancing light of the burning torch she held, it must have been like nothing she could ever have imagined, the work of something far greater than she. The woman was clever with her hands; she knew how to make things, and she was observant; she knew how things grew. But this stone was like no stone she had ever seen, it grew more like a tree or the roots of a tree. She could not know that these incredible formations occur because limestone is very slightly soluble in water, and that rain trickling through cracks in the rock brought tiny amounts of calcium carbonate here, and deposited them. But she would have known what bone was since she used it every day, and calcium carbonate is bone. It would take very little imagination for the woman to believe that she was deep inside the divine body of the Mother-Goddess.[64]

In many caves something fascinating has been found: handprints. These are handprints of women, men, and children, made

---

63 Paglia, C. *Sexual Personae: Art and Decadence from Nefertiti to Emily Dickinson.* Vintage 1992.

64 Caves with mouths in the shape of vulvae have been found, with the area around the entrance and inside painted with ruddle or ochre, to depict the menstrual blood of the Goddess. That these were places of cultic significance is incontestable.

by placing a hand covered in pigment onto the wall of the cave, or by placing the hand on the wall then spraying or daubing pigment around it.[65] Was this a form of worship? Or did placing the hand upon the wall of the womb of the Great Mother Goddess confer protection upon the person who did so, as if that person would be watched over as long as the print remained? If so, they were blessed, for their prints are still there. Or was it a rite of initiation into the tribe, like the Confirmation ceremony still performed by Christians, where a young person restates the promise to the religion that was made when she or he was baptised as a baby? We can only wonder.

Many caves also contain images of animals, of men with weapons, and of beings that are part human, part animal. These were the first male deities, deities of the hunt. They were ancestor animals, whose spirits had to be supplicated to forgive us for killing them. They were the precursors of later anthropomorphic male deities like Pan or Cernunnos, or wild men like the Sumerian Enkidu. Their realm was the woods and forests, the broad grassy plains. They lived with the beasts and often mated with them, and they were frequently beast-like or even part beast. Some were of the forest itself, like the Green Men of European folklore.

None of these, however, was a creation deity. That role was reserved for the Goddess.

# Celestial Conception

From the point at which we realised that procreation depends on the union of female and male, this concept became the foundation of every theist cult.

Our ancestors observed the world and explained it in terms they understood. If, for life on the human level to come into being, a woman must have sex, then, for life on a global or metaphysical level to come into being, the Goddess Earth must also have sex. Since the Earth was so vast and powerful, her consort must also be. The mys-

---

65 Spraying could be accomplished through the mouth or a hollowed bone.

teries of life would be explained by reference to astral objects that were invested with supernatural powers.

We know that the Earth orbits the sun, but the ancients did not. For them, the Earth was both more immediate and far larger. Its scale made it powerful and the relative difference between it and the sun made it natural to assume that the sun's movements were controlled by the Earth. This was so with the moon and the stars too. Since the Earth was identified with the Goddess, then she was controlling the movements of these objects, and thus time itself. Around these astral objects and their behaviour, complex mythologies were invented which related them to deities, and temples and observatories were constructed to allow the accurate observation of their movements.

The term 'solstice' means 'sun stands still', in the sense that it rises to the same height in the sky at noon. We know that this changes slightly every day; the sun does not 'stand still', so the term seems obscure. However, just because we know that this is so does not mean that we can *see* that it is; our knowledge comes from modern astronomical techniques which were not available to our ancestors.

For the ancients, the sun did appear to stand still for three days at the time of the solstices, and in a culture that measured time by the movements of celestial bodies, this meant that time also stood still. Christmas happens on the 25th of December, three days after the solstice, because it was on this day that the slow recovery of the sun could be observed. Similarly, the traditional Anglo-Saxon Midsummer Festival begins on the 24th of June, three days after the solstice, when the sun appears to begin to sink in the sky again.[66]

Discovering the exact date when the sun began to rise in the sky after the winter solstice came to be of enormous importance to the ancients. At first they would have lined the sunrise up with a reference point on the horizon, observed from a precisely marked position. Even this was not accurate enough for them, as is seen in the many elaborate devices for solar observation that they constructed. These devices allow a thin shaft of the rising sun's first light to pass between two uprights or through an aperture, onto a wall or a circle of stones. As the year comes to an end, this light will progress in one

---

66 Wallis, Faith. *Bede The Reckoning of Time; translated, with introduction and commentary.* Liverpool University Press. 1998.

direction; then, as the sun begins to recover, it will go the other way.

Megalithic structures designed to establish the exact moment of the solstice, when life's annual cycle begins, are found all over northwest Europe. Newgrange, in Ireland, is one such monument. Inside a circle of stones is a megalithic building, which is both temple and tomb, built 5,000 years ago. The entrance is a long narrow corridor which is aligned exactly so that at sunrise on the days of the winter solstice, a shaft of light penetrates into the very heart of the temple, the holy of holies. This signalled the moment at which the year began.

Henges – circles of stones, posts or trees – are not mere calendars or observatories, where highly-trained individuals could pronounce the moment the sun's journey changed course. They were temples for the propitiation of the Goddess, where people would gather to entreat her to release the sun from the darkness of her womb and allow the cycle of life to continue. Without that, time itself would stop; spring would not come; the world would not green, and the people would die. It was as simple and as terrifying as that. The ongoing progress of time was within the gift of the Goddess; only she could allow the sun to be resurrected. Without that resurrection, everything would die, not just for a period as it does every winter, but forever.

The crowds who gathered at sacred places across the world at the winter solstice were not there to entreat a distant and powerless, dead and pale sun to get up from his deathbed, but to beg the Goddess to release him and allow time and life to continue. The year is the Goddess; in Spring she is young and fertile, in Summer bounteous, but her third phase is the Crone, who washes the bodies of the dead in preparation for burial. In a cyclical conception, life comes out of the Goddess' womb and, at the point of death, there returns, to await the moment of rebirth; and that moment is for her to decide.

Astrotheology, which was the origin of astrology and eventually astronomy, developed as a means both to predict the seasonal progression of the year and to explain the movements of the sun, moon and stars. The celestial bodies were considered to move on a 'firmament', which was envisioned as a solid dome above the Earth, and were under the control of the Earth, personified as the Goddess. This mythological relationship is a reflection of the sociological relationship between women and men in the cultures that invented it.

# SECTION THREE:

# Settlement

The hunter-gatherers lived in an insecure world. Their groups were small, which provided little room for error. If there are only a handful of fertile women, a few more women dying in childbirth than usual or not enough girls making it through to their first pregnancy because of childhood illness may become a serious problem. In addition, children, who would normally be with their mothers, are an easier target for predators and so attract them. Here we see an evolutionary imperative in action: those tribes that keep their women safe from harm have a greater chance of surviving and passing on their genes.

The Taung Child is the fossilised skull of a young *Australopithecus africanus* discovered in 1924 in South Africa. The fossil is about three million years old.[67] In 2006, researchers identified marks on the skull as being consistent with the individual having been killed by an eagle. These marks are similar to those left on modern young primates who died in the same way, as the eagle tore their eyes out of their sockets. Horrible though this is, it was the reality of life; attack by opportunist predators was never far away and children are easy targets.

While the early death of a child is a tragedy, it would have been a much lesser disaster than the death of a fertile mother. The tribe would have invested far more in her, in terms of food and support, than in a child, and the woman could make another baby. A mother's death ends her ability to contribute to the child pool of the tribe, and her existing children become a burden on the others, impacting the overall viability of the group.

Protecting women and children and keeping close to a safe refuge is a basic impulse derived from the need to ensure the survival of our genes. This impulse led naturally to a desire to develop semi-permanent and then permanent homes, where the women and children were secure.

---

67 *Australopithecus* is accepted as the ancestor of modern humans.

# Göbekli Tepe

Göbekli Tepe sits on top of a mountain ridge in the south-eastern Anatolia region of Turkey, a few kilometres north-west of the town of Şanlıurfa. It is a tell, an artificial hill, about 15 metres high and 300 metres in diameter. The site was first noted in 1963, but not properly identified. In 1994 Klaus Schmidt, who had been studying a nearby site at Nevali Çori, investigated. He saw parallels between the initial finds at Göbekli Tepe and those he had been working on at Nevali Çori. He quickly discovered monumental pillars, weighing up to sixteen tonnes, and realised that this was a find of huge importance.

Further investigation revealed that the site was first established during the tenth millennium BCE, and activity there continued until around 7500 BCE. No pottery has been found in any of the levels, and all are consistent with Epipalaeolithic or Neolithic technology. The site is culturally fascinating and significant.

The best-known and most impressive features are the T-shaped pillars made from massive blocks of limestone. These required a co-ordinated effort to quarry, move and set up. Schmidt estimates that as many as 500 people were required to remove the pillars from the quarries and haul them to the site, a distance of up to half a kilometre. The pillars weigh between ten and twenty tonnes, with one still in the quarry weighing fifty tonnes. The stones, which were set up in numerous circles, were buried and then new circles built on top, with the last level, once again, deliberately covered over in a short space of time. The backfill is comprised of earth, stone chips, weapon points, bones and refuse.

No human remains have been found to date, but Schmidt believes these will be found, perhaps in niches in the rock. On the other hand, given that burial was to become a practice of great symbolic importance, it may be that the stones themselves were being buried in some type of ritual.

Although large numbers of animal bones, mainly antelope, have been found at Göbekli Tepe, the nearest signs of human settlement are several kilometres away. The site appears to have been purely symbolic or religious; it had no permanent population, but many people gathered there. Schmidt believes it may have been a cult centre that attracted worshippers from as far as 160 kilometres away. Such a large amount of food implies that the people working to build the site, and those who visited it, were being sustained by the efforts of others who continued to hunt, gather, prepare and cook food for them. Activities may have been seasonal, with the people coming together at certain times of the year to worship and carry out cult activities and celebrations, including the construction of the site itself. This level of organisation seems much higher than had previously been considered possible in hunter-gatherer culture at that time.

The stones are carved with many representations of animals. However, no acts of violence of any sort are depicted and there are no hunting scenes or images of prey animals. There are no pictures of warfare or even of armed men. The animals are all predators and not the antelopes, wild pigs and so on that the people hunted and whose butchered and cooked bones litter the site. This artwork is interesting, especially when we consider the examples of Lascaux and Chauvet, where hunting scenes are much in evidence.

It is possible that the stones, some of which have arms and legs and are anthropomorphic, represent clans. They may have had a funerary purpose, as totems for all the clan members who died and were not buried but were left to excarnate where they died, their remains being fed upon by the types of animals depicted on the stones. These totems were then buried. This explanation would suggest a very strong connection with the natural world, which is consistent with what we know of other hunter-gatherer cultures.

While the specific cult significance of the stones may never be known, the existence of this site tells us much about the people who made it. They were hunter-gatherers who were semi-nomadic, returning to this site over and over, but not living on it. It may have been a focal point that held together a culture of semi-sedentary people who returned to it annually. The sheer size of the megaliths and the difficulties of quarrying and moving them indicate that the society was organised, yet there are no signs of social hierarchy, of differences in status or even of a priestly class.

Building Göbekli Tepe was an ongoing process that lasted two millennia. It was not a chance coming-together or an isolated event. The monument is the product of a sophisticated culture that was successful for thousands of years.

The patriarchy, with its organisational structure based on male status, is often considered essential to the development of civilisation. It has been argued that without this system of chiefs and workers, the workforces required to build monumental architecture could not be made effective. At Göbekli Tepe we see exactly the opposite: a culture with no sign of patriarchal control organising itself in such a way that it could efficiently quarry, transport, carve and erect massive megalithic structures, requiring a workforce of many hundreds.

Wherever the patriarchy has existed, it has proclaimed its presence in the art it left behind. The depiction of war and violence is a sure sign that the culture has become patriarchal. We also see indicators of hierarchical status in wealth, habitation, diet and burial methods, the building of grand palaces and defensive works. There is none of this here, so we should be sceptical that the patriarchy was in operation and seek an alternative hypothesis. The people who built Göbekli Tepe collaborated like a workers' collective in order to do the work, not like an army of obedient workers directed by a hierarchy. There were no great chiefs or leaders, and everyone was equal.

By the time Göbekli Tepe was built, it is probable that people had been become semi-sedentary. Most likely each group had a small number of sites or camps that they moved among, depending on the seasons and the availability of food. The transition from semi-sedentary life, moving between caves or living in tents or similar shelters, to living in permanent, established homes was not so great a leap. The only requirements were permanent sources of food and water.

# From Nomad to Settler

The need to find a safe place to raise the children has always been a human imperative, not less so for our ancestors. As climatic and other conditions made perennial sources of food and water available, the impetus to wander must have been balanced against the advantages of sedentary life. Likely this was a slow process, with groups continuing to migrate for part of the year. Even once the women became settled in one location all year round, the men probably still organised hunting trips into their old territories. The egalitarian two-group structure we had evolved as wandering hunter-gatherers stayed with us and developed; it was not until much later that this changed.[68]

The adoption of sedentary lifestyle was not a smooth process and was dependent on the climate and resources available. In the early stages, while the people may have cultivated small gardens on patches that they revisited during the year, there was no widespread organised agriculture. Nevertheless the cultures were successful and long-lived.

## Natufians

The Natufians lived at the western end of the Fertile Crescent, in the Middle East and Anatolia, now Turkey, twelve and a half thousand years ago. During the 1920s, British archaeologist Dorothy Garrod excavated one of their sites, at Wadi an-Natuf near Tel Aviv, and named them after it.

The Natufians were nomadic hunter-gatherers, like thousands of other scattered groups of people such as those who built Göbekli Tepe. They had lived like this for tens of thousands of years, and their society showed little change. But in the hills of the Levant, they found

68 Dyble, M. *et al. Sex equality can explain the unique social structure of hunter-gatherer bands.* Science. 15 May 2015

wild forms of wheat and barley that could be cooked and eaten. They made crude biscuits from crushed grains mixed with a little fat and water and baked on a stone. It was the beginning of bread.

Grains have crucial benefits that set them apart from the other foods gathered by foragers, and the most significant is that they can be stored. Grains will remain good for a decade or more if kept dry.

While there is evidence that the Natufians did cultivate, they did not practise this on a large scale. For hundreds of years they continued to live as they had, gathering grains at harvest-time and storing them, and hunting antelope and other game. In addition, they were responsible for another development that remains with us today, the domestication of animals.

Dogs probably first entered human camps to scavenge for scraps of food that had been discarded, but soon the benefit of cooperation must have become obvious to both sides. Dogs would help with the hunt, scenting game, tracking it, and running it down. They would scavenge and clean up around the camp, probably making things more pleasant for everyone, and they would help the mothers mind the children. As modern-dog owners can attest, family pets are reluctant to see the 'pack' separated and they will try to bring a wandering child back. It has even been suggested that they kept the children's bottoms clean! We remain unsure as to whether dogs adopted us or we adopted them.[69]

Other animals may, like dogs, have partially self-domesticated; cats feeding on the rats and mice that lived on human refuse, and even goats, well known to be able to eat almost anything. Alternatively, perhaps hunters found young goats after killing the parents and took them home, or children adopted them as pets.

People cannot live only on grains. Without the sophisticated understanding of diet that modern vegans must have just to survive, meat is essential to a healthy life. We are omnivores for a reason. The domestication of prey animals was as great an innovation as the sys-

---

69 Richard Dawkins suggests that the domestication of dogs was a two-way process, with wolves self-selecting for tameness and willingness to approach the human habitation, and then humans continuing the process. He posits an intermediary stage that he calls the 'town dog' and suggests that these were not very different from the mongrels of feral dog populations today. (Dawkins, R. *The Greatest Show on Earth: The Evidence for Evolution.* Black Swan. 2010.)

tematic harvesting and storage of grains. It was no longer necessary to hunt for meat, although it is likely that this did continue.

The human habit of chopping down trees to clear land and for firewood and the goatish habit of eating all the young saplings combine to denude terrain very efficiently. Losing the trees makes the soil vulnerable to erosion and a vicious cycle ensues, with people clearing fresh land to compensate for this until the whole area becomes deforested. This has drastic consequences for the local ecology.

The Younger Dryas was a cold and dry period that occurred between 10,800 and 9500 BCE, characterised in the Middle East by extended drought. Archaeologists believe that a combination of this and the depredations of goats caused the fragile environment that sustained the Natufians to collapse into desert. Their lifestyle was brought to an end.

Amongst the items the Natufians left, archaeologists have found one that is fascinating: a tiny statuette of a woman and a man in sexual embrace. It is known as the Ain Sakhri Lovers and is in the collection of the British Museum in London. Precisely what the significance of this was we do not know, but it is clear that sex was something the culture felt strongly enough about to make into art. We see in the successor cultures that the act of sex became hugely important as a religious act in itself; this figure may be a precursor.

## Tell es-Sultan

The Younger Dryas appears to have made sedentary life precarious and people returned to nomadic wandering. They probably took their hunting dogs and herds of goats with them, and mixed a nomadic hunter-gatherer lifestyle with a wandering herder one.

When warmer and wetter weather came, settlement was re-established very quickly, suggesting that the people had remembered the advantages it gave through their oral traditions. In the Fertile Crescent, three important, large settlements were founded.

The first of these was at Jericho. The earliest evidence of settlement here dates to 10,000 BCE. It appears that the perennial spring, today called Ein es-Sultan, remained active through the Younger Dryas drought. From 9500 BCE onwards, the occasional campsite here became a more permanent settlement and eventually an established town.

The earliest phase of settlement is known as Pre-Pottery Neolithic A (PPNA). It is characterised by an absence of any pottery and small villages of circular houses made of sun-dried mud and straw bricks, thatched with brush and mud. These houses were usually around five metres in diameter. There were hearths both indoors and out.

The people who lived here left the earliest evidence we have of an important funerary practice that would later appear elsewhere. From the earliest times, they buried their dead within their homes.

The people hunted wild game but also cultivated cereals; they were carrying on the hunter-gatherer lifestyle, but were no longer nomadic. They had no need to wander because they could hunt, find, or grow enough to eat the whole year round. This transitional culture retained much of the previous lifestyle while introducing new practices and ideas. It is probable that, at least at first, the settlers lacked confidence that the droughts would not return, but as time went by their camps developed into organised, permanent settlements.

Estimates of the size of the settlement now known as Tell es-Sultan vary. Some sources believe it may have had as many as two to three thousand inhabitants at the peak of its success. Others suggest a much lower population, perhaps as low as two or three hundred at maximum. Tell es-Sultan has unusual architectural features: a stone wall 3.6 metres high and a tower of the same height with twenty-two internal steps.[70] These were massive structures and clear precursors to the monumental architecture that would come to characterise patriarchal cities. Their purpose remains enigmatic, but one explanation is that the wall was built as a defence against flood water and the tower for religious purposes.[71] Whatever their function, the effort required to construct them is estimated to have been at least equivalent to one

---

70 Mithen, Steven. *After the ice: a global human history, 20,000-5000 BCE* Harvard University Press. 2006.

71 Akkermans, Peter M. M & Schwartz, Glenn M. *The Archaeology of Syria: From Complex Hunter-Gatherers to Early Urban Societies (c.16,000-300 BCE)*. Cambridge University Press. 2004.

hundred men working for one hundred days.

After the PPNA period a new culture appeared, called Pre-Pottery Neolithic B (PPNB), characterised by rectangular houses built of elongated brick. Skulls, upon which the flesh had been replaced with moulded plaster, were found in these houses. It is believed that the skulls were buried under the floors of the houses long enough for the flesh to rot, then dug up and the plaster applied to form a likeness of the person in life. These skulls were then kept in the houses of the living, and may have been venerated, or regarded as having contact with the world of spirits. These are sophisticated artworks, which were not only plastered, but also painted. Shells were inserted into the eye-sockets to represent eyes, and even moustaches and beards were painted on. This elaborate process indicates the existence of a religious culture which may have been based on ancestor worship and the concept of life after death.[72] Most of the skulls that have been recovered are those of men, although some are of women and children.

According to Dr. Hamdan Taha,[73]

'The Neolithic Period at Tell es-Sultan represents the transformations during the first period of human history from a prehistoric subsistence pattern based on hunting and gathering, to a new subsistence pattern based on domestication of plants and animals of the first settled society. The production surplus of agriculture enabled human beings to free part of their time, which was dedicated in the past to securing food, for building houses and creating art. The material culture of this period indicates the growing social complexity of Neolithic society.'[74]

Tell es-Sultan is interesting because it appears to contain the

---

72 It has been suggested that these represent the beginning of the art of portraiture, but this is a dubious claim. However they are certainly the first evidence of portraiture of the dead as a central cultural element.

73 Dr. Taha was Deputy Assistant Minister for Antiquities and Cultural Heritage in the Ministry of Tourism and Antiquities of the Palestinian Authority.

74 http://www.thisweekinpalestine.com/details.php?id=3083&ed=181&edid=181 Retrieved 23/06/14.

precursors of the characteristics typical of later, violence-based, patriarchal cultures. Yet there is no evidence of generalised warfare or violence at this time and furthermore, all evidence of patriarchal culture vanishes for thousands of years afterwards. It is possible that this settlement was founded by people who had been displaced by drought and sought to predate on others using the perennial spring. This might explain the wall and tower. If this were the case, then the fact that it was a historical cul-de-sac might lead us to ponder whether this early version of the patriarchy was dependent on the presence of easy victims, and when wetter weather came and those potential prey went elsewhere, it died. This would speak to the parasitic nature of the patriarchy, the success of which depends on the exploitation of the vulnerable by the violent. If the tower and walls of Tell es-Sultan do indeed indicate the first incidence of patriarchy, then they show something else too: without easy prey, it collapses.

# Çatal Hoyuk

Elsewhere, a different and, initially at least, more successful societal model appeared. A thousand kilometres to the north and west of Jericho, near Konya in modern Turkey, is the next great example of early settlement. It is known today as Çatal Hoyuk, and it has been a far richer source of information about our early settled ancestors than Tell es-Sultan. Jericho, although abandoned for long periods, was settled throughout the Bronze Age, meaning that the earlier buildings were plundered. Çatal Hoyuk was never resettled after it was abandoned, and appears to have remained untouched until it was discovered in 1958. The British archaeologist James Mellaart led several expeditions to the site during the 1960s before becoming embroiled in a row with the Turkish government. This dispute led to the site being abandoned by archaeology until 1993, when the current investigations began, led by Ian Hodder, a former student of Mellaart.

Çatal Hoyuk sits on a tell, or mound, rising twenty metres. Some distance away from the larger settlement there is another mound that was settled at the same time. Neither has a defensive wall or fortifications. Between the two mounds, a branch of the Çarşamba River flowed. The fertile alluvial plain was well-watered and full of game. Eventually, this plain would be cultivated.

The houses were built together in such a way that they were like the cells in a honeycomb, with access via timber ladders or stairs, through hatches. They had no windows, and their roofs were effectively the roadways and public spaces. The materials were simple: sundried mud bricks and timber.

As is often the case, the settlement renewed itself by building on its ruins. Older homes were partially demolished into the space they occupied, and new ones built on top. Archaeologists have identified eighteen layers of such rebuilding.

Çatal Hoyuk was established around 7500 BCE, reached its peak five hundred years later, and was abandoned around 5700 BCE. This is a longer time than that which has elapsed since the collapse of the Western Roman Empire in Europe. Throughout this period, the pace of social change appears to be progressive, with no evidence of cathartic upheaval or any sign of war. According to Hodder, the difference between the oldest and youngest layers is considerable and points to the development of settled culture as a process that began with settlement and then moved to cultivation. The people initially continued their hunter-gatherer lifestyle while living a settled, communal life.[75]

The culture was simple and conservative, yet at the same time refined. Although population levels probably varied, it is estimated that Çatal Hoyuk was home to around 5000 to 8000 people.

The interiors of the homes in Çatal Hoyuk were rendered with lime plaster. Lime plaster has many advantages: it is relatively easy to make and apply and it is somewhat astringent, keeping the building healthy. The whiteness also would have brightened the windowless interiors. Because of the construction of the buildings, people, supplies and the smoke from cooking on the open hearths and in the ovens inside all had to pass through the trap in the ceiling. The open fires had no flues, so the walls and ceilings would have blackened quickly, which is probably the reason the plaster was frequently reapplied.

Mats woven of rushes covered the floors and were also used on the roofs. Inside, raised mud-brick benches served as beds and couches. The houses had storage spaces reached through low doorways, but family life appears to have been communal, with everyone sharing the same living and sleeping space. This shared space must also have been the space for sex, providing a link with the sexual practices in polyamorous matriarchal cultures and once again disproving the assertion that human sex is always private. Perhaps, in very hot weather, people moved onto the roofs to sleep, as they would later do in Uruk.

No public buildings have been found at Çatal Hoyuk and all the spaces are domestic. Some have intricate murals, but their significance remains obscure.

The flat space above the homes provided a safe place for children to play and learn. While it is unlikely that schools as we know them existed, it is almost certain that the mothers would have come together on the roofs of their houses to chat and work while their children were around them. On adjoining rooftops, people were perhaps

---

75 Hodder, Ian. *A Journey to 9000 years ago*. Cited by Ziflioglu, Vercihan. Turkish Daily News. January 2008. (http://www.hurriyetdailynews.com/default.aspx?pageid=438&n=a-journey-to-9000-years-ago-2008-01-17)

burning limestone or lime sand to make plaster, shaping stone tools, or carving wood for furniture and farming implements. The children would have learned the skills of adulthood in this place by watching and helping.

Also on the roofs were large ovens. It is possible that the roofs were, in part, a communal dining area, perhaps protected by from the elements by light structures. Perhaps this was a regular or even daily occurrence, or perhaps it happened on special days like the solstices or other celestial festivals. The flat roof of the town may have served in exactly the same way as market-places in later towns, with the advantage of being much more economical of land.

A feature of life at Çatal Hoyuk was the scrupulous cleanliness of the people. Archaeologists have found very little refuse or waste inside the houses, and there are middens outside the settlement filled with household refuse and large quantities of wood ash.

In Çatal Hoyuk, we are not looking at a 'primitive' culture, but a vibrant and sophisticated one. The people were house-proud and liked to make their homes beautiful, and their communal life was colourful and peaceful. It is very likely that the people extended the care they took in the appearance of their homes to their persons, and would have decorated themselves. James Mellaart commented on the obsidian beads he found, indicating that the people wore jewellery.[76] They may have dressed their hair. This was a thriving, successful and materially and spiritually rich society.

Early on in his investigation of Çatal Hoyuk, Mellaart discovered many female figurines. These were carved from marble, limestone, schist, calcite, basalt and alabaster as well as moulded from clay. Particularly well-known is a seated matron, flanked by two great cats, possibly lions. She is obese; her breasts are huge and pendulous, and her belly distended and sagging. Her expression is stern and impassive. Mellaart thought that these figurines indicated that the Great Mother was the principal deity of the culture.

In his book, *Çatal Huyuk: A Neolithic Town in Anatolia*, Mellaart says:

---

76 Mellaart, James. *Çatal Huyuk: A Neolithic Town in Anatolia*. Thames and Hudson. 1967.

'...statues of a female deity far outnumber those of the male deity, who moreover, does not appear to be represented at all after Level VI'[77]

Hodder also found figurines. Of one, he says:

'There are full breasts on which the hands rest, and the stomach is extended... the arms are very thin, and then on the back of the figurine one sees a depiction of either a skeleton or the bones of a very thin and depleted human. The ribs and vertebrae are clear, as are the scapulae and the main pelvic bones. The figurine can be interpreted in a number of ways – as a woman turning into an ancestor, as a woman associated with death, or as death and life conjoined. It is possible that the lines around the body represent wrapping rather than ribs... Perhaps (it) was related to some special role of the female in relation to death as much as to the roles of mother and nurture.'[78]

Here, Hodder appears to be unaware that the Goddess not only represents 'mother and nurture', but also old age, sickness and death. She is both loving and terrifying, the bringer of death as well as of life. The depiction of the Goddess as death, especially as death and life conjoined, is exactly what we should expect to find in a Goddess culture.

Renowned archaeologist Marija Gimbutas explained,

'Mother Goddess is a more complex image than most people think...She was giver of life...and at the same time she was the wielder of the destructive powers of nature.'[79]

Moving from the spiritual to the social-political, Hodder says:

---

77 *Ibid.*

78 Hodder, Ian. *New finds and new interpretations at Çatalhöyük.* Çatalhöyük 2005 Archive Report. Catalhoyuk Research Project, Institute of Archaeology. 2005.

79 Gimbutas, Marija. The Gods and Goddesses of Old Europe. University of California Press. (2nd Revised edition.) 2007.

'If one's social status was of high importance in Çatal-höyük, the body and head were separated after death. The number of female and male skulls found during the excavations is almost equal.'[80]

From this and other evidence, such as food remains, Hodder believes that at Çatal Hoyuk there was equality between men and women. This equality, he says, means there was no matriarchy.

This conclusion is flawed. Hodder's definition of a matriarchy is a patriarchal one. It assumes that in a matriarchal society, there will be exact equivalents to the hierarchical structure of power that is found in patriarchies. There will be queens instead of kings, women warriors instead of male ones. Civic governance will be by formal hierarchies of women; the laws will be made by women, and the judges and enforcers will be women.

There is no evidence whatsoever that, at any time in human history, such a society has ever existed. The matriarchy is not the patriarchy inverted. The definition of a phenomenon must arise organically, from our observations and other empirical evidence. We cannot predetermine the parameters that might define a phenomenon and then, because we do not find these, claim that the phenomenon does not exist!

Peggy Reeves Sanday has written:

'Defining matriarchy as the mirror image of patriarchy is based on two faulty assumptions. The first assumption is that women must be like men to occupy a central position in society. The second is that social prominence for either sex is founded only in social power as we know it, which always means power over people...Defining matriarchy either in terms of female rule or by reference solely to mother goddesses blinds us to the social complexities of women's actual and symbolic role in partnership societies...mainstream scholars looked no further and proclaimed universal male dominance. *This is a mistake.*'

---

80 Hodder, Ian. *A Journey to 9000 years ago.*

(our italics.)[81]

Hodder, in common with many others, is making the presumption that the matriarchy is exactly like the patriarchy, but with women in charge and men playing a subservient role. Were this misrepresentation true then it would indeed be hard to see why men, with their greater physical strength and tendency towards violence, would put up with the subjugation.

Within the patriarchy there is a self-reinforcing agenda which holds that the only viable structure for a developed society is the pyramidal, hierarchical, top-down, elitist patriarchal model, based on a military command structure. The patriarchy promotes this as the only natural form of human culture; not merely one possible model. But this is a deception; other models have existed and still do, even today, despite millennia of the patriarchy attempting to destroy them.

These other models exhibit no trace of the patriarchy, or restrict its influence to the society of men. To understand the social order that is operating in these cultures, we must first observe and note the common factors. Among the most significant of these are: women's complete control over their bodies and fertility; non-proprietorial human bonding arrangements; the open acceptance of transgender people; the acceptance of same-sex bonding; the absence of organised military structures; the absence of monumental buildings and the absence of elevated status for either men or women. When we see these factors we can say that the patriarchy is not in control. Once we take away all that defines the patriarchy, then we are left with another, different system, and that system defines itself as the matriarchy.

From this standpoint, of observation rather than presumption, we can offer a supported definition of the matriarchy: it is a collective culture based on independent, but interdependent, often closely related mothers who organise society for the safe upbringing of their children. The matriarchy is not the patriarchy with women in place of men, but something altogether different.

Observation of wider human society reveals that, although there

---

81 Sanday, Peggy Reeves. *Matriarchal Values and World Peace: The Case of the Minangkabau.* Paper delivered to the 2nd World Congress on Matriarchal Studies, Texas, 2005.

may be variations in the appearances of specific models, there are in fact only two cultural alternatives. One is based on violence and competition and is hierarchical, with males always having higher status. The other is based on peaceful cooperation, is firmly egalitarian, and in it women and men are of equal status. These are the patriarchy and the matriarchy.

At Çatal Hoyuk, there is no evidence of kingship, a ruling hierarchy, war or violence; there is no city wall, no defences at all. The settlement is in plain sight. There are no palaces or grand dwellings, and women and men are of equal status. This culture is not representative of the patriarchy. Therefore, we may conclude that a matriarchy was operating at Çatal Hoyuk.

When people began to settle, the two cultural groups within hunter-gatherer society, one based on mothers and gatherers and the other on male hunters, came together more permanently. Each had its internal hierarchy and neither was dominant over the other. We now know, from the findings at Çatal Hoyuk as well as discoveries in other parts of Anatolia, that the first settlers were hunter-gatherers, and continued this lifestyle for hundreds of years. They developed agriculture slowly as a result of settlement, not the other way round. Because of this, it is very likely that they maintained the social structures they had established over thousands of years of wandering. In other words, women and men were equals but they had different spheres of authority: women within the home and family and men outside.

Hodder points to another hypothesis, which is that the houses in Çatal Hoyuk were clustered according to extended family units. The people buried their dead inside their homes, and he believes that when the oldest person in the family group died, the house was ceremonially caved in on itself, locking the dead into the remains. This begs the question 'who was that oldest person?' Was it a patriarch or a matriarch?

In traditional society as it currently exists in the Philippines, parts of Africa, Southern Europe and elsewhere, we see extended families based around a matriarch. In the Philippines, one reason for the existence of this matriarchy appears to be that so many of the men work away from home.[82] This is a parallel to the two-group social structure we see in hunter-gatherers, adapted to settled living.

Frequently, in such Filipina homes, several members of the family may sleep in the same room, which is often the main communal living area. Three or more generations live together this way, with the head of the household being the grandmother, who is often also the owner of the property. Grouped together in one 'compound' may be several such homes, and frequently the women at the head of each family thus housed are sisters. Sometimes the compound is owned jointly by them, or it may be owned by a great-grandmother or even more senior mother, who has granted permission to her daughters to construct homes. In even older examples, there may be no distinct properties within the compound at all, just one big, rambling house, shared by everyone.[83] Decisions about the families, about common repairs to the properties and other communal matters, are made by the group of mothers.

In Çatal Hoyuk, there were no written codes or contracts because the people were not literate. Thus, it is likely that land tenure followed a similar model, and that this was the standard model in early settled cultures. It may be that this structure first appeared in settlements like Çatal Hoyuk and has simply persisted, overlooked or ignored by a patriarchal world-view obsessed by notions of 'legal possession'.[84]

When we take these factors into account, the picture of life at Çatal Hoyuk comes into better focus. In all likelihood it was little different from the domestic matriarchies we see today in much of Asia, Africa and Latin America. Hodder's suggestions about the extended family living in one sedentary locus do not in any way conflict with the notion of the matriarchy, as long as we understand what the core concept of matriarchy is – the extended family based on the oldest mother.

---

82 This is similar to the situation which has caused the matriarchy to be maintained amongst the Minangkabau of Indonesia.

83 The basis of property tenure of Filipina homes like this may seem strange, at least to Western eyes. The reader should remember that Western property laws are based on the patriarchal system of ownership, and upon written codes.

84 The patriarchal system of property ownership is one of the principal means by which the patriarchy divests the majority of wealth and concentrates it in the hands of a few.

The above helps us to contextualise the question of whether the oldest person whose death provoked the demolition and rebuilding of homes in Çatal Hoyuk would have been a man or a woman. The answer must be that there is no good evidence to suggest that it could only have been a man. Rather, given also that women do, on average, live longer than men, the probability must be that most if not all would have been matriarchs.

The form of matriarchy present at Çatal Hoyuk would have been simply a development of how people lived in the nomadic hunter-gatherer era. The group of mothers lived and moved together with the children and formed the nucleus of the culture, while the men wandered far in search of game. The impetus for settlement came from women, who wanted a safe place in which to bear and raise their children with their families united around them. They settled first, while the men continued to travel far in search of game.

This interpretation also suggests that civic governance at Çatal Hoyuk was in the hands of women, who defined the matriarchal groups that were clustered together. Like the system of property tenure, this was probably an informal arrangement without the defined hierarchy that characterises patriarchal systems of government. There was no formal organisation, simply, as Hodder says, family groups 'doing their own thing' – and led by the matriarchs.

A number of figurines found at Çatal Hoyuk show a twinned pair of women. Each has four breasts and two heads. These may symbolise the sisterhood of women that was the basis of the culture, and Hodder has theorised that these figurines indicate the 'extended family'. This observation fits exactly with the others and supports the idea that the culture was composed of clans centred on women.

There are no palaces or other public buildings because these are a function of the display of status that is central to the patriarchy. In a matriarchy, they are not required since there is no hierarchy of status; the society is collective and cooperative and founded on sisterhood. It is only within the patriarchy that status is seen as a hierarchy of power, whether that is in military, political or economic terms, and the legal possession of property. In the matriarchy, it is seen in terms of motherhood and family.

The evidence of Çatal Hoyuk, far from challenging them, confirms the existence of both Goddess culture and a matriarchy.

Although Çatal Hoyuk was ultimately abandoned, the same agrarian, settled lifestyle appeared in many other areas and there it took hold.[85]

# Ain Ghazal

Ain Ghazal is a large Neolithic site that was first established around 7250 BCE. It is located in what is now Jordan, near Amman. The peak of its success appears to have been around 7000 BCE, and the site was abandoned 2000 years later. The site was discovered in 1974 by engineers building a road, but unfortunately excavation did not begin until 1982, by which time much damage had already been done. The site is now under threat from urban development. Nevertheless it has been a rich source of finds and information.

The population rose to about 3000 by 7000 BCE, was sustained for about 500 years and afterwards it shrank to around 300. This fall has been attributed to environmental circumstances that may have been partly caused by the goats the people herded.

Like Tell es-Sultan and Çatal Hoyuk, no pottery is associated with the settlement. Hunting and gathering were pursued alongside cultivation, and the reasons for settlement are probably the same as at the other two: perennial water and natural food supply. The people cultivated cereals, peas, beans and chickpeas, and hunted antelope, wild pigs and horses, as well as hares and other small game.

The rectangular houses were built of sun-dried mud bricks. The exteriors were rendered with mud and the interiors with lime plaster, which was regularly renewed. They were built in terraces on a hillside overlooking a valley. Each had one main room and an anteroom. As

---

85 The reasons are obscure but probably had to do with climate change or soil erosion or exhaustion caused by a combination of unsophisticated farming techniques, the systematic clearing of trees and the depredations of domestic goats.

at Çatal Hoyuk, no evidence of defensive architecture has been found or any large civic buildings. It is probable that the people lived in extended family groups which, once again, would probably have been centred on a matriarch.

The burial practices at Ain Ghazal remain somewhat mysterious, but they reflect those first seen in Natufian culture. Some people were buried inside the homes, and of these, some had the heads later removed and re-buried in separate pits. Why only some were chosen for this treatment and not others is not clear. We do not know whether the heads spent some time between the interments on display, but they may have. It is possible that the dead were buried quickly because of the corruption of the body, to avoid the foul smells and risk of disease. After a while, the heads may have been dug up to allow the family time to mourn and pay their respects.

So far, everything fits the overall pattern of settled Neolithic life that was appearing in many parts of the region, as illustrated at Çatal Hoyuk. However, Ain Ghazal has revealed one fascinating development. Thirty-two figurines made of lime plaster moulded onto bundles of twigs have been found. These are approximately half life-size and have cowrie shell eyes with bitumen pupils. Fifteen full figures have been discovered, along with fifteen busts and two partial heads. The figures were not scattered about the site but were in two discrete locations.[86]

Strikingly, three of the busts are two-headed. These call to mind the two-headed figures of women found at Çatal Hoyuk, but do not have breasts, so their gender is uncertain and may represent a woman and a man. They are not sexualised, as was the tantalising Natufian figure of a couple making love, but gaze straight ahead at the viewer. They might suggest a shift from venerating the Great Goddess as the supreme deity, to accepting two, or at least a binary deity, the female/male partnership. The two discrete groups of hunter-gatherer life were joined in settled society, and this may be the cultural expression of that.

This interpretation of the figurines is supported by later mythology. There was first a Great Mother, who conceived life without

---

86 Unfortunately, because of the damage to the site, many others may have existed but will never be found.

requiring a mate. Then the first Great Mother, known by a host of names across the planet, and represented either as the Sea or the Earth, gave birth to twins, one female and one male. These twins were both sister and brother, and woman and consort; the single unitary deity had become binary.

Çatal Hoyuk and Ain Ghazal represent a societal stage that persisted in Mesopotamia for thousands of years. During this horticultural phase, crops were raised in small gardens, principally by women. Foraging and hunting remained the primary methods for acquiring resources. The lifestyle continued as before, mixing hunting and gathering with horticulture and limited animal husbandry, but now people had discrete, permanent living spaces. The genders remained equal, and there is no evidence of warrior culture or endemic violence.

# Drawing a Parallel: The Toraja

The Toraja people live on the island of Sulawesi in Indonesia. They are agriculturalists and produce a variety of crops, especially rice. While their culture has been badly damaged by the activities of Christian missionaries, in modified form their traditional beliefs are still followed by about thirty percent of the population, or around 100,000 individuals.

The core of the culture is called 'Aluk To Dolo'. This is a complex tradition that involves ancestor worship, animism and other beliefs. The Toraja believe that in the beginning the Earth and Sky were married, and there was darkness; then they were separated and there was light.

From the marriage of Earth and Sky were born the deities.[87] This has close similarities to other ancient mythologies, particularly the Sumerian, suggesting that there may be a common origin.[88] The Torajan pantheon contains both female and male deities. The cycle of life

---

87 http://www.philtar.ac.uk/encyclopedia/indon/toraj.html (Retrieved 14/11/2014.)
88 We will discuss Sumerian mythology in depth in the next Section.

is separated into a part of fertility, light and life, and a part of death, decay and darkness. These are identified with the upper and lower worlds respectively.

The University of Durham's *Philtar* site provides this description:

> '(Humanity's) role is to help maintain equilibrium be-
> tween the upper world and the underworld by rituals.
> There are two divisions of rituals. The 'Rambu Tuka', the
> Rising Sun or Smoke Ascending rituals are associated
> with the north and east, with joy and life. This includes
> rituals for birth, marriage, health, the house, the com-
> munity, and rice. The 'Rambu Solo', the Setting Sun or
> Smoke Descending rituals are associated with the south
> and west, with darkness, night, and death. Healing ritu-
> als partake of both divisions. The most important Ram-
> bu Tuka ritual is the Bua' feast in which the buraka, a
> priestess or hermaphrodite priest, petitions the gods of
> heaven to look after the community. The Merok feast
> is for the benefit of a large family. Rambu Solo' rituals
> include great death feasts at funerals conducted by the
> death priest. These funerals are now the main feature of
> Toraja religion.'[89]

It is important to the Toraja that the 'great feasts' and other fu-
nerary rites are properly respected, and in Toraja terms, this means spending large amounts of wealth on them. Many animals will be sacrificed and eaten. Since the Toraja are relatively simple hill-farm-ers, the families of the deceased may have to save for years to pay for these ceremonies. This leads to a phenomenon that is of interest here.

After death but before the official death feast and funeral, the dead are carefully wrapped in layers of cloth and placed temporar-ily under the tongkonan or family home. This causes their bodies to mummify. The corpses may remain there for years while the fami-ly saves for the funeral. Every August the bodies are unwrapped by the families in a ceremony called 'Ma'Nene'.[90] They are washed and

---

89 http://www.philtar.ac.uk/encyclopedia/indon/toraj.html (Retrieved 14/11/2014.)
90 As a result of tourism, this ritual now also happens at other times of year.

their clothes are repaired and changed and their hair gently tended. The mummies are then walked through the lands – always in straight lines – by their relatives. They are placed in positions of honour at the community feast, as observers, before being re-buried.

Finally, after their funerary celebrations, the dead are placed in coffins, which are buried in one of a number of ways, either in caves carved out from cliffs or suspended on ropes attached to them. The coffins of children may be hung from trees.

The parallels with what we have seen in Natufian, Çatal Hoyuk and Ain Ghazal cultures are striking. The dead are temporarily laid to rest under the family home. They are later exhumed (perhaps many times) and interact with their families and friends. They walk through their lands as they once did, assisted by family and friends, and then they are re-buried. While we cannot precisely know what specific rituals were being carried out in the ancient cultures, the Toraja provide us with a fascinating glimpse of what they were possibly like.

The division of life into two equal halves, that of life and light, Rambu Tuku, and that of death and darkness, Rambu Solo, is fundamental. Although Rambu Tuku has been suppressed because of the influence of Christianity and Islam, the two were once equal, symbolising harmony and balance. When this equilibrium is achieved, then harmony and peace will prevail. When one part of this is suppressed, the culture becomes unbalanced. Typically, this imbalance will allow bad things to happen, like natural disasters, famine, disease or crop failure.

Rambu Tuku, the half that deals with light, life and birth, is under the control of women. This is made clear by the gender of the officiating clerics. They are either natal women or 'hermaphrodites'. Since genuine hermaphrodites, who possess in full both female and male sexual and reproductive organs, are vanishingly rare in humans, this probably refers to transgender or possibly intersex women.[91]

We saw how the Red Lady of Pavilland may have been a transgender priestess, and the same phenomenon is seen here. Why are transgender women involved in rituals such as this? The answer may be that transgender people symbolise change, evolution and trans-

---

91 Intersex refers to a range of conditions which may result in indeterminate sexual organs or parts of both female and male organs, not the complete possession of both.

formation: transition. Transgender women represent the death of the male and rebirth as a woman, through the rejection of manhood and the embrace of femininity.[92] In a fundamental sense, they are never fully one or the other and so represent the state of transition itself.

Transition is a recurring constant in life yet it is deeply mysterious. It exists at the point of birth and also of death, when we are neither one nor the other. Transition is a fluid state of being that defies rigid rules and classifications, and for most of us it is fleeting. Transgender people, on the other hand, are permanently at this point, constantly in transition. Because they personify this potent yet mysterious phase, they are not vilified in Goddess cultures but instead are revered as shamans, priestesses, bringers of good luck and blessing, and as servants of the Goddess.[93]

Rambu Tuku, then, is a celebration of the Divine Feminine, the Goddess as bringer of light and life. The other half of Aluk To Dolo, Rambu Solo, is concerned with death, decay and darkness. In pre-agricultural cultures, this was also under the aegis of the Goddess and the rituals would have been presided over by women. The Goddess was in charge of everything that had to do with the home life of the people, from birth to death, and this was a cycle: death leads to birth just as birth leads to death, and women are the key to this. One early expression of the transferral of power is that male deities take control of the afterlife.[94] Rambu Solo death ceremonies are presided over by a male death-priest.

From all of these clues, we can identify the developmental point at which the overall Torajan culture sits, or at least sat before it was damaged by Christian and Islamic interference. It is sedentary, indeed

---

92 We should emphasise that this is not by choice. While the specific causes of transgender are still unknown, it is now accepted that it is not a mental condition but a form of intersex. The American Psychiatric Association, along with other similar bodies, no longer considers it a 'disorder'. (American Psychiatric Association. *Diagnostic and Statistical Manual of Mental Disorders, Fifth Edition (DSM-5)* American Psychiatric Publishing. 2013.)

93 Transgender is relatively common in many parts of the world such as Asia, where later religious traditions like Christianity, Islam and Buddhism have been overlaid, often by force, on pre-existing cultures that had transgender people at its heart. In Indonesia such pre-existing traditions are called adat and may be accepted; see for example our discussion of the Minang people.

94 See the relationship of Nepthys and Set in Egypt for comparison.

settled, and agricultural, yet it has not developed the obsession with building 'monumental architecture' that patriarchal historians believe defines a 'civilised' culture. Torajans know the concepts of property, personal possessions and money, but they are bilineal, meaning that both material property and names are inherited through both maternal and paternal lines.[95] The female and male elements of the culture are equal, and within the society women and men are equal.

Their understanding of marriage is more one of partnership than possession, and it occurs within the context of extended, already-related families. The society is extremely close-knit, and Torajan villages are each effectively one extended family.[96]

Given the artefacts and what we know of how the people of Çatal Hoyuk and Ain Ghazal lived, as well as their precursors, the Natufians, it is reasonable to suggest that their cultures were similar to the Toraja. But this begs a question: if models like the Torajan have existed since at least the time of Çatal Hoyuk, why are they not the norm today?

As we explore the cultures that followed Çatal Hoyuk, we will see how gradual changes occurred, changes that eventually caused seismic shifts in the balance of power within the society. We will unravel the tale of how men, instead of sharing authority and status equally with women, assumed dominance over them. This resulted in millennia of war, genocide, colonial invasions, imperialism and plunder. Whole populations were killed or enslaved and any non-conformity or dissent punished with brutal severity. Within this new phase, men took control of everything. Through violence and the threat of it, they seized all political and religious power and material wealth. They destroyed the Goddess and deliberately, overtly, denigrated and devalued women. This phase is called the patriarchy, and it is important that we understand it; we live under it today.

---

95 This power to name – both in the sense of the name given to children and the title they earn by their life's efforts, is significant. It is regarded in many traditional societies as a way to confer special attributes or ward off evil spirits.

96 Torajans have special rules to prevent the marriage of those who are too closely related and whose offspring might be at risk of congenital defects.

# SECTION FOUR:

# The Sacred Marriage

## Changing Perceptions of Sex

Why do we think the way we do about various kinds of relationships? The fascinating answer to this question is closely connected to, in fact inseparable from, the gradual cultural development of our species, from the earliest hunter-gatherers to today's post-modern society.

Currently, same-sex relations have been documented in over 450 different animal species. They can result in superior care for offspring, and alleviate tensions within reproducing pairs. The existence of this behaviour is quite prevalent, and may confer certain evolutionary advantages.[97]

We saw amongst the hunter-gatherers that same-sex bonding is a natural and potentially beneficial part of the human condition as well. Sex fulfils a variety of roles including bonding, compassion, reward and simply pleasure, and the specific sex of the partners is not relevant for these interactions.

How then, did the prevailing attitudes about sex and partnering come to be?

At some point in our history the relationship between sex and conception became understood, not just as secret 'women's wisdom' but by everyone. This began a subtle transformation in the way we thought about sex.

Once sex was understood as the vehicle through which life was created, it came to be seen metaphorically as an essential factor in

---

97 Comments by Arash Fereydooni referring to research by biologists Nathan W. Bailey and Marlene Zuk, University of California. (*Do Animals Exhibit Homosexuality? Yale Scientific.* March 14, 2012.)

the annual regeneration of the seasons and thus the assurance of the fertility of the land and the ongoing passage of time. Natural events like the changing seasons and the rise and fall in the declination of the sun became connected in mythology to divine reproductive sex.

While Goddess cultures and those cultures based in them remain very tolerant of different expressions of gender and sexuality, the idea that the Goddess needed to have divine sex in order to assure the continuance of time meant that reproductive sex acquired special status.

One of the most interesting and culturally significant expressions of this is in hierogamy, or the Great Rite.

In the earliest form, the Great Rite was an affirmation of female reproductive power. It was an act of sex consummated in public, in a place of devotion, by a female shaman and a male partner. The function of this rite was to cause the shaman to conceive. Because she was identified as the Goddess incarnate during the ritual, her conception meant that the Goddess also conceived and so would give birth to a new year and ensure the ongoing passage of time.

Conception of new life became the imperative that drove Goddess societies. They were not only birth-oriented, but also conception-oriented.

This is a subtle, but significant transition. Originally, the Goddess gave birth independently, so conception was not an issue. Now, sex that could lead to conception was venerated not just as a pleasure, reward or bond, but as a religious and culturally affirming act in itself. Reproductive sex, in other words, became an act of divine significance, of worship.

# Heirogamy: The Great Rite

In the Great Rite, a female shaman played the role of the Goddess, to whom she was closely bound through prayer, meditation and other ritual practices, such as the use of alcohol and narcotics. The bond was profound, for in her travels into the spirit- realm, the shaman literally became the Goddess; she was the embodiment of this mighty power, the source of all Creation and of time itself.

A partner was chosen from amongst the young men. Likely, as was continued in later versions, the choice was a matter of profound spirituality that required the satisfaction of many rules. Auguries would have been cast, meditations practised and arcane lore known only to women discussed in the search for the right partner. It is likely that the shaman was surrounded and assisted by the other women in making the choice, since similar phenomena are seen in later, similar cultures. It is possible that the boy had to be a virgin; we see an inversion of this in later cultures where the bride must be untouched and this is by no means the only such inversion we will discover.

Once selected, the boy would have been lionised. He had been identified as the Goddess' consort, and thus was a central figure in the culture. His semen was required to fertilise the Goddess, in the form of her earthly avatar, and so assure the continuation of time. This would have been a great honour for him and for his family. He would have been anointed with oils and unguents and dressed in ceremonial robes, while his family would have been rewarded with blessings and favours.

The shaman, and later the High Priestesses who inherited this role, would also have prepared herself as she did for a journey into the spirit world. She would ingest drugs, chant or dance. She would be perfumed and adorned with her jewellery and her hair coiffed. Her face and eyes would be made up, making her features the more striking.

It is possible that hierogamy was the portal into the life of a shaman amongst the sisterhood of women. In other words; perhaps conceiving new life was an original 'rite of passage' through which a girl not only became a woman, but also part of a powerful caste of female shamans.

On the other hand, the shaman might have been an older, more experienced woman, perhaps even the 'first amongst equals', the matriarch herself.[98]

Resplendent in her beauty, wearing the ornate finery placed upon her by her sisters, already in an altered state of consciousness as a result of the preliminary rites, the shaman would appear before the tribe. She was the Goddess now, the power of Creation personified, and the focus was her womb and her vagina. Likely her breasts were bare – we know that in later Goddess cultures this was commonplace and a sign of power – and indeed, she may have been naked or nearly so, apart from her adornments.

She would proceed to a prepared bed and there wait while her consort was brought to her. He too would also have been made-up, oiled and prepared. Possibly, through the use of herbs and drugs or by other means, he was already erect; later images depict the Goddess' consort with a naked, erect penis.

While the other women chanted and in the dancing light of fires, the young man approached the bed where the shaman lay. This was a highly sexualised and charged environment, full of music and drums and perfumed smoke. The atmosphere would have been as conducive to a successful sexual union as possible. Both parties knew what to do and had most likely been rigorously coached in how to perform, since it was essential that the ritual should be enacted properly for its power to have effect.[99]

Then, before the gathered people and while ritual verses were chanted, the shaman and her consort would come together in sexual union. This moment, at which the phallus and womb come together, had huge cultural significance – and would have for millennia.[100]

---

98 The later literature provides evidence for both models, as will be discussed.

99 In these societies sex, while often surrounded by cultural rules and rituals, was and remains a very open part of everyday life. People, uncorrupted by the bizarre and arbitrary rules surrounding sex that are only a part of later cultural baggage, do not feel the need to hide sexuality or sexual behaviour. Sex was not an exclusively private act; within homes with more than one generation and many children living in communal, large rooms, it was rather a shared expression of love.

100 The Egyptian ankh, for example, depicts the moment at which the phallus and womb come together, thus symbolising creation and life.

The Great Rite was not just spiritual but shamanistic in nature. The act was highly ritualised. The chanting of poems and words, the carrying out of specific acts, including bathing and changing clothes, the couple lying together in specific ways, and the presence of not only an audience but assistants to the principal couple, all carry the hallmarks of shamanistic rite. Since the imperative was that the shaman should conceive and this ritual was so important, the couple would have remained together until the woman's menstruation stopped and she knew that she was with child.

Sex releases into the blood natural stimulants that not only heighten our pleasure, but also cause us to step outside our everyday consciousness into a metaphysical world. Sex is an out-of-body experience, which produces a union of the physical and spiritual and which, when shared with someone we love, reinforces and revitalises that love.

But the relationship between sex and consciousness has other implications. The physiological changes that engender the psychological pleasures we enjoy during and after sexual acts are very similar to those achieved by fasting, by meditation, or by ingesting certain narcotics.

The so-called 'Passion Cycle' of desire, lust, sexual passion, orgasm and sexual bonding depends on a complex interplay of chemicals produced in the brain.[101], The same chemicals are involved in the mind-state changes experienced during transcendental meditation. Similar effects are found in those using narcotics and mind-altering drugs,and in the brains of people deliberately altering their consciousness for religious or spiritual ends.[102]

The Great Rite was specifically designed to tap into all of this and to be a transcendental experience for the participants, in which

---

101 'Dr Jim Pfaus, a psychologist at Concordia University, in Montreal, says the aftermath of lustful sex is similar to the state induced by taking opiates. A heady mix of chemical changes occurs, including increases in the levels of serotonin, oxytocin, vasopressin and endogenous opioids (the body's natural equivalent of heroin). "This may serve many functions, to relax the body, induce pleasure and satiety, and perhaps induce bonding to the very features that one has just experienced all this with", says Dr Pfaus.' (http://www.oxytocin.org/oxytoc/love-science.html)

102 Bujatti, M. & Biederer, P. *Serotonin, noradrenaline, dopamine metabolites in transcendental meditation-technique. Journal of Neural Transmission* Springer Wien, 1976-09-01 (pp257-267)

they ceased to be their mortal selves and instead literally became the Goddess and her consort.

Perhaps, after the main ritual, the others in the crowd came together themselves. Such a communal act of sex, especially in a culture where polyamory was practised, would have reinforced the bonds that held the whole tribe together through the process of sexual reward. While this would have been a culturally important ceremony, there is no reason to suppose that the participants did not enjoy it!

Tikva Frymer-Kensky notes that,

> 'Sexuality is such an important force for renewal because Sex unites. Sacred Marriage is about union, about the coming together of the many elements that together make a fertile world. Through this act, renewal and regeneration occur when the male component of fertility (Dumuzi) combines with the female component (Inanna), thus unifying the various aspects of cosmos. Male and Female appear as the interlocking pieces which combine to open the riches of the universe. The union of the two principals that Sacred Marriage signifies, expresses and effects the meeting of the male-female axis of the world.'[103],[104]

It was intended for the partners in coitus to be united entirely with the holy couple; that is to say, in the truest sense, to 'become one with God', by a process of psychological transmutation.

# Sacrificial gods

In the earliest times, the shaman or High Priestess' consort was a young man. Over time, as cultures changed, the deities became an-

---

103 Frymer-Kensky, Tikva. *In the Wake of the Goddesses: Women, Culture and the Biblical Transformation of Pagan Myth*. Ballantine Books. 1993.
104 We shall discuss Inanna and Dumuzi in detail in subsequent chapters that explore Sumerian mythology.

thropomorphised but the male partner remained less significant, not a powerful deity comparable to the Goddess.

One of the recurring myths about male gods is that they are killed and their bodies cut up and scattered over the land. This is usually taken to be a reference to the harvesting and sowing of grain, which is certainly part of its meaning. The young man would have been ritually taken as sexual partner by the priestess, to serve her. He would have been treated with the highest respect and veneration. Is it possible that he was sacrificed at the end of his term so that at the next spring equinox, the High Priestess could take a new consort to bed?

Tales of such ritual sacrifice have left widespread, tantalising traces across the mythology of Goddess culture throughout the Middle East and to Carthage and beyond.[105] There are references to it throughout mythology and we have direct evidence of male human sacrifice in early cultures.

Sacrificing the High Priestess' partner after a year ensured that he could not become powerful enough to threaten the hegemony of the shamans or priestesses. His fate was known; he would die, yet he would come back to life as the next year's consort. We will see this reflected in the mythologies of the 'dying and rising gods', who were sent or conducted into the Underworld by the Goddess, and then resurrected through her. The Goddess was in complete control of the god's life, and the human Priestess was in control of her consort's life.[106] This is unlikely to have arisen in a culture wherein women were subjugated by men!

Men were important; without their labour, the agricultural surpluses that paid for the development and building of the early Goddess-cities of Sumer would not have existed. They were also beloved

---

105 Burials at Ur show that human sacrifice was indeed practised in Sumer. In the 1920s, British archaeologist C Leonard Woolley discovered sixteen tombs containing up to 70 ritually killed bodies near Ur, to the west of Uruk. The bodies had been carefully laid out in the tombs, which were then sealed. At the time of Woolley's discovery, many were quick to suggest that these were ritual 'kings' and 'queens' who had been killed after their purpose had been served. However, Woolley himself disagreed, pointing out that the timescale of the burials was quite limited and furthermore, such ritual sacrifice should have been annual, but there simply were not enough tombs.

106 It is unsurprising that little archaeological confirmation of the mythology has been found since the stories often speak of the body of the sacrificial consort god being cut into small pieces and scattered over the land.

by their mothers and lovers. Sacrificing one man might have been sufficient symbolic affirmation that the Goddess governed the earth and time, and women ruled the home and society.

There is evidence that, at least in certain cultures, the boy consorts may not have been physically killed and that their 'death' was instead metaphorical. Transgender priestesses, called gala in Sumerian and kalu in Akkadian, were present in the temples of Inanna. A tradition of transgender women serving as priestesses exists throughout Goddess culture from the time of Sumer and probably long before, until today.[107]

The boy's castration may have been a ritual 'death' through which he was reborn to serve Inanna, no longer as a consort, but as a priestess.[108] In the developing Sumerian pantheon, even the male gods were served by priestesses. Since only women were permitted to serve in this role, the boy's male genitalia had to be removed. The power of the consort to assist the Goddess in the conception of the Divine Child was seen as residing solely in his genitalia, so it would have been enough that the genitalia were removed – killed or sacrificed – rather than the whole person.

While we may find this horrific, the boys who passed through this ritual sacrifice of their genitalia became valued members of society, themselves shamans or priestesses, which provided them with considerable status and temporal power.

*Galli* served the goddess Cybele in the kingdom of Phrygia in Anatolia, the region north of Mesopotamia, and the custom was recorded in Roman times. Initiates castrated themselves during an ecstatic celebration in early spring. These were transwomen, who wore women's clothing, mostly yellow, bleached their long hair and wore makeup, pendants and earrings and a small headdress. It is clear that this was a voluntary station because when Cybele was officially adopted as a Roman goddess in 204 BCE, Roman citizens were prohibited from becoming *Galli* until the emperor Claudius lifted the ban.[109]

---

107 Wolkstein, D. with Kramer, S.N. *Hymns to Inanna*. Harper Perennial. 1983.

108 Teppo, S. *Sacred Marriage and the Devotees of Istar*. Published in Nissinen, M and Uro, R. (edit.) *Sacred Marriages*. Eisenbrauns. 2008.

109 Vermaseren, Maarten J. *Cybele and Attis: the myth and the cult*, translated by A. M. H. Lemmers. Thames and Hudson, 1977

There is logic in having only priestesses, either natal or transgender, serve the deities. The child resulting from the Great Rite would be very special indeed. The other priestesses were free to have all the lovers they wanted, but having males other than the chosen consort in close company with the High Priestess/Goddess would have potentially been problematic in assuring that the 'divine' child was a result of that union.

Over time, as we shall see, the focus of the Great Rite changed. As the consort transitioned to a powerful Priest-King, the paternity of the child would become significant. Might the later tradition of patriliny have been encouraged by the Great Rite?

## Of Boys, Bulls and Kings

In many cultures, another substitute for the actual sacrifice of human males was the sacrifice of animals, notably bulls. Bulls play a hugely important part in world mythology, albeit one that is frequently overlooked or misunderstood. They are a central motif in Goddess culture.

In the Sumerian myth *Inanna's Descent to the Underworld*, the goddess Inanna intentionally enters the Underworld, which is the realm of Ereshkigal, her alter-ego and the dark goddess. Her ostensible reason for this visit is to bring news that Ereshkigal's husband, the Bull of Heaven, has died and Inanna wishes to pay respect.[110] In the myth, Inanna herself dies and is reborn from Ereshkigal. The reference to the Bull is often seen as mysterious but, in fact, the explanation is simple.

Ereshkigal is the Goddess Earth in her dark aspect. She is night, darkness, death and the power of creation. When she was given a consort, he had to express all the potency of male sexuality. Both bulls and male goats became identified with this but in two different ways. The goat became satyrs and similar mythical beings, more

---

110 The Bull of Heaven in Sumerian mythology is under the control of An, who is the Sky-father and consort of Ki, the Goddess Earth. The bull is a physical aspect of the deity.

mischievous and tricky than dangerous. The bull, however, came to represent not only male sexuality but male physical power and later, aggression.

The Bull was adopted to give the Goddess a consort who could match her own sexual potency. Bulls express masculinity in a more profound way than any other domesticated animal, even stallions, because of their sheer size. The bulls that were used as the original models were even more impressive than the largest seen today. They were aurochs, *Bos primigenius*. These now-extinct beasts stood two metres tall at the shoulder and could weigh 1000 kilogrammes (one tonne). They had huge, spreading horns up to a metre from point to point and were famous for their violent and aggressive tempera-ments.[111] Aurochs naturally ranged across Europe and Asia and they were domesticated in various cultures independently.

In Mesopotamia this domestication occurred around 6,000 BCE.[112] This fits the timeline of the beginnings of settled culture in Mesopotamia, so the metaphor of the aurochs bull was available to represent the seminal force of masculine sexuality. The Goddess, at least once she had devolved from the original transcendent singular-ity, was the quintessential, ultimate expression of women's sexuality, fertility and reproduction. It followed that her consort should be as powerful a totem of masculinity, and the aurochs bull was ideal.

Because bulls represent the quintessential power of male virility, they could be sacrificed in the place of a human male, to assure the Goddess' annual regeneration.

Helen Benigni observes:

> 'The Goddess embodies the form of an omnipresent force of Nature, even in her bride aspect. Although her later associations with deities in the Iron Age in Greece, such as her name as Eileithyia, Britomartis, and Ariadne, are presented in maiden form, this does not take away from the fact that the bride aspect of the Mother Goddess of the Bronze Age was in fact a maiden about to join forces *through the sacred marriage with the male in the form of*

111 http://www.lhnet.org/aurochs/ retrieved 03/12/2014
112 *Ibid.*

*a bull to regenerate the cycle of the moon and the sun.*[113]
(our emphasis.)

This suggests that the practice of sacrificing a human boy was supplanted by that of an aurochs bull, and this latter certainly continued for millennia. In northern Europe, for example, young men were ritually killed and their bodies placed in bogs that were sacred to the Goddess, and aurochs skeletons have also been found there.[114]

Although the origins, in the sacrifice of bulls to ensure the annual regeneration of the Goddess and the continued passage of time, are all but forgotten, the ritualised killing of bulls persists to this day in many cultures, notably those surrounding the Mediterranean, as in Spain and France.

---

113 Benigni, Helen. *The Goddess and the Bull: A Study in Minoan-Mycenaean Mythology.* University Press of America. 2007.
114 Iping-Petterson, M.A. *Human Sacrifice in Iron Age Northern Europe: The Culture of Bog People.* (Doctoral Thesis) University of Leiden. 2011.

# Cultural Significance of the Sacred Marriage

The moment we gave the Goddess a consort to help explain the changing seasons and cycle of the year, we had begun to spin a new strand into the thread of our cultural development. The Great Rite persisted in the stories of the ancients, handed down through oral traditions. Once we settled and invented writing, the stories were recorded, and we know that this particular ritual remained central to later cultures for millennia. In fact, as we shall see, its echoes still affect us today.

In the early, shamanic rite, it is likely that once the shaman conceived and everyone knew time would go on, the key participants returned to life as usual. When we settled and began to grow crops, the annual harvest worked its way into the stories and, unfortunately for the consort, his role became sacrificial. Gradually, as we began to build towns and the role of men became more central, the sacrifice became symbolic.

Whether the young men who served as consorts to the shaman/ High Priestess were killed or castrated or their place taken by bulls, the balance of power in the relationship between the representative of the Goddess and her consort remained the same. The woman had all the power; her consort was a callow youth who would be killed or emasculated at the end of his year.

Even in the temple ritual, in early Sumerian mythology the Goddess' consort was not the great sky-god who would later be invented in order to control the Goddess, but a simple shepherd lad who would sexually serve the mighty Inanna, the Queen of Heaven.

Is it conceivable that such an arrangement could have continued to exist under the later, male-dominated warrior culture?

By the time we established cities, the shaman/Goddess had become a cadre of priestesses who retained huge power and influence. However, as the early cities developed they changed. Walls and great buildings were erected and, alongside this, the Great Rite became the Sacred Marriage. This ritual was an elaborate spectacle, highly orchestrated and conducted in a palatial temple. Its cultural significance was different from that of the earlier version. Instead of affirming the sexual independence of the Goddess and women, through their ability to choose partners as and when they liked, the Sacred Marriage would bind individual women to a specific male, for life. The reasons for this will become clear.

*Why Men Made God*

# SECTION FIVE:

# The Advent of Agriculture

## Sumer

Until the 19th century, no-one in the modern world knew that Sumer had ever existed. Scholars in the West, trained in the classical tradition, believed that the first flowering of civilisation had been in Ancient Greece.[115] Even Egyptology was in its infancy, and was challenging, and challenged, in turn. These views were dramatically overturned by the discovery of Sumer, where a refined and developed civilisation had been established at least a millennium before the earliest on the Nile.

Sumer was in Mesopotamia, Greek for 'Land Between Two Rivers'. It was situated in what is now Iraq, on a plain between the Tigris and Euphrates rivers, which flowed out from the mountains to the north-west. These rivers had deposited a thick layer of fertile alluvial soil. They provided good water, abundant with fish and other wildlife. The riverbanks were thick with reeds that could be cut to make shelters, baskets and cradles. The land close by the river was bountiful, and there would have been much for the foragers to find. There was game, too, especially on the grassy steppe that lay further from the rivers.

The Sumerians invented the Eurasian arch, which uses a keystone, as well as the wheel, writing, and codified laws. We have recovered much of their mythology, yet the people themselves still seem mysterious. For the first thousand years of its life, the major

---

115 Until the 18th century and the identification of dinosaur fossils, the age of the Earth as stated in the Bible, some 6,000 years, was generally taken as correct. This meant that scholars could not comprehend the existence of cultures older than that, and even where they found evidence of them, considered them to be later. (The true age of the Earth is 4.5 billion years.)

Sumerian city, Uruk, had no wall. This is significant, given that some of the earliest examples of catastrophic warfare were to appear here, and the entire region was to be ravaged by genocidal savagery in later centuries.

## The scene is set: Ubaid

A simple, agrarian culture appeared in eastern Mesopotamia around 5,500 BCE. It has been named 'Ubaid'. The Ubaidians lived in scattered hamlets and villages, with very little in the way of infrastructure. They cultivated patches of land, probably irrigating them with water carried from the river in reed buckets. They constructed floating islands of reed bundles and on these they built distinctive houses, also of reeds. This lifestyle persisted for at least seven millennia. The people who lived there until the 1990s, still building reed houses, fishing the river and cultivating the soil, are called the Marsh Arabs. Their world was known as 'Eden'.[116]

At some point early in its development, Ubaid culture was changed by the arrival of nomadic Semitic herders. Where had these nomadic herdsmen come from, and how did they become herders? Since the domestication of animals began in settlements, there are several ways in which this may have happened. Perhaps wandering hunter-gatherers came into contact with those who had already settled and either traded for or stole the animals, or perhaps they came from settlements with domesticated animals that had been abandoned due to crop failure or loss of water resources. We know that climate change brought about the demise of many proto-agrarian settlements in marginal areas. Those settlers probably did not die out but returned to a wandering life, taking their animals with them.

It has been suggested that the unification of the two cultures was through invasion and conquest, but this view is speculative. It is more likely that it was a result of cooperation.

---

116 They would doubtless be there still, but after the first Gulf War, Saddam Hussein determined to exterminate the Marsh Arabs, and used engineers to achieve what hostile gods and soldiers could not: he drained their wetlands and destroyed Eden.

There are mutual advantages for a culture based on arable farming to meld with a pastoral one. Meat, and particularly fat, is very high-energy food that is easy for us to digest, especially once it has been cooked. It can give humans the full set of amino acids necessary for a healthy life. In addition, animals like sheep and goats provide milk, leather, wool and many other products.

On the other hand, as omnivores we cannot live on meat alone. Humans cannot synthesise vitamins and must ingest them as a part of their diet. Meat and fat provide the fat-soluble vitamins A, D, E, and K, but we also require vitamins B and C, which are obtained from fresh fruit and vegetables.[117] Many other products of arable farming are also attractive to herders, such as bread, beer and flax for weaving. Also, it is unlikely that the shepherds would have been in a position to overwhelm populous settlements defended by fit men armed with scythes, sickles and other farming implements.

In addition to providing animal produce, the nomads fulfilled another need of the burgeoning agrarian culture; a workforce to help with the seasonal harvest. The necessity for such a workforce persists today and without it even modern agriculture would be severely handicapped. This seasonal help would have been vital in a non-mechanised system. Thus the settled farmers had something else to tempt wandering, herding people to stay: work.

Rather than a by conquest then, for which there is no archaeological evidence, the original Ubaidians and the Semitic herders probably came together in an alliance of mutual benefit based on trade and barter. Formalising their relationship would have given them access to one another's produce, and defined areas for arable farming and pastoral grazing. This suggests a process of alliance wherein the settled, farming people remained in control, not one in which they succumbed to war and conquest.[118]

These factors, often overlooked, present convincing evidence that the Ubaidian and Semitic cultures came together more or less

---

117 Vitamin C is essential to cell replication and insufficiency results in the disease known as scurvy.

118 A similar process, where we have much more archaeological evidence, has been described in the highlands of Canaan, thousands of years later, by Israel Finkelstein and Neil Silberman. This explains the symbiotic relationship between the settled people and the nomads. (Finkelstein, I & Silberman, N. *The Bible Unearthed: Archaeology's New Vision of Ancient Israel and the Origin of Its Sacred Texts.* Touchstone. 2002.)

peacefully. Their association was clearly successful, because it attracted another group towards the end of the fifth millennium BCE. The newcomers were the Sumerians, who were to give their name to the entire culture and region.

## The Sumerians

We do not know much about the Sumerians before they appeared in southern Mesopotamia. We think they spoke a language that suggests they came from the area around Anatolia to the northeast, where Çatal Hoyuk had been. However, exactly where they originated or why they had wandered so far remains unknown. Again, there is no evidence that their association with the pre-existing Ubaid-Semitic culture was a warlike invasion. There are no burned settlements, a common indicator of warfare, nor are there warlike references in the early art or mythology.

So we are left with a mystery. However, there are other examples we may draw on to give us clues. One such was in Europe, thousands of years later, when Celtic culture spread in waves emanating from the centre of the continent. For many years, it was thought that these waves were actual migrations of people. Now, thanks to exhaustive DNA sampling, we know that this did not occur. Celtic culture spread through technology, in particular, metallurgy. Small numbers of Celts travelled far and wide, taking their art, technology and culture with them. People became Celtic because the culture was useful and attractive, not because of war and imperial conquest.

In all the Celtic cultures there existed a shadowy caste of people called Druids, who were shamans, priests, doctors, lawyers, musicians and poets. Although it is often thought that their role was principally religious, this is an oversimplification. Druids were the intelligentsia of the culture. They played the same role as a modern educated class plays. It is likely that the metal-smiths were also Druids and their techniques were amongst the closely-guarded secrets that formed the core of druidic learning.

This group carried their intellectual, religious and artistic culture with them, and spread it through Europe. And yet, to this day we do not know where druidic culture originated. The Celts may have invented it, or it may be much older. It is possible that the Druids came from a long line that stretched deep into the past, conserving the mystical knowledge of the ancestors and carrying it forward. This would have made them extremely useful in a world without writing.

Were the Sumerians like this? A group that moved from place to place, perhaps trading and entertaining, offering advice and religious teaching, ministering to the sick, offering judgement in disputes? Were they warriors or teachers or perhaps even both? Mercenaries or doctors and lawyers? Poets and bards? Builders or engineers? Or all of these? Did they support themselves by force of arms or by the knowledge and expertise they brought? At present, we may only speculate.

Whatever their history, and whatever brought the Sumerians into the Ubaid/Semitic milieu in southern Mesopotamia, soon after their arrival a cultural revolution occurred. From scattered, small villages of subsistence farmers, a civilisation full of art, poetry, science, literature and philosophy burst into being in a way that has astonished researchers ever since. Before long, the economic power of Sumerian settlements became strategically important. Large-scale agriculture was established and soon, city-based civilisation began.[119]

The Sumerians saw beyond their immediate needs. They realised that if they could harness the natural world to their will they would not only be fed, but also become rich. They built miles of huge canals that linked the Tigris and Euphrates rivers, irrigating the land and turning it green. This was civil engineering on a grand scale that would continue for thousands of years. Along with their language and culture, the Sumerians probably brought to the Ubaidian milieu their mythology and pantheon of deities.

---

119 We cannot be absolutely certain that these were the very first cities but if there were earlier ones they vanished without leaving any trace, whereas Sumer and its culture can trace a line of descent via the Middle-East, throughout Europe and across the world. Sumerian culture is still with us.

## Eridu to Uruk

The first truly Sumerian settlement we know of was called Eridu. It followed the developmental profile that we saw in Çatal Hoyuk and Ain Ghazal. It had no great public spaces or monumental buildings. This absence is typical of Goddess cultures and, as we have already seen, a powerful indicator of a matriarchy.

Eridu was eventually supplanted as the premier settlement of the area by another, which would be called Uruk. This would become the world's first 'true' city, and the birthplace of a cultural tradition that remains with us and has become globally dominant.

Eridu was the cult centre of the god Enki. Mythically, he was the son of a union between Nammu, the eternal Mother, the Sea, and her first-born, An, the Sky-god. Ki, in Sumerian, means the Earth and is the name of the Sumerian Earth Mother, and En can mean 'lord' or 'priest'.[120] Enki, throughout Sumerian mythology, is the closest of the deities to the Goddess and repeatedly comes to her aid. He also is more sympathetic to humans than the other male deities.[121]

Uruk became the cult centre for the most iconic anthropomorphic goddess in the history of the culture. She was called Inanna. She was beautiful, sophisticated and mercurial yet fickle and wilful. She was a goddess of women, love and sex, fertility and war and, at least in her earliest forms, was completely independent of male control.

In some versions, Inanna is Enki's niece but in all their interactions, throughout the mythology, she is stronger than he. Enki's role in relation to her is of a loving (if sometimes tested) benefactor. He is Inanna's first hero and protector, and at the same time he is the Goddess' son, a prior deity, powerful in his own right.

Enki's mythological relationship to Inanna reflects the relation-

---

120 Scholars such as Samuel Noah Kramer suggest that the element 'ki' is a corruption of 'kur' which would mean 'lord of the underworld'. Others interpret it as 'Lord of Sweet (i.e. fresh) Water'. All three have roughly the same significance, since the Earth, water and the Underworld are all representations of the Goddess.

121 In the *Myth of Atrahasis*, the model for the Biblical story of Noah, it is Enki who forewarns Atrahasis that the other gods are planning a mighty flood to kill the humans.

ship between Eridu and Uruk. Uruk became far more powerful and wealthy, yet Eridu 'gave' civilisation to it. This is reflected in verses from the *Epic of Gilgamesh*.[122] The English historian Michael Wood has translated part of it thus:

> 'The goddess Inanna brought the arts of civilization from the god of wisdom, Enki of Eridu, but it was like a Pandora's box. Here were the delights of society, exquisite craftsmanship, beautiful clothes, the arts of sex and music. But civilization has a darker side, which has to be accepted along with the good. The art of being mighty, the art of being kind, the art of straightforwardness, the art of deceit; the art of kingship, justice and the enduring crown; the resounding note of a musical instrument, the rejoicing of the heart; the kindling of the strife, the plundering of cities, the setting up of lamentation, fear, pity, terror – all this is civilization and you must take it all, you cannot refuse any of it. And once taken, you cannot give it back.'[123]

This relationship is interesting. It is repeatedly made clear in the mythology that Enki is the protector of the Goddess, yet she is far more powerful than he. Enki may represent an ideal of the early male hero, who does not seek reward in his own name, but in service of the Goddess. Alternatively, his avuncular relationship to Inanna may directly reflect the society that invented this myth. We have seen that in many matriarchal cultures, the male parental role is performed not by fathers but by maternal uncles. This is compellingly similar to Enki's relationship to Inanna.

After it was established, Uruk rapidly outstripped Eridu. All that was beautiful, all that was rich, was poured into it over the thousands of years of its existence. It was a city of arts and crafts, of beauty and the good life. Its buildings sparkled with blue-glazed tiles, and it was the original 'City of Light'. All around her city, Inanna caused the

---

122 The *Epic of Gilgamesh* itself is a later work which appeared in the third millennium BCE. However it was syncretised from earlier traditions.
123 Wood, Michael. *Legacy*. An Island World Presentation Central Independent Television. 1991.

fertile earth to bring forth crops, the animals to reproduce and be healthy, the rivers to be full of fish and the countryside to be full of game.

When the Sumerian civilisation of Uruk reached its peak, in the middle of the fourth millennium BCE, the people built the first monumental structure, a stepped pyramid called a ziggurat, in the centre of the city. On top, they built a beautiful home for the great goddess who had brought them so much: the Eanna Temple, the House of Heaven. It rose high above the rooftops, so that it could be seen from afar. This was not only the home of the Goddess, but the centre of the religious life of the city, the seat of political power and the courts. It was where laws were made, and justice dispensed. It was also where business was conducted. This was the greatest era of Uruk's history, long before it was ravaged by war and became subject to the violence of men.

# From Horticulture to Agriculture

In a hunter-gatherer worldview, where one simply harvests Nature's bounty, time is effectively limitless. There is no pressure to do something today or tomorrow or even this or next year.[124] Agriculture required that things be done on time: the fields ploughed, the seed sown, the earth hoed, the harvest gathered and so on. Huge areas of land had to be cleared, tilled and irrigated, and this required an organised workforce of physically strong workers, a workforce of men.

People already knew how to mobilise workers; Göbekli Tepe is the proof. There, the large workforce had been motivated by religion. In the agricultural phase a new reward system was invented, which put material value on time and effort, in other words, on work.

The men would own the harvested produce that grew on the

---

124 The phenomenon of a complete failure to understand the urgency that animates Western life has frequently been noted – usually pejoratively – by those meeting such cultures. A sympathetic, if puzzled observation of this was made by John Steinbeck and E. F. Ricketts. (Ricketts, E.F. and Steinbeck, J. *Sea of Cortez: A Leisurely Journal of Travel and Research*. Penguin Books. 2009.)

land they worked, and this could be shared and traded. Those who put in the time and effort most effectively, or who had been fortunate enough to begin working the best land, had the most successful crops. Some began to amass more wealth – in terms of produce surplus to their needs – than others. A new economic model was born, based on surplus produce and its accumulation as wealth. Gradually, the wealthiest were able to buy produce from the others and market it themselves. The market economy and the establishment of individual property rights soon followed.

Increased trading led to the invention of money, which appeared in Sumer in the fourth millennium BCE. Money could be saved, stored and transported more easily than produce, and, most importantly, it meant that commerce was no longer reliant on barter. Money could be traded for anything.

The inevitable result was that everything was given a monetary value. Even the land, rather than being held communally, was divided up so that it could be bought and sold. Instead of a 'workers collective' owning and cultivating the land, some men became owners and some labourers. Ultimately, this led to the development of a culture in which all material wealth and power was concentrated in the hands of a small number of men. To protect their 'rights' to money and land, these men invented systems of law that defined what property was, who owned it and what would happen to those who usurped these rules. The divisions between rich and poor were established here.

This model was so successful that large amounts of surplus were soon being created. This allowed the building of ever larger and more sophisticated settlements.

## Wealth, Status and War

Men acquired wealth and status and appropriated power initially through agriculture, then through the development of growth economies and ultimately by the adoption of warfare.

The invention of writing allowed the codification of strict legal codes and the establishment of legally binding contracts. These documents provided an effective means of social control. Central to these codes, wherever they appear, is a concern with property rights.

In the matriarchy, women not only had the power to choose their mates, but also had authority over their own reproduction. In hunter-gatherer and even horticultural societies, women were self-sufficient; they could gather or grow enough for their needs. Agriculture changed that. Once men controlled the land and the production of food, women became dependent on them, which gave men control over women. A new kind of contract called Marriage was invented. Now men could appropriate exclusive rights over and access to women's fertility through the use of written laws.

Other than water and land, which it had in abundance, the principal requirement for the development of Uruk was labour to build the canals and work the fields. The easiest way to find labour – absent a ready source of slaves – is to increase the birth rate. Women found their bodies, sexuality and fertility shackled to one man through the institution of marriage. In an extension of this, their reproduction was bound to the economic needs of the city. The cultural ideal that Sumerian women were expected to live up to was to be beautiful, sexually seductive, highly desirable – and produce many babies.

As male assertion of social control increased, women's political voice was progressively reduced and ultimately silenced. Although their subjugation took many years, by the end of the third millennium BCE women had become second-class citizens and worse was yet to come.

# The Goddess in Transition

## Nammu: The Sumerian Great Mother

Prior to her devolution, there was only one, transcendent, Great Goddess, who brought everything into being alone. The Sumerians called her Nammu, the Goddess of the Sea.[125],[126] She was singular, supreme, unchallenged and unchallengeable, indeed beyond the scope of human comprehension. She was the primordial mother; she had always existed, alone. 'In the beginning the whole universe was a sea.' Samuel Noah Kramer said of Nammu:

> 'first was the primeval sea (Nammu.) Nothing is said of its origin or birth, and it is not unlikely that the Sumerian conceived it as having existed eternally.'[127]

Nammu is the goddess of the hunter-gatherer woman. She creates life without the aid of a consort. This reflects a time when it was believed that women created life without male assistance. There were no other deities in the pantheon before or beside her, so she was a monotheistic deity.

Reflecting human understanding of reproduction, Nammu bore a pair of deities, female and male twins, Ki and An.[128],[129] Originally, these were equals, born at exactly the same instant, locked in coitus. They are an essential pair, which, together, forms a singularity.

---

125 MacKenzie, Donald A. *Myths of Babylonia and Assyria*. Gresham. 1915.

126 'And the Earth was without form, and void; and darkness was upon the face of the deep,' Genesis 1:2. This is a reference to a primordial sea and likely contains a memory of Nammu.

127 Kramer, Samuel Noah. *History begins at Sumer*. University of Pennsylvania Press. 1981.

128 Ki is also known as Ninhursag, and sometimes, today, as Ninhursag-Ki.

129 We use the Sumerian form 'An' rather than the later 'Anu' in order to differentiate from the much later Celtic deity also called Anu.

Ki, the Earth, was the Great Mother, the Creatrix from whose body everything living flowed. She received the fertilising rain and produced life.[130] An was the sky, from which the rain fell; rain was his metaphorical semen. He impregnated her with the seed from which life would be born, and this correlated to the fresh sweet water that flowed in the rivers. It should be clear that this version of deity is very much informed by the agricultural society that developed it.

> 'The Great Earth made herself glorious, her body flour-ished with greenery. Wide Earth put on silver metal and lapis lazuli ornaments, adorned herself with diorite, chal-cedony, carnelian, and diamonds. Sky covered the pas-tures with irresistible sexual attraction, presented himself in majesty. The pure young woman showed herself to the pure Sky, the vast Sky copulated with the wide Earth, the seed of the heroes Wood and Reed he ejaculated into her womb, the Earth, the good cow, received the good seed of Sky in her womb. The Earth, for the happy birth of the Plants of Life, presented herself.'[131]

This passage describes and sexualises the relationship of the fer-tile Earth to a rain-bearing sky. The parallel is between the fertility of the land and the fertility of women.

The arrangement seems benign: the Sky God cannot make life alone but needs the willing help of the Earth Mother. He does not plunge down from on high and rape the Earth Mother, forcing her to his will as he might if he were all-powerful and dominant.[132] In-stead, he courts her, charms her, seduces her. That is because his pow-er, great though it may be, does not govern the Earth. The natural world may reject humanity's control by storms, catastrophic floods, droughts and other disasters. In mythological terms, An must woo Ki, please her and care for her, in order for the world to be fertile and the people to prosper.

Every farmer and gardener knew that to bring forth crops it was

---

130 The Sumerian word for 'water' is the same as that for 'semen', literally, 'a man's water'.
131 Dijk, J. Van *The Birth of Wood and Reed*, Acta Orientalia 28. 1964.
132 And as the later Greek sky-god Zeus would repeatedly do.

not sufficient simply to scatter seed on the ground and hope for the best. The soil had to be tilled, watered and nourished, and weeds hoed. The Earth has the power to bring forth life but it is up to her whether she does or not, and the only way to ensure this is to respect her, to treat her with love and care. The relationship between Earth Mother and Sky-Father reflects that between land and farmer in the horticultural stage.

In the myth-cycle, however, all was not well for the couple, Ki and An:

> 'Before all time, as they lie together, his phallus clasped in her vulva, in the liquid womb of Nammu, a sigh of love escapes them, and rests between their bodies. They make love again and again and Ki is filled with the seed of An; but then the sigh takes the form of Enlil, who becomes greater and greater. Enlil is the Master of Wind, the god of the Air, and as he stretches to separate the Sky from the Earth, he makes it impossible for the lovers Ki and An ever to come together again. An weeps for his lost sister and lover, whom he can never again touch, and his tears drop into the Sea, Nammu. Nammu feels her son's anguish and reaches out for him, and for the first time, mother and son make love. From their union, a pair of twins is born, male and female, Enki and Ereshkigal. Enki we have already encountered: he is lord of Magic, Crafts and sweet water, and Ereshkigal is goddess of knowledge within and becomes the mistress of the Underworld.'[133],[134]

In the timelessness of their lovemaking within the womb of Nammu, Ki, the Earth, was filled with An's seed, making her forever fertile. Although he was born of their love, Enlil is not one of their children, in the sense that the seed An plants inside Ki would become. Enlil represents the life the lovers must wake into, chaos and

---

133 Leick, Gwendolyn. *Sex and Eroticism in Sumerian Literature.* Routledge. 1994.

134 The early Sumerian tongue was not gendered, but many of our records are written in Akkadian, which was. An and Anu refer to the same deity, An in Sumerian, Anu in Akkadian.

filial disobedience. He is powerful and unruly, an elemental force.

After Enlil separates Ki and An, Nammu compassionately has sex with An, her son, resulting in the birth of another female/male pair, Ereshkigal and Enki. Ki and An were the transcendent representations of the original deity Nammu, divided into female and male elements. Ereshkigal and Enki are the anthropomorphic successors to them.

Ki and An together with Enki and Ereshkigal form a Divine Tetrad, group of four closely-related deities. They are mother and father, daughter and son, all born of the original Great Goddess Nammu. After giving birth to them, Nammu essentially disappears from Sumerian mythology, and her place is taken by Ki.

All the deities, from the original tetrad above to the whole pantheon of Sumer, were not only born of the Great Goddess but were a part of her. The male gods were simply the male part of what was once a transcendent, singular deity that contained all the power of creation, both female and male.

These mythological changes reflected cultural changes brought about by the adoption of agriculture and permanent settlement. Ki and An, born together, are equal. In time, with the rising power of men, being equal would not be enough, and the Sky Father would take on different characteristics.

# Transcendent to Anthropomorphic

With the advent of agriculture, we had a new relationship with nature; it was at least partly under our control. And with this we see the arrival of anthropomorphic deities. These are more powerful and more beautiful than we, but they resemble us. They can be reasoned with; they are close to us. Indeed, they seem to like us, and all the more if we propitiate them. Furthermore, they could be loyal to specific groups of us, which reflects the emergence of settlement and city dwelling. Each settlement could have a goddess or god of its own, who might be persuaded to live there and give it her or his protection. We built homes for them, which we called temples, and provided food or other offerings for them.

Eventually there was a veritable tribe of goddesses and gods, each responsible for some or other facet of life. Each of these was a dilution of the power of the Great Goddess, the Eternal Mother, for it was from her, originally, that all of their powers came.

The relationships between the goddesses and gods thus created reflect the relationships of land to men. The Earth, the land, was increasingly seen as the possession of men, to be cultivated and made profitable. Similarly, the Goddess, little by little, was made subordinate to new male gods. The new male deities were increasingly assertive and demanding of obedience. They were lords and masters, patriarchs and warriors. They controlled the Earth and, by implication, the Goddess, in whichever form she appeared.

For women, this had severe consequences, because the triad Goddess-Earth-Women contains human women. The three elements of her subjugation, taming nature through large-scale agriculture, controlling the Goddess by placing male gods above her, and disempowering women by making them the chattels of men, are indivisible.

As the Sumerian polytheism developed, both goddesses and gods were served by priestesses. Having priestesses in a position of power retained a balance in the broader culture. In any society where the right to rule is conveyed to a monarch by the deity via the hands of a prelate, the priestly class has great influence. While women's control over their sexuality and fertility was no longer absolute, collectively they retained political power through the priestesses.

Although the Goddess would persist, the first fateful steps that would lead to the systematic exploitation and subjugation of over half the world's population had been taken.

# The Underworld: Ereshkigal

The Goddess is both light and dark, day and night, life and death.

When the Goddess became anthropomorphic, she required two forms to convey this. In Sumer, the dark is Ereshkigal, the Queen of the Underworld, and the light is Inanna, the Queen of Heaven. They are the light and dark aspects of the Goddess; they are the same being, two halves of one whole. Inanna is concerned with the world of the living and life and Ereshkigal with the dead and death. One cannot exist without the other because this is a cyclical conception. An understanding of Ereshkigal depends on knowing Inanna.

Inanna, alongside Ereshkigal, was the most important anthropomorphic deity of Mesopotamia. In Assyro-Babylonian culture, Inanna became Ishtar, who is cognate to the Northwest Semitic goddess Astarte, the Greek Aphrodite (and Roman Venus) or Athena, Egyptian Aset, also known as Isis or Hathor and the Etruscan Turan. She is Eve and she is Mary. She is Asherah, the consort of Yahweh, the Hebrew god. She is the sacred Earth-Mother of the Celts. She is Kali. She is Cytherea and Cyprus.

Inanna and Erishkigal, life and death together as an inseparable concept, appear everywhere. When we are not alive, we are inside the Underworld, in the great void which is metaphorically the Goddess' womb. We are born from women and when we die we return to the Earth. Since women are one physical manifestation of the Goddess, and the Earth is another, this is a cycle. The portal between life and death is the vulva, in both divine and material forms. The entrance to life is through women's material birth canals and the exit from it is through the opening of the grave or tomb, into the body of the Goddess, the Earth itself.

Ereshkigal is the Underworld; she is the oblivion after death and also that before life. Therefore, she symbolises not only death but also the route to rebirth. This idea of reincarnation is so central to Goddess culture that we will come across it many times.

# SECTION SIX:

# The Devolution of the Goddess

Although Inanna is a manifestation of the transcendent Goddess, she is anthropomorphic and thus comprehensible to the human mind. As the Queen of Heaven, she can walk in the world and commune with people and at the same time intercede on their behalf with the other deities. She lives amongst them, in the 'Temple of Heaven' which is her home. The form that she takes is that of the most beautiful, desirable, fecund young woman imaginable. It is significant to note that Inanna is a form of the Goddess designed to appeal to men.

Because she is a deity initially conceived while women had real power, Inanna is extreme. As goddess of fertility, love, protection, fate, sex, hunting, storms and war, her mood swings are ferocious. She can be a ruthless killer and a spectacular lover. She holds all other authority in contempt and refuses even to be guided by male deities, much less controlled by them. She is so brave and haughty as to enter the Underworld herself, and so vindictive as to send her husband Dumuzi there when she discovers he had not mourned her while she was dead. She can be imperious and demanding, wayward and hard on her lovers, unafraid of her sexuality and sexual power. She can be loyal and supportive too, and refuses to allow her loved ones to come to harm. She is multifaceted and complex; a super-woman, indeed, but 'just' a woman.

# Inanna's Mythology

## Inanna's Descent

Resurrection is at the core of the most significant story about Inanna, which deals with her descent into the Underworld.[135] In this story, Inanna dies, becomes Ereshkigal, and then, as Ereshkigal, gives birth to herself. The story is therefore a metaphor for the cycle of the year and the passage of time, and this identifies Inanna as a 'year' goddess – in other words, the Great Goddess.

Inanna decided to enter the Underworld knowing that, at least for everyone else, there was no return from it. She girded herself with her regal clothes, her turban, her measuring rod and line, egg-shaped beads and lapis lazuli necklace, a breastplate and a wig and make-up, which are the symbols of her power, and she set off with her minister Ninsubur, who was a woman. Before entering the Underworld, Inanna carefully instructed Ninsubur to mourn with great grief for her for three days. Then she was to seek, in turn, the help of three of the gods: Enlil, Nanna and Enki. She said that only Enki would help, but Ninsubur must go to all three.

Inanna arrived at the Palace Ganzer, the entrance to the Underworld. She 'pushed aggressively' and demanded of Neti, the doorman, to let her in. Neti asked who she was and why she wanted to enter. Inanna told him that she brought news that her sister Ereshkigal's husband, the sacred Bull of Heaven had died, and she wished to honour him at the funerary rites. This is important, as it may be a reference to the ritual sacrifice of a bull, which would have been the moment when the annual ceremonies to ensure the rebirth of the year would begin; this contextualises the rest of the story.

Neti told Inanna to wait and went to tell Ereshkigal what had happened. Ereshkigal 'slapped her thigh and bit her lip'. She even-

---

135 The original version is at: ETCSL translation; t.1.4.1: *Inana's Descent into the Nether World*. http://etcsl.orinst.ox.ac.uk/cgi-bin/etcsl.cgi?text=t.1.4.1

tually told Neti to let Inanna enter. At each of the seven doors she had to pass through, one of her divine powers was to be removed, and when she was delivered before the throne without them, all her clothes and jewels would be taken away.[136]

Inanna found herself before her sister's throne, crouched and naked. Then something strange happened: she caused Ereshkigal to rise from her throne and sat there herself. The Anuna, who were the judges, looked at Inanna 'with the look of death'. She died, and her body was hung to rot on a hook on the wall.

After three days, loyal Ninsubur, who had been carrying out the rituals of grief, 'lacerating her eyes, cheeks and buttocks', set off as instructed to get help. As Inanna had predicted, the first two of the three gods she asked, Enlil and Nanna, refused to help. Her troubles were Inanna's own doing and they could not break the rules of the Underworld. Enki, however, agreed to help, showing his special relationship to the Goddess. Taking the dirt from his fingernails, he created two entities, the kur-ara and the gala-tura. To the kur-ara he gave the life-giving plant. To the gala-tura he gave the life-giving water.

Enki told them to go to the palace of the Underworld, to slip in like flies and phantoms, and there they would find Ereshkigal, lying in great distress. Enki warned the spirits that Ereshkigal would tempt them with offers of great gifts, including a river full of water, but they were to ask only for the corpse hanging on the hook and take nothing else.[137] Enki warned them that Ereshkigal would be reluctant, but they were to insist.

When the spirits arrive before Ereshkigal, the text tells us:

'The mother who gave birth, Ereškigala, because of her children, was lying there. Her holy shoulders were not covered by a linen cloth. Her breasts were not full like a šagan vessel. Her nails were like a pickaxe upon her. The hair on her head was bunched up as if it were leeks.'[138]

---

136 This is the origin of the famous *Dance of the Seven Veils* in which a female dancer removes seven items of clothing to end up, at least in earlier times, naked.
137 The theme of temptation established here is an important part of this and successor cultures. The underlying message emphasises the importance of loyalty and obedience.
138 http://etcsl.orinst.ox.ac.uk/section1/tr141.htm

Ereshkigal was suffering the throes of parturition and asked the spirits for help to relieve her pain.[139] As Enki predicted, she offered them great gifts in return, but they refused, saying they only wanted the corpse on the hook. As Enki had said she would, Ereshkigal released her sister's body. The spirits sprinkled the life-giving plant and water on it, and Inanna was reborn.

However, as she was leaving the Underworld, Inanna was seized by the Anuna, who had condemned her to death. They said that no-one could leave the Underworld, and if Inanna was to break this rule, she must provide a substitute.

The demons of the Underworld accompanied Inanna,

'the one in front of her, though not a minister, held a sceptre in his hand; the one behind her, though not an escort, carried a mace at his hip, while the small demons, like a reed enclosure, and the big demons, like the reeds of a fence, restrained her on all sides'[140]

First they came across Ninsubur, waiting outside the gate, and the demons would have taken her, but Inanna refused this, because of Ninsubur's loyalty. Then they went to the city of Umma, where Sara threw himself at their feet. Again Inanna refused the demons, saying 'Šara is my singer, my manicurist and my hairdresser. How could I turn him over to you?'[141]

So they went on to Bad-tiriba, where Lulal presented himself.[142] Once again, Inanna refused to let him be taken, saying that he was her loyal follower. She told the demons to proceed to the great apple-tree in the plain of Kulaba. Here they found Dumuzi, draped in finery, surrounded by wealth and riches, sitting on a great throne and, apparently, not in the slightest concerned about his bride's death.

'(Inanna) looked at him, it was the look of death. She

---

139 This is a metaphor for the human suffering of labour which can only be ended with the delivery of the baby into the world, or by death.

140 http://etcsl.orinst.ox.ac.uk/section1/tr141.htm

141 In some versions, Sara is described as Inanna's son, but whether this is meant in an honorary or a literal sense is not clear.

142 As with Sara, Lulal is sometimes referred to as Inanna's son.

spoke to him, it was the speech of anger. She shouted at him, it was the shout of heavy guilt: "How much longer? Take him away." Holy Inanna gave Dumuzi the shepherd into their hands.'[143]

Inanna appears to have immediately had a change of heart, for she was distraught at the death of her husband, tearing her hair and clothes. Eventually, 'a sister', possibly Dumuzi's, agreed to take his place in the Underworld for six months of the year. This allowed Dumuzi to return to the world in the spring and go back to the Underworld in the fall. In this telling, Dumuzi would be married to the Queen of Heaven for half the year and the Queen of the Underworld for the other half.[144]

This story expresses the annual resurrection of life. Inanna, the Earth as Maiden, enters the Underworld at the end of the year. There she meets Ereshkigal, who is another aspect of herself: the Mother, the source of life, death and rebirth. Through Ereshkigal, Inanna is resurrected, born again, and rises once more to the world of the living, as the year passes its nadir and the sun begins to rise in the sky again.

The relationship between Inanna and Ereshkigal is established: they are two aspects of the same goddess. Inanna became Ereshkigal to mount her throne, and as Ereshkigal, gave (re)birth to herself. At the same time, Ereshkigal is Ki (Ninhursag) the Earth-Mother-Goddess, the giver and taker of all life.

The Goddess as Inanna determines when she will die, and as Ereshkigal, when she will rise again. While the Winter Solstice, the marker that determines the exact point at which the regeneration of the annual cycle happens, is a solar event, it is not the sun, typically viewed as a male deity, nor the sky that causes this to happen, but the Goddess. The Sumerians were not sun-worshippers; the sun was just the calendar they used. The Sumerians worshipped the Goddess and considered the movements of the sun, moon and stars to be under her control.

Inanna (as Ereshkigal) gives birth to herself. We do not know

---

143 http://etcsl.orinst.ox.ac.uk/section1/tr141.htm

144 Inanna, Ereshkigal and Dumuzi bind together life and death, and fertility and resurrection, the foundations of the culture.

when the part of the story that concerns Enki was introduced, but it is probably a later overlay on an older myth in which the power of life, death and rebirth was entirely within the gift of the Goddess. This later version of the story requires the approval and assistance of a male god, Enki, for the Goddess to resurrect herself.

At this early point, male power is tentative; two male gods are powerless to help and only Enki, ever the champion of the Goddess and closest to her, can. He does not storm the Palace Ganzer with the terrible demons at his disposal, however, which must indicate that they are powerless against the Goddess. Instead, he creates two meek little beings, from the body of the Goddess herself (the earth under his fingernails) and sends them to beg Ereshkigal for Inanna's resurrection. Power remains with the Goddess.

The fact that Inanna spends three days in the Underworld is an expression of triplism. This concept derives from the three days when the sun appears to be still at the Winter Solstice, before rising again, and the three dark days of the lunar cycle.

In the conclusion to the tale, the familiar pattern of seasonality is re-established, which is what the story was probably originally meant to convey. Inanna controls her own resurrection, the cycle of the year, marked by the Solstice, as well as that of Dumuzi, the cycle of the seasons.

## The Huluppu Tree

This myth reveals a shift in the balance of power between Goddess and God, reflecting that between women and men. It is probably based on an older myth but appears to have been updated during the third millennium BCE. It features a new character, Gilgamesh, who is part man and part god. Gilgamesh appears in the *Sumerian King List* during the third millennium. While we cannot be certain if this was one man or a dynasty of kings, it seems probable that his character was based on a real man. It is likely that the story sought to legitimise the mortal ruler by association with a powerful deity.

This is a well-known phenomenon that mythologists call 'euhemerisation', after a Greek writer who placed historical figures in contact with deities.[145]

The myth discusses Inanna and her special Huluppu tree:

'The woman tended the tree with her hand, placed it by her
    foot,[146]
Inanna tended the tree with her hand, placed it by her foot,
"When will it be a fruitful throne for me to sit on,' she said,
"When will it be a fruitful bed for me to lie on,' she said.
The tree grew big, its trunk bore no foliage,
In its roots the snake who knows no charm set up its nest,
In its crown the Imdugud-bird placed its young,
In its midst the maid Lilith built her house –
The always laughing, always rejoicing maid,
I, the maid Inanna, how I weep!" [147]
Her brother, the hero Gilgamesh,
Stood by her in this matter,
He donned armour weighing fifty minas about his waist –
Fifty minas were handled by him like thirty shekels –
His "axe of the road" –
Seven talents and seven minas – he took in his hand,
At its roots he struck down the snake who knows no charm,
In its crown the Imdugud-bird took its young, climbed to the
    mountains,
In its midst the maid Lilith tore down her house, fled to the
    wastes.
The tree – he plucked at its roots, tore at its crown,
The sons of the city who accompanied him cut off its branches,
He gives it to holy Inanna for her throne,
Gives it to her for her bed.'[148]

---

145 Euhemerus, also spelled Euemeros or Evemerus; (Ancient Greek: Εὐήμερος, Euhemeros, happy; prosperous; late 4th century BCE), was a Greek mythographer at the court of Cassander, the king of Macedon.

146 This refers to the common practice, when planting a tree, of compacting the soil around the roots with one's foot.

147 The maid Lilith and the maid Inanna are not one; other versions of the poem make this clear, as does the subsequent text of this one.

148 Kramer, Samuel Noah. *The Sumerians: Their History, Culture and Character.* Univer-

The poem associates the Huluppu Tree with the Tree of Life, an ancient concept that appears across the world and in many religions. It connects the Underworld, through its roots, with Heaven and Earth, through its branches and so represents a cyclical conception of life. The fruit of the Tree of Life conveys immortality. Its counterpart is the Tree of Knowledge, whose fruit, amongst other things, confers the wisdom and authority of rulership. Both trees are powerful Goddess objects.

The Lilith Maid is a *lilitu*, a female demon who preys upon women and new-born children. The translation 'Lilith' here suggests that this is the same creature as appears in Hebrew tradition, with the same characteristics.[149] Patai describes the Lilith-Maid as having no milk in her breasts and as unable to bear children.[150], [151]

Lilith, the dark maid and she-demon who is constantly cackling at Inanna's plight, is the fear of all women: of childbirth, of its terrible pain and of the possibility that it may result in the death of the woman or her child. She also represents the fear of sterility, the inability to conceive. Lilith cannot have her own children, so she kills mothers and takes theirs. Childbirth is difficult, dangerous, and extremely painful for humans. At this time in history, despite the fact that women would have had their first babies when their bodies were young and supple, fear of the pain and danger must have preyed on their minds. Conquering this fear is clearly a rite of passage, a step from the world of the girl-child to the mature mother. Parturition is a moment of death and rebirth: the death of the girl and her rebirth as a mother, alongside her newborn.

The Imdugud-bird is a reference to the storm demon Anzu who:

---

sity of Chicago Press. 1963.

149 In that tradition, Lilith was the first wife of Adam, created as he was, from the earth. When she refused to be subservient to him, she was cast out of Eden and replaced by Eve, who was created from his rib. Enraged, Lilith transforms into the demon.

150 Patai, R. *The Hebrew Goddess*. Enlarged edition. Wayne State University Press. 1990.

151 In a fascinating hint that these oral traditions are indeed very ancient, in the Philippines there exists a belief in shape-shifting spirits called *Aswang*. One class of these, the *manangganal*, are self-segmenting winged female horrors whose torso separates from their lower bodies at the waist, leaving the legs standing and then, trailing their intestines, they fly onto the roofs of houses where pregnant women live and suck the foetuses from their wombs by passing their long prehensile tongues though cracks. Is there here an echo of the *lilitu*?

'had a lion's head and body, huge wings, and could walk on two legs like a man. Anzu was called Imdugud, and among other things was known for being able to create whirlwinds, thunder, and sandstorms with his wings, and for stealing the tablet of destiny.'

The Imdugud-bird is an elemental force of chaos, violence and destruction, which could raise desert storms and cause the rivers to flood the land. The catastrophic flood of the Old Testament may have its origin in one that occurred in Sumer around 3500 BCE, causing huge damage and almost certainly massive loss of life, and depositing a layer of mud nearly two metres thick. The menace posed to agriculture and civilisation by untamed nature is very real.

In the roots of the tree lives a serpent, the 'snake who knows no charm'. Its presence is another indicator that this story is a precursor to the Biblical one of Adam and Eve. It is immune to Inanna's attempts to evict it with the force of her magic, but Gilgamesh simply strikes down the snake with his axe. This is a statement that the masculine power of force of arms is greater than the feminine power of magic. It is the clearest indicator in the text that the warrior patriarchy is now ascendant.

The snake can be interpreted as Enki, the Lord of Craft and Knowledge, who was Inanna's greatest ally. The implication is that Gilgamesh has overwhelmed even this mighty deity. Enki may have given Inanna the *Mes*, the gift of civilization, but war could take it away. The Goddess must now depend on the military power of kings.

Snakes are associated with knowledge and with the Goddess. Through the phenomenon of shedding skin, they represent growth, transformation and rebirth, and snakes were identified with magic and shape-shifting. Snakes, along with dragons, represent the Goddess' untamed natural forces. In earlier times, these forces were recognised as powers of the Goddess. While her other qualities may be represented by other manifestations, snakes, serpents and dragons are always the most dangerous, chaotic and destructive aspects.[152] As a consequence of their refusal to be tamed by the power of men, snakes and the Goddess are represented within patriarchal cultures in the worst light as, again, in the Hebrew myth of the Garden of

---

152 In a later myth-cycle the Goddess transforms into the Serpent of Chaos, which is killed by a later god-hero, Marduk, in a clear restatement of the theme here: by strength and force of arms, men rule over nature, the Goddess and women.

Eden.[153]

The wild and destructive elemental power of nature is as much a part of the Goddess as her ability to create. Inanna must find a way to reconcile these two parts of her own nature if her city is to prosper. In order to do this, the Goddess and the Hero must come together to form a partnership of woman and man. Just as women need men to fertilise their bodies and the land needs the sun to bring forth crops, the Goddess needs the Hero to make civilisation. Inanna cannot charm the snake – the wild and destructive force of creativity that is central to her being – but Gilgamesh, with his great axe, can smite it and bend it to his will.

Inanna's reliance on Gilgamesh to rid the Huluppu tree of the demons and her pleas for someone – some man – to 'make her a bed' indicate that, far from being a strong independent female force, she had been tamed and put under the control of a male hegemony. Or at very least, that the effort to do so was under way.

The Tree of Life is connected by its roots to the Underworld; it connects the cycles of death and life. By cutting down the tree, Gilgamesh severed that connection. Johanna Stuckey says:

> 'Inanna was now goddess only of the heavens and the Earth, and the cycle of life had suffered irreparable damage. The destroying of the Huluppu tree meant that human beings could no longer count on Inanna and the World Tree to maintain the cycle of life and death. Instead, they were now facing a terrifying, linear world. The old cyclical understanding of death as merely one stage in the eternal round of birth, death, and renewal, symbolized by the tree, had been replaced by a linear perception of life with death and the underworld as the end.
>
> 'The seemingly innocent poem "Inanna and the Huluppu Tree," then, constitutes an androcentric account of the reasons for Inanna's involvement in the "Sacred

---

153 The original suspicion of snakes likely derived from the dangers of their venom, but mythology frequently dramatises. Interestingly, in some cultures, spiders are invested with the same qualities as snakes, probably for the same reasons.

Marriage," both as herself and as furniture. It shows well how myth can be remade to serve ideology! A powerful goddess subject, the sacred World Tree, had, over the centuries, been reshaped into limited goddess objects, a bed and a throne, while the goddess herself was co-opted into seeing this limited role as powerful. Independent Inanna had become feminine, a woman reliant on males to get her out of trouble. The extant poem probably echoes an earlier story, one in which Inanna and the World Tree had very different roles.'[154]

Stuckey suggests that the story describes a point at which a cyclical understanding of the life and death cycle was replaced by a linear one. That would place much greater authority in the hands of the priestly class, who would define how a person would fare after death.

The shift in cultural practice and belief from a cyclical model of existence to a linear one could not have happened without argument, nor quickly. We know that the pace of social change in early civilisations tended to be far slower than that to which we have become accustomed in the modern world. There would have been a period, perhaps many centuries long, where the two sides were in opposition.

In a linear model, a better after-life is possible only through approved behaviour in this one. In a patriarchal theocracy that would mean obedience to the king and his laws: spiritual and political subservience. Once again, we see the intimate relationship between belief and power. Individuals had specific roles and had to obey laws that were no longer agreed, but were imposed. Social stratification was a natural, perhaps inevitable, consequence of this.

The struggle for ultimate authority would become focussed on the spiritual and political elites who would gain temporal power. The spoils of this power were rich and tempting: there were going to be winners and losers.

---

154 Stuckey, J. *"Inanna and the Huluppu Tree": One Way of Demoting a Great Goddess.* http://www.matrifocus.com/LAM05/spotlight.htm

## Temple Life

There are sparse details about temple life before 3000 BCE. However, by 2350 BCE, the temples had grown into large, well-organised operations with 1000 or more permanent staff.[155] These included the priestesses, but also many men, who worked as labourers and animal herders. There were even slave women.[156]

Overseeing the temple was the entu (originally en) or High Priestess. She had the ear of the deity. In the private Holy of Holies, that part of the temple reserved for the deity and her servants, the priestesses could serve and confer with her. In the earliest temples, this was a real garden and even in much later representations foliage is often part of the decoration of such spaces. The idea was adopted into Hebrew Scripture as a source for the Garden of Eden, where Jahweh liked to walk and talk to the humans. This close relationship with the deity gave the priestesses political power.

The outer part of the temple was a busy place. In addition to the priestesses and worshippers, there would have been traders, business people and political leaders, all seeking the blessing of the deity through the intercession of the High Priestess. To those with whom she sympathised would come financial and political reward and success; but for those who were rejected, only the bitter ash of failure. It would be naive to imagine that the priestesses did not appreciate the gifts that might buy their support.

At the same time, the Temple of Inanna was a place where the priestesses indulged in sex, in public. We have drawings of specially-designed couches that allowed the woman to recline in comfort while the man, standing, penetrated her. This practice has often been pejoratively called 'Temple Prostitution'. What was really going on?

Many pleasures were available in the Temple. Beer, for example, was much loved by the Sumerians and by 3400 BCE they had already

---

155 Lerner, Gerda. *The Creation of Patriarchy, Volume 1.* Oxford University Press. 1986.
156 It is possible that the Temple 'slaves' were women who through misfortune had become destitute and had turned to the Temple for shelter and help. In the later period, when war became endemic, there may have been many women whose husbands had been killed in combat and who had to turn to this solution.

established the cultivation of opium, which they called Hul Gil, or 'the joy plant'.[157] The air would have been fragrant with perfume and incense, and there would have been music. This was a holy place, and while human pleasures were certainly indulged in and enjoyed, these would have been under the eye of the senior priestesses, who would have maintained order and decorum. Most of all, this was a place of women, where their sexuality was celebrated and not under the control of any man.

The Eanna Temple or House of Heaven was a place in the living world where women could savour all of the pleasures of life in the company of the great goddess Inanna, personified by her priestesses. It was run by women for women, but men could and did enjoy the pleasures it offered.

Temple sex was probably a lingering echo of a time, a thousand years before and more, when women really were in control of all aspects of their lives and reproductive sex was seen as a holy act of worship. The Temple harked back to a time when women had been free, in the matriarchal groups that were at the centre of earlier cultures. There they could enjoy the company of other women, in the presence of the Goddess, and if they felt like it, enjoy sex with a stranger who caught their eye. Perhaps it was where women would go to meet their lovers, knowing that jealous husbands could not intervene, and where they were supported by a matriarchal sisterhood of women, led by the High Priestess.

Sumerian women had already been disempowered by the middle of the third millennium BCE. They remained, for all of their lives, the property of their fathers but were held on long-term lease by the men to whom they were married.[158] In the main, these were arranged marriages, which were probably negotiated on their behalf without their permission and, as is the case today, settled on the grounds of the mutual benefit of the men involved. And so what does a woman, married to a man for whom she has no sexual desire but still has the needs of any woman, do? She goes to the Temple and sips some potent liquor, smokes some narcotics and there, in the perfumed anonymity

---

157 Booth, Martin. *Opium: A History*. Simon & Schuster. 1996; also Latimer, Dean, and Goldberg, Jeff. *Flowers in the Blood: The Story of Opium*. Franklin Watts, 1981.

158 This arrangement may reflect a limitation of a husband's rights over his wife, since she could appeal to her father in the case of abuse.

of the sisterhood of the Goddess, she enjoys carefree, blameless sex with a handsome stranger whom she will never see again.

The women having sex in the Temple of the Goddess in Sumer – which were equally houses of all sorts of mortal pleasure – were not doing this to make money or because they were coerced, but because they wanted to. Women in Sumer were proud of their beauty, fertility and seductiveness, and they chose to have sex in the Temple because it was legal, while having adulterous sex with a neighbour was not.

Most women were virginal, sexually intact until their marriage as teenagers, and baby-factories after that. They had no choice in this. In the Temple, they could relax, be beautiful, watch as men surveyed them, perhaps meeting and physically enjoying men to whom they were far more attracted than the husbands chosen for them. In this place, they knew that they were desired and knew that this gave them power. And here they were protected by the Goddess herself.

This freedom, maintained for thousands of years in defiance of an increasingly controlling and misogynistic patriarchy, represented the last bastion of women's power. Until Roman times and beyond, the right of a woman to control her own sexuality was a central plank of Goddess culture, and one reason why the Goddess was so hated by the male priests who eventually came to power, and the patriarchy that supported them.

Goddess culture is not, as monotheist apologists have so often ranted, about the 'pleasures of the flesh', usually stated in such a way as to imply that there might be something wrong in that. There is no moral dimension in sex; that is an invention of the patriarchy. Goddess culture teaches that our purpose should be to have a full and complete life here on Earth while we are alive. It implies a concern for the living, for the people around us and the world in which we live, indeed the planet itself. Amongst them and in this place must our happiness be found, for there is no other place or time that it can be. Goddess culture does not trade off the slavery of mindless 'obedience' to a distant and harsh god, through his cadre of priests, against the unproven and unprovable promise of happiness after death. Instead, it implies a desire for balance and moderation, protection and nurture here and now.

# Sacred to Profane Marriage

Sex in early Uruk was considered a sacred act of creation. After the emergence of large-scale agriculture, sex, while retaining the pleasures that it affords, became an agricultural practice. Men fertilised women to make babies, and women eagerly complied, exhorted by the mighty and quintessentially seductive Inanna herself.

We have already seen how the phenomenon of reproductive sex became hugely important to our culture, and how the formal institution of marriage bound each woman's fertility to one specific man and placed him in control of it. Divine marriage placed the official stamp of the culture on that relationship. Changes were made to the Great Rite that transformed it into the Sacred Marriage so that even the gods and goddesses reflected the same arrangement.

When the power went from the Goddess to her consort, society had fatefully changed. This evolution occurred during the third millennium BCE. Once a symbolical rite that affirmed women's power of reproduction and fertility and at the same time their central role in society, hierogamy became a formal marriage ceremony binding the Goddess to the God, Priestess to King and woman to man. The mythology provided both a reinforcing model and a standard for behaviour.

Johanna Stuckey notes that during the course of the third millennium BCE, a significant change in the balance of power between women and men occurred. In the beginning, the High Priestess chose her male consort but by 2300 BCE, this right had been taken by the king. This is a clear indication of the general downward trend of women's status during this time.[159]

Although the aspects of the Sacred Marriage relating to fertility and the role of sex in ensuring its continuation were retained, the later versions of the Sacred Marriage ritual placed the Goddess under the control of a god. He was represented by a priest/king, who then exercised the divine power of the Goddess himself.

---

159 Stuckey, Johanna. *Inanna and the 'Sacred Marriage'.* http://www.matrifocus.com/ IMB05/spotlight.htm Retrieved 21/08/2014.

Sacred marriage was not merely a royal practice. Throughout the Tigris and Euphrates valleys there were many temples to Inanna, of which the greatest was in Uruk, and to the other deities, many of which also appear to have practised it. In Sumerian mythology, the Goddess Ki, the Earth, is 'the broad field' and the 'great cow'. Women were like the cultivated fields or the 'good cows' to be fertilised and make babies as often as possible. They were no longer wild, mysterious and dangerous, wielding the limitless power of the Goddess. Like the land and animals now under the control of men, their powers had been tamed.

Sumerologist Douglas Frayne cites a French translation of a 'tablet of the ritual of the *entu*-priestess of the storm-god Emar.'[160], [161]

'The ritual took place over seven days. On the first, jars (for divining the identity) of the new priestess, presumably using oil drops, were placed...in the temple of Ninurta. The god chose one of the daughters of the citizens to be the new *entu* priestess. The new priestess was anointed. The next day the priestess was elaborately coiffed. The next day the consecration ceremony *mallulu* took place when the red garment of Ninkur was put in the house of the new priestess' father. The second day of the *mallulu* various sacrifices and ceremonies were made. At evening the *entu* priestess was made to sit on a throne and various presents were made to her. These included earrings, a red turban, a bracelet and a pectoral. The next day the *entu* priestess ate and left her house. They covered her head like that of a fiancée. Before evening more food was consumed and the elders presented to the priestess a new garment, a bed, a chair and a stool. They spread a coverlet on the bed and more food was provided. While the singers chanted *hulelu* the priestess' sister washed her feet.[162]

---

160 The term *entu* is an Akkadian derivative of the Sumerian *en*, which means 'highest person'. The use of *entu* indicates that this is a later Akkadian text.

161 Even today the Catholic Church is a symbolised Goddess, and Catholic priests are married to her, which is why they cannot take human wives.

162 Note the similarity between hulelu and the Judaeo-Christian hallelu, which is part of hallelujah. This is another indication that the later cults borrowed heavily from Sumerian

The *entu* priestess went up and lay down on the bed.'[163]

Since marriage was such a cornerstone of the nascent patriarchy, it is not surprising that this would be reinforced on the public stage. Thus, incidentally, was born the tradition of grandiose royal weddings that persists to this day. These are performed by religious authority, evidence that the priestly class still retains considerable power. Not only do they confer legitimacy on the monarch, since no king can be taken seriously without a fertile bride to continue his line, but they also reinforce, in very deliberate terms, the subjection of women to the patriarchy. Queens and kings, amongst their other roles, are meant to show an example to the people they rule.

In Goddess culture, menstrual blood is holy and revered.[164] The time when a woman is bleeding is that of her greatest power, when the mark of the Goddess, the creatrix of all life, is upon her. Whenever we see one group attempting to overrule or wrest power from another, we also see propaganda and vilification. When the patriarchy began to overthrow the matriarchy, they also began to devalue the sacred, life-creating power of women. Women became mere vessels for the creative seed of men. By the end of the first millennium BCE, in many cultures and certainly all those in the Eastern Mediterranean, the Levant and the Middle East, women were deprived of any voice and regarded, particularly when menstruating, as being 'unclean'.

By 2000 BCE the Sacred Marriage had become an uncompromising statement about the balance of spiritual and temporal power between the genders. The Goddess had been tamed by a priest-king-god, just as ordinary women were made subservient to ordinary men. Male authority over women was a central part of later Sumerian society and of many successor cultures, and it became essential to the development of Western culture itself.

With the change from Great Rite to Sacred Marriage, the edifice

---

originals.

163 Frayne, Douglas. *Notes on the Sacred Marriage Rite. BiOr 42.* 1985.

164 It is the Goddess' drops of menstrual blood on the holly-tree, its red berries, that make it important at our winter festivals.

of matriarchal power was dealt a blow from which it would never recover. As dynasties of kings established control over society, the oppression of women increased, power began to be wrested from the priestesses, and the attempt to destroy the Goddess began.

# SECTION SEVEN:

# The Emerging Patriarchy

## Sumer to Akkad

At its peak, Uruk grew to have more than 50,000 inhabitants, a metropolis by ancient standards, and was the dominant city in Sumer. Huge volumes of trade flowed in and out of the area and many settlements grew to populations of more than 10,000, becoming city-states in their own right. There is remarkably little evidence of a warlike culture anywhere in Sumer in its first millennium, and the cities were not walled.

The first period of truly Sumerian culture was named after Uruk. The condition of women in this era was far better than came to be the case later, and the society prospered. For peace to last so long was a great triumph for the Goddess and her culture. It was not force of arms or the greed of men that finally brought ruin, but an enemy that no wall or army could defend against: climate change.

The end of the Uruk era was brought about by a dry period called the Piora Oscillation that lasted for 300 years, from 3200 BCE to 2900 BCE. The city's wealth, built upon the agriculture of the fertile plain around it, diminished, and its population went hungry. Had their beautiful but fickle Goddess Inanna turned against them? Though the times were hard, Uruk somehow survived, but it was much changed. After this time, in what is called the Early Dynastic Period, Uruk became much more like the city-state model with which we are familiar. This is the time of the epic hero-king Gilgamesh. He was said to have built the great city walls that still encircle the remains of the city. According to the *Sumerian King List*, Gilgamesh, the hero, was the fifth king of Uruk and lived around 2,500 BCE.

This period may have been glorious for Uruk, but it was less so for her goddess. Inanna had ignored the city's pleas for an end to the drought for hundreds of years, and this brought about a shift in the mythology.

Most telling is the replacement of a peaceful, biddable shepherd-boy, Dumuzi, as the consort of the Goddess, with Gilgamesh, a warrior-king and adventurer who bedazzled his subjects and took whichever woman he fancied, by rape if she resisted. He glorified the city and built huge battlements as well as high ziggurats. He was part god, part man: bombastic, vainglorious, in short a bully. His best friend was a wild man called Enkidu, who lived and mated with animals, until Gilgamesh sent a priestess to seduce and tame him.

In sending a priestess to have sex with a wild man who practised bestiality, the story of Gilgamesh and Enkidu demonstrates a sea-change in the status of women. Instead of being able to choose with whom they would have sex they must now submit to the will of men, even if that means mating with a beast-lover. The balance between men and women in Uruk had been fatefully shifted.

After the end of the Piora Oscillation, the climate was drier than it had been, and this, among other things, brought greater change. The *Sumerian King List* now includes references to two other cities within southern Mesopotamia, Ur and Kish.[165] Uruk had become but one of many rival cities and it seems probable that a great deal of its economic power evaporated during the long period of drought.

This period is increasingly characterised by evidence of war and the dominance of warrior culture. We see this in the Epic of Gilgamesh and in the practice of building walls around cities while smaller, undefended villages were abandoned. The original culture of Sumer was absorbed into an Akkadian warrior culture, which lessened the influence of the Goddess and the status of women, especially once the Akkadian supreme god Marduk was put at the head of the pantheon.

From the middle of the third millennium BCE, war persisted with hardly a break throughout Mesopotamia. The Goddess cultures, which were characterised by their peaceful nature, gave way to a new world order dominated by uncompromisingly aggressive men

---

165 Ur is perhaps better known in its much later guise of Ur of the Chaldeans, when it became an empire in its own right.

such as were idealised in Gilgamesh. Battle and glory were set above the gentle, sensual pleasures of early Uruk.

The tumult of war broke out with a vengeance when Eannatum, king of the city-state of Lagash, annexed most of Sumer, including Uruk, Ur, Umma and many other cities. He was violent and bloody and deliberately tortured and abused his defeated enemies, perhaps the first recorded use of terrorism in human history. After Eannatum's death, his empire collapsed. Lugal-Zage-Si, the priest-king of Umma, destroyed the remnants of Lagashi power, then conquered Uruk and made it his capital. He proclaimed his Empire from the Gulf to the Mediterranean but eventually was defeated by an Akkadian king, Sargon, in 2270 BCE.[166] War raged periodically after the time of Sargon, as succeeding waves of conquerors swept through, and lasting peace was never to return to the area.

It is not surprising that the cities that were the targets for violence soon developed the arts of defence and war for themselves. Before long, the first thing people would do when laying out a city would be to build a wall. Soon they too would be raiding, recovering that which was theirs and punishing aggressors, nipping potential threats in the bud. They would soon have realised that force of arms could win great wealth. We know that Uruk prospered for a thousand years without any wall; the decision to build one for protection, a massive undertaking, was not made lightly.

There was Uruk before its wall, so the Goddess was there before the violence began. Her city was peaceful, a wonderful place of art and music, with traders bringing goods, lovely and precious things, from hundreds of miles away. This was truly the Goddess in her happiest role, at least in civilisation. Loving creatrix, benefactrix, goddess of fertility, of sex, of love, and patroness of the arts, she brought her people such largesse.

Then, strange men came to Uruk, not to trade or spend their

---

166 Sargon is interesting not only because he marks the shift in political balance away from the Sumerian south-east to the Akkadian north-west but also because, according to legend, he was placed in a basket made of rushes by this mother and allowed to float onto the river Euphrates, where he was found by a woman drawing water and taken to the home of Ishtar, as Inanna had become, who raised him and trained him in the skills of kingship. The motif of the future king being placed in a basket in a river, rescued and raised by a deity or ruler was used in the story of Moses, who was mythically raised in the house of the Egyptian king.

wealth on the pleasures of the city, but to rape and kill and steal everything they could. The young Inanna, so beautiful, so charming, so innocent yet so mischievous, so full of love and delight in life, so replete with joy at her own fecundity, turned into a screaming she-devil of war. She killed with utter savagery and bloodlust any who stood before her, cutting a swathe through the enemy ranks and leaving only death behind. What force could make a woman do that? The menace to her children, the killing of her beloved, the destruction of her home. She was the lioness who turns on the hyenas who threaten her cubs, and she was just as ferocious.

The advent of warrior culture brought about not only the rise of warrior kings, but also changes in the Goddess herself. She became a warrior too. As gentle as she was in love would she become violent in her unleashed destruction; magnificent, awe-inspiring, utterly terrifying. Because war became such a prevalent part of human history, this is a familiar face of the Goddess. We see her again and again, as Boudicca, as Zenobia, as Tamara and Jeanne d'Arc. She is Liberté, her breasts exposed and hair flying, bearing the tricolour flag in one hand and a musket in the other as she leads the French Revolutionaries' charge in Delacroix' epic painting.[167]

As warrior culture took hold, protection from attack became so important that it soon overshadowed all other concerns. There is little point in growing food, making children and building cities if these cannot be defended, if enemies can just come in and take everything. This was when the patriarchy became absolutely dominant. Within it, war was as important as agriculture and trade; killing, plunder and destruction had become an economic model.

We would soon see the development of the conventional, pyramidal hierarchy which built the Roman Empire and which exists today. Power flows downwards from one divine and absolute ruler, through layers of individuals less divine and powerful, to the common citizen-soldier, who must only obey and pray. Within this rigidly structured society, there was no place for women. They lost all political voice and their role of ensuring the survival of the culture through motherhood became increasingly less valued than that of men enriching it through war.

---

167 Delacroix, Eugène. *Liberty Leading the People*. Oil on canvas. 1830.

# Inanna to Ishtar

Although the Sumerians, particularly after the early third millennium BCE, became capable warriors, the Akkadians, a Semitic people who took their name from Akkad in northwest Mesopotamia, seem to have been tougher and more aggressive from the very beginning, and this was reflected in their deities.

Ishtar is usually identified as the successor to Inanna within the Akkadian culture that overtook Sumer. The Akkadians drew on their own oral traditions, which differed somewhat from the Sumerian ones, in their depiction of her. Many different versions of the myths surrounding Ishtar exist, and this leads to contradictions. As we have discussed, this phenomenon is very common, and we will see other proliferation of myths in Greece and elsewhere.

Ishtar's mythology is similar to Inanna's but changed in important ways. Poems and hymns are truncated and Ishtar, for all her ferociousness, is less wilful and audacious than Inanna. She seems to be more controlled, at the behest of men or at least male deities. She is like a caricature of herself, an attenuated strain, and this fits with what we know of the warlike, patriarchal nature of Akkadian culture. While Ishtar's role as a fertility goddess remained important, her other one, of war-goddess, came to the fore in Akkadia and persisted in successor cultures.

Ishtar would become Eostre or Ostara, the goddess of fertility, from whose name we derive the word oestrogen, the female hormone, and the springtime festival Easter. This festival was tied into the life and death cycle of Ishtar's consort, Tammuz, who, while also a product of Akkadian culture, shared many characteristics with the Sumerian equivalent, Dumuzi.

Ishtar's relationship with Tammuz is a modified restatement of the bond between the pastoral and arable farming methods on which the culture was based. Tammuz was a mortal shepherd boy with whom Ishtar fell in love at first meeting.[168] This feeling was recip-

---

168 This is subtly different from the earlier version, where Inanna is at first reluctant to accept Dumuzi the shepherd, preferring instead to marry a farmer.

rocal; hardly surprising since Ishtar was the embodiment of female beauty and sexuality and Tammuz asked for her hand in marriage. Ishtar accepted. In this, the initiative is with Tammuz; in the earlier Sumerian versions, it was with Inanna.

## Ishtar's Descent

Whereas Inanna was in control of her descent into the Underworld and rebirth into life, Ishtar is constrained.

As Ishtar's consort, Tammuz is a metaphor for the passage of time in the agricultural year. One myth, largely derived from Inanna's Descent into the Underworld, but much modified, says that in the burning heat of summer, during the month to which he gave his name, and which still bears it in the Jewish calendar, people came to the fields where Tammuz stood and savagely cut him down with sickles and scythes, scattering his flesh in many places. This represents the harvest of the grain crops, a critical moment in the agricultural year. Ishtar is distraught when she hears of his disappearance and wears herself out with grief. For months, she searches and she and the world pine for the lost lover Tammuz. She was the goddess of fertility so during her distress all procreation ceased. Trees and plants withered and died, and humans and animals became sterile.

Having searched everywhere else, Ishtar knew Tammuz must be in the Underworld. To enter the Underworld is to die, even for a deity, yet she does not hesitate. Ishtar descends into the Underworld and, after three days, returns with Tammuz, who is born again into this world. Tammuz' birthday is three days after the winter solstice; his return to glory is on the spring equinox, and he is cut down three days after the summer solstice with the crops ripe in the fields.

These three dates are still celebrated, and there is no doubt of their origin: the 25th of December, three days after the solstice, is the day that Tammuz, as weak as a baby, begins his return; Easter, the spring equinox, is when he rises into the world in his majesty and is wed to his beautiful Bride, the Queen of Heaven, the Goddess; and three days after the summer solstice he is cut down again and the cycle continues.

In this version, instead of a 'year' Goddess and a 'seasonal' consort, the cycle all revolves around the male, Tammuz. Ishtar's role is to rescue him and bring about his resurrection. In the Sumerian tale of Inanna, Dumuzi is sent to the Underworld after Inanna has been resurrected, by Inanna herself. The entire focus of the earlier myth is on the Goddess, in the form of Inanna and her annual resurrection, while in the latter, the Goddess is merely the protector and saviour of the deity. In the Sumerian myth, the Goddess is in absolute control, albeit in later versions requiring the aid of Enki. In the Akkadian she has become the God-King's bodyguard and it is axiomatic that in any such relationship the bodyguard is less important than the guarded. We will see this again and again.

As ever with oral traditions, the story evolved. In some versions, Ishtar and Tammuz were born together in embrace, adapting the earlier story of An and Ki into their own, and in others, Ishtar herself gave birth to the baby Tammuz. Thus, when Tammuz came back into the world, it was not as a man, but as a baby contained within Ishtar's womb. Therefore, Tammuz is Ishtar's husband, and also her brother and son; a neat expression of the triple aspects of a deity. Nevertheless, the focus is always on Tammuz.

In another version of the tale, Tammuz was killed either by anonymous 'people' with scythes and sickles, or by a wild boar, a symbol of untamed chaos. Ishtar covered her head in ashes for forty days, giving up all pleasure and food.[169] She then discovered that she was pregnant. She says that this must be a divine conception (recalling the divine parthenogenesis of Ki and An within the womb of Nammu), and has a golden egg made to celebrate the event. She searches all over the world and again finds Tammuz in the Underworld, where she rescues him. Tammuz is resurrected in all his glory, and summer and fertility return. This particular version persisted into Babylonian times, when Ishtar had transformed into the goddess Shammuramat, perhaps better known by her Greek name, Semiramis.[170]

---

169 A tradition which Christians still follow, calling it Lent, as do Muslims, as Ramadan.
170 This goddess has been identified with a real historical figure, the Assyrian Queen Shammuramat, but some scholars dispute this. The historical figure may simply have adopted the name of the goddess.

In yet other tellings, Ishtar (sometimes Shammuramat) herself is born from a bloodstained egg that lands in the Euphrates at sunrise. While, predictably, patriarchal monotheists have invented many gruesome tales about this, the real explanation is simple. The egg represents the holy womb of the Divine Mother and the blood her menstrual flow. Seas and rivers represent the creative waters of the Goddess, in which all life was formed, and the tale, by placing the egg in the river, restates that the power of creation and re-creation of everything, including herself, is reserved to the Goddess.

There are differences between the stories of Inanna and Ishtar, partly due to the ongoing effect of oral tradition but mainly to the great socio-political changes that were under way. Nonetheless, there are important commonalities. At either the Vernal Equinox or the first full moon after it, Tammuz rises into glory accompanied by his consort/wife Ishtar. The Sacred Marriage took place all over Mesopotamia during this festival, uniting Inanna/Ishtar with Dumuzi/Tammuz. This was the most important celebration of the year, now a formal marriage between the King and the High Priestess. It is the foundation of the traditional May Day celebrations which persist in the West to this day, where young men and women dance around symbolic trees – Maypoles – in fertility dances.[171]

Tammuz dies and rises again every year, just as the sun appears to.[172] Even here, when we know that the patriarchy was already deeply entrenched, the deity cannot rise without the Goddess' intervention. She must resurrect him, for she is the Goddess, who both takes and gives life.

Changes in mythology follow changes in culture, as a means to explain and enforce them. Although this was now a patriarchal culture, the prevailing mythology was still strongly Goddess-based.

This would change.

---

171 Maypoles are often seen as phallus symbols that impregnate the Earth, ensuring a bountiful growing season.

172 The sun is not being worshipped here. It is simply a measure of the passage of time.

# Babylon

Desert irrigation contains the seed of its own destruction by depositing salts in the soil. There is not enough natural rainfall to leach these out again. Progressively increasing salinity in the soil around Uruk, caused by many hundreds of years of artificial irrigation, began to cause problems. Crop yields fell, and a change was made from the production of wheat to barley, which is more resistant to salt. The people tried flushing the land with fresh water, but ultimately there could be no cure and climate change, over-intensive agriculture and salination of the soil turned the fertile plain of Sumer into a sterile desert. Uruk collapsed and now sits abandoned in desolation, with no sign that it was once the greatest and most beautiful city on Earth and one that was truly of the Goddess.

By that time, war had scourged the land for hundreds of years, and the centre of power had shifted from the Sumerian south east of Mesopotamia to the Akkadian north west. Ishtar remained a goddess of love, but she was increasingly seen in her role as goddess of war. She was no longer just the lioness who bares her teeth in defence of her family, but the hunting lioness leading a great horde of armed men on the path of pillage and spoil. She embodied the military power of Babylon. Fearsome armies marched out through the Gate of Ishtar, and she was their Great Goddess. She was revered and worshipped by her people and, more importantly, hated and feared by Babylon's enemies.

From the third millennium BC onwards, not a century passed without catastrophic warfare within the territory. As a result of this turmoil, we see evolving religious beliefs. Son and daughter gods overthrow old gods, usually replacing them with even more brazen warriors. Inanna might have been the lioness who defended her children, but Ishtar had acquired the patriarchal characteristic of territorial aggression.

It would not be long before a male god was put in charge and women deemed as being 'half the value' of men, and allowed no access to power in military, religious, political or spiritual areas of life.

Men would stand tall over the bloody wars that they caused, venerated as heroes and their violence and fighting ability celebrated. For thousands of years to come, those at the top of the hierarchy would subjugate those at the bottom. Many male warriors would die, but the principal victims of this ongoing carnage would be women and the children they sought to protect, the old, the ill and the weak.

The patriarchy had come of age.

## The Patriarchy's Greatest Fear

Kings have always taken counsel from prelates and in Sumer this was undoubtedly so. Sumerian cities were theocracies, where political and religious powers merged.[173] The king's religious, spiritual, and temporal consort was the High Priestess. The priestesses had great power, for they had the ear of the king; power flowed from the Goddess to the King, and the Priestesses were the Goddess incarnate. They had the ability to influence events, to see those they favoured rewarded and those they did not cast down.

As cities developed, so did formalised systems of government and regulation. The Sumerians invented the contract and a type of cylinder-seal that could be rolled into a clay tablet to perform the same function as a notary's seal. This being a theocracy, the lawyers who drew up contracts and the bureaucracy that administered them would have been of the priestly classes. Control over that bureaucracy, and control over the treasury that would pay for everything, was the remit of the main temple of the city's patron deity.

But temporal and political power is coveted. Like the other Mesopotamian cultures that followed it, Sumer was polytheistic, with both male and female deities. In the early culture, these were all served by priestesses, but as the patriarchy developed some of them began to be served by male priests instead. They were jealous of the

---

173 Jacobsen, Thorkild (Ed.). *The Sumerian King List.* Oriental Institute of the University of Chicago. 1939.

political power of the priestesses.

As the wealth of the Sumerian cities increased, notions of class status arose; a function of the burgeoning patriarchy. For the first time society had its rich and its poor. An unequal distribution of wealth naturally led to an unequal distribution of power. With the rise of warrior culture, men, especially men of the lower classes, were expected to fight and die not only to protect their city and their families but also to expand the wealth of their kings and the powerful men at the top of the hierarchical pyramid. The patriarchy weighs most heavily on women, but also on men.

The fundamental tool through which the patriarchy exercises control is by legally binding each woman, as property, to a man and punishing her for any transgression. We still see today, in some cultures, how women who have been the victims of rape may be legally flogged for 'sex outside marriage' and those who dare to have extra-marital sex willingly are judicially murdered in public.[174] There is nothing as important to the patriarchy as the control of women's ability to create life. Even today in the West, a constant battle must be fought against the repressive forces that try to limit women's rights over their own reproduction. The appropriation of property rights, by men, over women's bodies, and the entrenchment of this through law and custom, is the cornerstone of the patriarchy.

This is why right-wing religious demagogues and the groups they animate today are so militant in their opposition to what they see as the dilution of the institution of marriage. They hate the idea of people 'just living together' because it undermines their power over society. For marriage to have meaning, *they must approve it*. Think how much more galling it must be for them, to see same-sex marriages permitted and honoured! Marriage, in their minds, exists as a mechanism for the enslavement of women to men, and so it must be *between* a man and a woman.[175] For them, a woman marrying

---

174 In Islamic law, adultery is a crime of property and all women belong to a man. A woman who willingly has sex outside marriage denies either her father or her husband's possession of her sexuality. However, a man only commits adultery if he has sex with a woman who 'belongs' to another man. If he has sex with a girl or woman who is orphaned, widowed, abandoned, captive, 'dishonoured' or not Muslim, this does not count, since there is no right of property established over her sexuality. Yet, of course, such a woman can still be whipped or killed for having sex outside marriage.

175 Notice that in today's polygamous cults, such as Islam and Mormonism, only men

another woman confers the right of marital slave-ownership upon a woman, an unthinkable contradiction in terms. Even more insufferable to them is the idea of marriage between two men since, for them, marriage is not a profession of deep and sincere love of two equals but an arrangement by which one is put under the dominion of another. It is invidious, to this mindset, to see two men marry because, once again, it undermines the power structure inherent in the patriarchal concept of marriage.

But the patriarchy's fantasy is just that, for in truth, women do not need men at all. They just need semen, and everything else they can happily manage for themselves. One man can make hundreds of women pregnant, given the opportunity and energy, but once his purpose as impregnator is served, he has no further function. Women are perfectly capable of managing society, finding or growing food and bringing up their children without the assistance of a man, and the way they do this is to come together in matriarchal groups. That is something that the patriarchy goes to immense lengths to prevent.

This is why it punishes single mothers and their children, once condemned as 'bastards', and lesbian women who live in partnerships of mutual support. Above all else, the patriarchy fears sexually and reproductively independent women, supported by their sisters. A man who is promiscuous may be occasionally called a 'womaniser', but more often he is admired. Consider what a woman who is similarly in control of her sexuality is called – whore, tart, loose woman, slut – the litany of obscene names is long. Lesbian couples who use the seed of an unknown donor to conceive children and then raise them, never once knowing a father's 'authority', are likewise condemned.

Without the establishment of men as figures of power, dominant over women, the whole facade of established patriarchy crumbles into nothing.

---

are allowed multiple marriage partners. This speaks volumes about how these cults see women.

# SECTION EIGHT:

## The Proliferation of Deity

In the beginning was the Mother Goddess, The Sea, who became the Earth as we moved inland. We have seen how she divided into a binary male/female form when we understood procreation, and from there produced Tetrad families when we settled. When we developed agriculture, The Goddess took multiple anthropomorphic forms whose natures meant that they could relate directly to humans, and her omnipotence was divided amongst them. As people spread across the world, representations of deity proliferated. Each was a little different, reflecting the cultural values of the societies that adopted them; yet they all stemmed from the Goddess.

In these cultures the physical and spiritual were two dimensions of the same space. The supernatural world affected every aspect of human life from birth to death, love, sex, marriage, business, even war. Religion and politics were similarly indivisible.

Everything that occurred in the mortal world was governed by the will of the deities. Priestesses, and later priests, who could influence them, thus held great temporal power. Just as our hypothetical grandmother-shaman of the beachcombers had behind her the unlimited and unimaginable power of the Sea Mother Goddess, so the later clerics could wield the power of the deities and influence events in the physical world. In a time full of superstition, no ruler could challenge them. There was good reason for the proliferation of deities: their priestesses and priests were both spiritual and political leaders, and the cults themselves equated to political parties. The link between spiritual and political power became increasingly evident, and its importance continues, even to the present time.

By the time of Sumer, we had left behind the older, more organic and less organised shamanistic cults. Religion, as well as being politics, was business, and it could be very big business indeed. We have only to look at the massive wealth accrued by the Roman Catholic Church, the Church of England or the many Evangelical churches in

*135*

today's United States to see that religion remains profitable.[176]

Essential to the development of religious cults is popular appeal. New and exciting, fashionable versions of the deities were sought to promote each cult and so acquire both political power and material wealth. People did indeed fabricate religions in order to become rich and powerful, and their completely fictional deities were believed in by thousands of gullible people.[177] A striking example of this is the well-documented case of Alexander of Abonoteichus, a fraudster who invented the cult of the snake-god Glycon.[178]

The cultures of the early cities were not meritocracies where the gifted or hardworking could, through their own efforts, become wealthy and powerful. One way to acquire wealth and, possibly, status was to join the city's army and be paid a share of the booty if you survived. The other was to find a new god who could help you: in other words, to invent a religion.

Religiosity and a willingness to suspend disbelief in the promise of a better life after death remain an essential, if problematic, part of the human condition; there are always followers to be had. Moonies, Scientologists, Mormons, Christian Scientists, Baha'i – history is replete with cults, every one invented by hopeful career preachers. An awareness of this tendency was one reason the Roman Catholic Church so severely persecuted heresy. In its collective consciousness was a memory of the second and third centuries CE, when Christianity had struggled against myriad other cults to be selected as the official religion of Rome, and win wealth, status and power.

Organised religions exist for thoroughly materialistic reasons. The more followers a cult has, the more the money it makes and the more political influence it can wield. Thus, there is pressure for religions to 'be fruitful and multiply', and to evangelise and gain more

---

176 It has been estimated that the income, via donations, of religious groups the US is 100 billion dollars per annum. (http://www.statista.com/statistics/296336/revenue-religious-organizations-in-the-us/ retrieved 28/08/2014). Because these organisations do not pay tax on this income, their investments or property, the taxpaying American subsidises them to $71 billion per annum. (Cragun, R *et al. Research Report: How Secular Humanists (and Everyone Else) Subsidize Religion in the United States. Free Inquiry.* May 2012. (http://www.secularhumanism.org/index.php/articles/3149 retrieved 28/08/2012.)

177 We would not like the reader to infer from this that there are deities other than fictional!

178 Lucian of Samosata. *Alexander or the False Prophet.* (*c.* 180 CE)

converts – by both peaceful and violent means.[179] At the same time, they must retain members even if that requires threats of death for apostasy.

The other face of the coin of evangelism is the condemnation of every cult but your own, something that has led, throughout the millennia of human civilisation, to unimaginable horror and bloodshed. This is ongoing and shows no sign of relenting.

If the deities prove unwilling to help a priestly class achieve its will, an angry mob stirred up by ranting prelates will often do the trick, something we have seen countless times over the centuries. Consider Savonarola, the demented priest whose vitriolic condemnation of the Medici dynasty that governed Florence in the Renaissance led to its downfall. The Romans, too, well knew that the person who controls the mob controls the city; it was how Mark Antony turned the tables on the conspirators who had assassinated Julius Caesar. Hypatia, the Alexandrian mathematician, was murdered in 415 CE by a Christian mob stirred up by clerics bent on silencing women.

Religious cults proliferated throughout the Eastern Mediterranean and the Near East in the last millennia BCE. In Akkad, Babylon, Assyria, Canaan and elsewhere the Sumerian tradition evolved. In Egypt, other traditions appeared which, while likely derived from the same original sources, were significantly different. In Greece, much of the Sumerian mythology was adopted but merged with indigenous traditions. All of these were crucially important for the later development of the Abrahamic religious traditions and cultures.

All of these cultures show the same phenomena: the suppression of the Goddess and the appropriation of her powers by male deities alongside the suppression of women and the reduction of their status. The establishment of male gods as rulers over the goddesses is a direct parallel for the objectification of women, their transformation into the property of men, and male control over women's sexuality and reproduction.

As always, the wealthy ruling elite, which included the priestly class, would have had the wherewithal to travel to other lands. They

---

179 This is the real reason why the Catholic Church decries birth control and the US Evangelicals are so violently opposed to abortion. World overpopulation and the struggles of families with more children than they can afford do not matter as long the cult keeps growing.

would have seen and recognised effective strategies for the maintenance of their authority. We will see how these strategies proliferated across cultures, with only minor modifications. First, women had to be controlled by assigning them to individual men and restricting their freedom. Then the Goddess had to be mastered by the gods, to indicate that female subservience was a universal, ideal, 'natural' state. Once this had been accomplished, a new model for the understanding of life had to be invented, one that filled the hearts of all the people with a terror that might only be alleviated by absolute obedience to the ruling class and the patriarchal status quo.

If we examine the mythologies, we see that the differences are merely marketing. The deities themselves are the same. Humans create gods in their likeness so all deities are human in an idealised form. The Goddess, no matter how many forms she takes, is always Woman, and the God is always Man. Myriad expressions of deity have appeared all over the world and throughout history but in all of these we find the same essential human core. It could not be otherwise because we invented all the deities we have ever worshipped. We cannot invent something that is beyond our conception, so all deities, in the end, are a reflection of ourselves.

# The Goddess in Egypt

Egypt was a strange country, full of contradictions. Long and thin, it depended entirely on the narrow fertile strip along the banks of the Nile. The river flooded every year, soaking the soil and depositing alluvium, rich in loam and nutrients.[180] The country was divided into northern and southern kingdoms, and their agricultural wealth supported one of the greatest civilisations of the ancient world.[181]

In Egypt, there were many representations of the Goddess: Aset (Isis), Bastet, Hathor, Ma'at, Nekhbet, Nephthys, Nut, Sekhmet, Selkhet, Taweret, Tefnut, Uadjet and more. These are cognate to similar deities in the Sumerian pantheon, which points to a common source. From our point of view, the most interesting is the one the Egyptians called Aset. She is better known by her Greek name: Isis.[182]

Aset/Isis adds something that Inanna never had, the role and image of the nursing Mother. Inanna is a goddess of fertility rather than of birth and motherhood, and while the two are closely related they are not quite the same. We do not see Inanna as a mother until much later, by which time she had become the Babylonian Ishtar, and even then it is a limited role.

The Egyptians had a Great Mother of their own. Nut, the goddess of the Sky, was born from Shu (Air) and Tefnut (Moisture), and was the sister/wife of Geb (Earth). Her star-covered body stretched across the heavens, and her arms and legs were the pillars that held up the sky.

In an interesting parallel to Ki and An being separated by Enlil, many images show Nut and Geb being held apart by the Air god, Shu.[183] Nut's name, in hieroglyphs, contains the symbol for a pot, which is also a symbol for the womb.[184] Nut swallows the sun, Ra, every night and gives birth to him in the morning. The movement

---

180 This continued until the completion of the Aswan Dam in 1970.

181 'Kingdoms' because the Egyptians did not use the term 'Pharaoh' to describe their kings; that is a Hebrew word.

182 Ions, Veronica. *Egyptian Mythology*. Paul Hamlyn, 1968.

183 Campbell, Joseph. *The Mythic Image*. Princeton University Press. 1974.

184 Pots, wombs, motherhood and women are strongly associated in many early cultures.

of the sun – and, therefore, time itself – is thus under the Goddess' control, a meme that we have seen previously. By the time the great civilisation of Egypt evolved, Nut had already become remote, just as, in Sumer, Ki/Ninhursag had. The divestment of the Great Mother's powers so that they could be given to new deities was well under way by this stage.


## Aset


Aset/Isis is the daughter of the Earth, Geb and the Sky, Nut.[185] She is one of a pair of goddesses with her less beautiful sister, Nephthys. They have two brothers, the gods Osiris and Set, who are also, respectively, their husbands. They are a Divine Tetrad, a linked group of four deities, which is associated with the development of settled agrarian living. Aset and Osiris symbolise day, light and the organised and productive farmland of Egypt, while Set and Nephthys are night and darkness as well as the chaotic desert with its sandstorms and droughts and the destructive yet life-giving power of the annual Nile floods. The sisters Aset and Nepthys clearly parallel Inanna and Ereshkigal.

Aset's name, in hieroglyphs, contains the symbols for a throne and an egg. In her earliest depictions, Aset's headdress is a throne, although later, after she had been syncretised with Hathor, she wore the sun-disc and horn headdress of the latter deity as well, with the throne on top of the disc.[186] Again this parallels Inanna, whose headdress was of horns.[187]

The identification of Aset with the throne is important and rep-

---

185 Note that the genders of the Earth and Sky are inverted from the Sumerian version.

186 Hathor's head-dress, with the sun held by cow's horns, symbolises that the sun is under the control of the Goddess. She controls time.

187 The horns are sometimes described as 'bull's horns' but this is incorrect. They are cow's horns. The Sumerian Ki, the Goddess Earth, was 'the Good Cow' and Inanna, as an anthropomorphic representation of Ki, wears cow horns. Hathor was also the 'Divine Cow' and is represented as such at Hypostyle Hall of the Chapel of Hathor, 'Temple of Millions of Years' of Queen Hatshepsut, West Uaset-Thebes. Bulls and their horns represent the male element in goddess thealogy.

resents a significant development of the mythology concerning kingship. In Sumer, Inanna conferred the power to rule through the Sacred Marriage. In Egypt, the power to rule is conferred in the form of the throne itself.

Nearly all the representations of Aset place her in close proximity to the throne, either through her headdress or a real throne. In the latter cases, she is almost always seen behind the throne and the seated king. Frequently, she is accompanied by Nephthys. Together, they are the Goddess.

When Aset is depicted standing behind the throne of Osiris or the king, the throne part of her head-dress usually disappears and, instead, the monarch is sitting on it. The Goddess, through Aset, confers the power to rule to the monarch, by giving him the throne and her blessing. Thus the Goddess is not merely protecting the king, but creating him. She is, literally, the king-maker.

The king is acting in Aset's name and by her divine authority. This device has been a useful political tool for monarchs for millennia. It is the origin of the claim 'divine right to rule'. Her authority is what gives the king's deeds and words legal and religious sanction and what protects him against usurpers.

Egyptian kings were transformed into Osiris through ritual and culture. They became the consort of the Goddess, and it was this relationship that gave them the power of monarchy. The difference between the Sumerian and Egyptian cultures is only that the ritualised sexual element of the union is far more emphasised in the former. The underlying cultural meaning is the same.

At the temple of Seti I at Abydos in Upper Egypt, a carved relief illustrates the point. Here, Ramses II is depicted wearing Osiris' tall, bulbous headdress, symbolising the identity of king and deity. He is sitting on the throne, and Aset stands behind him. As usual in images like this, the throne element of her head-dress is missing, since the king is sitting on it. Her right hand is raised, not in defence or warning, but in blessing, and in her left she holds an ankh.

The ankh is a form of a cross with the upper element formed from the shape of a womb, egg or fruit. The lower is a phallic element, here penetrating the womb. It symbolises the union of the sexes that makes life possible and, because it represents both male and female elements, it symbolises the power of creation.[188]

The ankh in Aset's hand is an important part of the gift she brings. She has given the king the throne of Osiris to sit on. With the ankh, which contains the Fruit of the Tree of Knowledge, she gives him the divine wisdom necessary for a king to rule – to be the earthly representation, indeed incarnation, of the good and wise Osiris.

## The Mythology of Isis and Osiris

The best-known account of this story was written down by the Greek historian Plutarch, who lived from 46-120 CE. However, the story he codified had been known since at least the Middle Kingdom, which lasted from 2055 BCE to 1650 BCE.

Osiris was king of Egypt and Isis, his sister-wife, queen.[189] By marrying Osiris, Aset conferred on him the power to rule. Osiris, by the grace of the Goddess, was a good king and governed justly, and his brother Set was jealous of him.

The Great Mother was once the ruler of the Underworld and in the relationship of Nephthys to Set we see a transfer of her powers to a male god. It was probably Nephthys who originally ruled the Underworld, powers she was made to give up to Set as a result of the developing patriarchy.

In Sumer, Inanna took a husband who is in some ways similar to Osiris and about whom there are equivalent myths. Ereshkigal's husband is only mentioned in passing, as the Bull of Heaven. He has no particular association with darkness, although the bull is a

---

188 The ankh has many references to the Goddess. For example, another is that it represents the rising sun over the Nile, with the upper oval the sun, the horizontal bar the surface of the river and the lower upright being the light reflected from the water. This is a parallel with the blood-coloured egg of Shammuramat rising at dawn over the Euphrates, making it a symbol of Goddess resurrection. The ankh is a hugely potent Goddess object.

189 The marriage of a monarch is an event of political significance and it has always been a requirement that a king's brides should be of the blood royal themselves (the limited pool of such stock makes inbreeding practically impossible to avoid, a trait which is reflected in the European royal families to this day.) The mythologies mentioning this provide a justification for the practice.

symbol of unrestricted masculinity. In the Egyptian version, the two husbands are very different: Osiris is associated with light and the power of good and Set with darkness and evil. This distinction is not made in the Sumerian mythology; it contains no independent concept of 'good' and 'evil'. To a Sumerian, order and stability were good and chaos and disorder evil. The Imdugud-Bird that infests Inanna's Huluppu Tree is evil only in the sense that it brings storms and torrential rains that destroy crops and fields. It is not a focussed, wilful form of evil, just the wildness of untamed nature. The lilitu in the same story is the evil of pain and death in childbirth but once again it is random, wild, unfocused and unregulated.

The evil represented by Set is specifically malign and driven by hate.[190] It is not only personalised, but also directed; it is subject to will. Osiris is good because he does good things. He treats his subjects fairly and brings them the rewards of prosperity and happiness. Set is an evil king who does the opposite. Here, good and evil are not, simply, on one hand the maintenance of order and on the other the chaotic forces of nature, but derive from personal intent. Good and evil are no longer abstract but are consequent on human thoughts and actions. This distinction marks an important change because it contains the essential core of modern religious morality. One may decide to be good and live a good life and reap the promised reward, or one may decide to be the opposite and spend eternity in darkness with the source of all malignant evil, the dark lord himself, in this case, Set.

Darkness was ever the place of the Goddess, from the original Great Mother through her daughters like Ereshkigal and Nephthys. In the caves that were her first temples, it was dark. It is in the darkness of night when the Moon shines its gentle silver light, and the Moon is closely associated with the Goddess through the parallel between its phases and the menstrual cycle of women. The Celts, who remained loyal to the Great Goddess longer than any other European people, always counted time in nights rather than days. In Goddess culture, darkness does not equate to evil, but to the time when the Goddess is most close.

---

190 The initial reason for this hatred was that one dark night Osiris mistook Nepthys for Aset and as a result of that illicit union she bore a son, the jackal-headed Anubis.

Again and again the apologists for the patriarchy, both in political terms and in the mythologies they invent to justify their actions, portray the Great Mother Goddess as deceitful, dangerous, chaotic and manipulative. This is how real women are portrayed in these cultures and the mythology exists to justify men's treatment of them. Ascribing to darkness an association with evil and then placing a male in charge of that evil represents a double blow to the status of the Goddess and women.

In the Egyptian tale, Osiris decided to throw a great banquet and invited everyone, even his evil brother, Set. This gave Set the opportunity he had long sought and he devised a plan to kill Osiris. He secretly obtained the measurements of his brother's body and had a beautiful sarcophagus made, of precious wood and gilded, exactly to fit. At the banquet, Set boasted about the casket and Osiris asked to see this magnificent thing. Set had it brought in and said that he would give it to whichever person it fitted, knowing that it would only fit one: Osiris. When his brother tried it, Set and his accomplices slammed the lid shut, nailing it down before anyone could intervene. While his men held back the rest of the court at sword-point, Set had the coffin thrown into the Nile. Osiris was killed, and Set proclaimed himself king.

Isis was distraught: she cut her hair and tore her clothes. Overcome with grief, she set out to find Osiris' body. The sarcophagus had floated down the Nile to the land of Byblos, where it came to rest, and a tree grew up around it. Because the tree held the body of a god, it became mighty and famous, so the king of Byblos decided to have it cut down and built into his palace.

Isis, following the trail, three times came across groups of children who told her they had seen the coffin and at length she arrived at the palace of Byblos. Entering, she laid claim to the tree, showing herself in her true form as the Goddess.[191] The king, awed by her magnificence, complied and Isis had the coffin cut out, to the wonderment of everyone. Leaving the tree, Isis blessed the king and the palace and took Osiris' body back to Egypt.

---

191 It was widely held in the ancient world that no mortal could look on the true nature of a deity and live; this explains why deities adopted so many other forms, from idealised humans to pillars of fire. It is not explained how the King of Byblos survived seeing Isis. In some versions of the story Isis first appears to the Queen, in disguise.

She and Nephthys hid the coffin in the marshes, but Set, out hunting, found it. Enraged, he had Osiris' body dragged out and chopped into many pieces, which he had scattered all over Egypt.[192] Boastfully he claimed that he had truly killed a god.

Isis set out to find all the parts of Osiris' body, for until they were reunited, he could not pass on to the next world. After many months she had found them all except one, his penis. But Isis took the clay of Egypt and made a penis for her husband. With all his parts together, she performed magic that brought Osiris back to life, complete with his new phallus. They made love, and she conceived a son, who would become the god Horus.[193] Osiris could only stay on Earth as long as Isis' magic lasted, (in some versions, three days), and he then passed on to the next life.[194]

Like Dumuzi and Tammuz, Osiris is an agrarian, 'dying and rising' god. He represents the fertile land of Egypt, which is why his body is scattered into every province. His death and resurrection describe the cycle of the agricultural year. He needs Isis to bring him back to life and to ensure the continuity of the cycle of all life. At the same time, for all her magical power, Isis cannot conceive without the seed of a god, so must fashion a penis for her husband and make love with him. This emphasises the interdependence of man and woman, saying that both are needed to make life, just as the fertile land of Egypt needed the annual flooding of the Nile to bring forth its riches.

It is from Aset/Isis that Osiris derives his power. He is laid low and emasculated; his penis, always the symbolic source of male power, is lost, and so he has none. Isis, by her divine craft and using her own body, since the clay of Egypt is the body of the Goddess, gives him a functioning penis, delivering back his manhood and his power. The metaphor is clear: the Goddess gives the king all his power, including that which allows him to rule.

---

192 Compare this to the story of Dumuzi/Tammuz.

193 Horus is one of the many models for Christ.

194 Egyptians believed that the celestial event which symbolised the moment that Isis conceived Horus was not the dying and rising of the sun, but the annual reappearance of the star Sirius, which disappeared below the horizon for 70 days. The moment the star appeared over the horizon again was taken as the beginning of the annual cycle of life because it coincided with the beginning of the Nile floods.

While the similarities between the Egyptian and Sumerian my-thologies suggest a common earlier derivation, the Egyptian tale has adopted a more linear understanding of life than the Sumeri-an versions, consistent with the broader cultural belief. Osiris must complete his journey to the Afterlife, after the three days which the reader will have come to understand symbolically. The Goddess as Isis is unable to enter the Underworld herself. She remains behind and, within her, Osiris grows again and is reborn, as the infant god Horus, the Light of the World, the Lamb of Heaven.

This tale retains cyclical elements, despite its apparent linearity. It is derived from the agricultural model in which the god is born in spring, grows up over summer and then is cut down and scattered, and the goddess brings him back to life.

Isis is not only Queen of Heaven but also the Great Mother God-dess. In Sumer these roles were kept separate, with Inanna in one and Ki, or Ereshkigal, the other. Isis' child Horus is the Son of a god and himself a god, so she is, literally, the Mother of God. It is this form of the Goddess that would be at the heart of one of the great-est monotheisms the world has seen, and through it she would once again ascend the throne of Queen of Heaven.

The Egyptian life was not a cycle of life-death-rebirth, but of birth-life-death-afterlife. What does this shift mean and why has it occurred? The change from a cyclical to a linear understanding of life and death allows for a very important concept to be introduced: obedience. Those who obey the rules will have a better afterlife than those who don't. In Sumer, the Underworld was unpleasant for every-one, a place of cold and dread. In Egypt, this changed, and souls were tested before passing on. Testing implies judgement, and that judge-ment is on the performance of the individual – that is to say, her or his obedience – in this life.

# Heaven and Hell

Those of us brought up in cultural traditions shaped by the Abraham-ic cults of monotheism are used to the idea of an afterlife in Heaven. We are allowed entry if we are good and obey the code central to the religion here on Earth. In other words, Heaven is a promised place of reward, after death, for our behaviour in life.[195]

Since the time of the Natufians, through the Sumerians and all the other ancient cultures of the near east, and for the Greeks and many others, the afterlife, both for humans and deities, was through the Underworld. This was regarded as a temporary resting-place be-fore the soul was reincarnated.

The Sumerian deities lived in Heaven, an invisible realm which was contiguous with the real world. This realm was restricted to the deities; humans could not enter it. Human life was spent in the World, and while Heaven was very close, it was inaccessible to us. When goddesses and gods died, they left this spiritual plane, just as humans leave the physical plane, and entered the Underworld.

Sumerian mythology proposed no reward after death for any-thing one might do in life. Its focus was on behaving well according to the expectations of the culture and society, and being rewarded while one was still alive. The desired behaviours were to work hard and have many children. The ultimate reward, in this cultural view, was to be surrounded by a large and loving family. For your efforts in raising them well, your children would take care of you and show-er you with love. They would work to keep you when you become old and even after you died, they would pray for you so that your discomfort in the Underworld would be minimised.[196] Their prayers after your death were not to secure for you a place in Heaven, but to ameliorate the grim time in the cold, dank Underworld.

The Egyptian understanding is not cyclical, but linear. One life on Earth is offered, and how we behave in it will determine how

---

195 This idea of reward after death did not appear until much later in Mesopotamia, but was more fully developed in Egyptian culture from early on.

196 This can still be seen in many Asian cultures, where children are expected to 'repay the mother's milk' or in other words, to support their parents.

we spend eternity. But if we cannot rise again, and there is only the horror of the Underworld, where is the incentive to live a good life? Clearly this was not satisfactory. So the Egyptian myth-makers invented a solution: a paradise to which the souls of those who had been good in life would pass after death.

The Egyptians called this place the Fields of Aaru or the Fields of Reeds and it was ruled by Osiris. By living a good life and learning the answers to certain questions which would be asked after death, by certain funerary rites including mummification and embalming, but most of all by having commissioned a Book of the Dead, one might pass all the tests and arrive in the Fields of Aaru. There one would spend eternity in grace, in the company of the good god Osiris.

In the Goddess cultures, where life was essentially egalitarian and the joys and pleasures of life were celebrated, simply returning to life on earth was reward enough. And there was always the opportunity to do even better if one tried harder next time. To an Egyptian, as well as to all the followers of the later Abrahamic cults, this was simply not available. There was no reincarnation into the world of the living; no chance to try again, to do better. Mortal life was just a passing preliminary phase in which one established whether one would pass an eternity of suffering or joy.

The idea of Heaven as a wonderful paradise where obedient humans might go is an invention of the patriarchal death cults; indeed it is central to their reward system. In more developed versions of these cults, it is paired with an opposite, which we call Hell.

Hell is not the same as the Underworld; it is a perversion of the idea. Grim and forbidding though it may be, the Underworld is not a place of punishment, while Hell has no other function. Hell is designed specifically to intimidate the living, so its horrors are grotesque.

In the patriarchal death-cults, life became a one-way street: birth from oblivion, a life of struggle and work, and then death.[197] Only in the death-cults do we see 'terrifying linearity' at the core of the entire

---

197 Although Catholicism is one of the death-cults, it retains much of birth-oriented, Goddess culture. Here we see a phenomenon called Purgatory, which means 'the place of cleansing'. It is much more like the earlier understanding of the Underworld, from which it was probably adopted. Purgatory, like the Underworld in Goddess culture, is a place of temporary, not permanent, residence.

tradition. There is one life, and failure to pass the tests will result in suffering an eternity of torture and misery. On the other hand, conforming to the rules laid down by the culture will be rewarded with everlasting bliss.

For this idea to have any persuasive power, the relative positions and qualities of Heaven and the World had to be changed. Heaven became accessible to humans, albeit only after their deaths. Mortal life was represented as a 'vale of tears', and Heaven divorced from it and made fabulous in the scale of its rewards.

The patriarchal death-cults proscribed all earthly pleasures as sinful. They denied them to people whilst they were alive, while promising delivery after death, but only to those who did as they were told. For those who did not obey, they promised an eternity of torture, often preceded by a horrific death. Every act in life would be judged. This became the most effective form of social manipulation humanity has ever invented.

# Greek Mythology

In the West, Greek cultural influence is so pervasive that we often are unaware of it. Most of the foundation of our philosophy comes from Greeks like Plato and Aristotle, and our enlightened view of science from others like Lucretius and Democritus. Our mathematics was first established by those like Pythagoras and Euclid. Many of the words we use are Greek in origin. Greek examples shape our ideas about art and culture. It is not an exaggeration to say that we see the world through Greek-tinted glasses.

Greek culture spread throughout the Middle East during the second half of the first millennium BCE. Initially, this was done by the Greeks themselves, through trade and conquest. Alexander the Great established Greek cities like Tarsus and Alexandria throughout the region, as well as dynasties of Greek rulers such as the Ptolemy Pharaohs in Egypt and the Seleucid Empire which stretched from modern Turkey to India. The Romans, who adopted Greek culture, reinforced its influence in the Middle East and eastern Mediterranean, and spread it across their empire.

Greek mythology shows clear similarities with the others we have already discussed, from Sumer and its successors and from Egypt.

Did the Greeks, or at least the proto-Greeks, directly borrow from the Mesopotamian tradition in the way that Akkadia did from Sumer? Walter Burkert is convinced that some tales were directly borrowed. He points to similarities between the rendition of the Story of Atrahasis in the *Epic of Gilgamesh* and the part of Homer's *Iliad* where Poseidon, who is a parallel to Enki, claims the right to 'become active' on the plain of Troy, saying:

> 'There is hardly another passage in Homer which comes so close to being a translation of an Akkadian epic. In fact it is not so much a translation as a resetting through which the foreign framework still shows.'[198]

---

198 Burkert, W. *The Orientalizing Revolution – Near Eastern Influence on Greek Culture in the Early Archaic Age*. Harvard University Press. 1998.

The close relationship between Greek and Akkadian mythology is important because both had a great influence on the later cult of Christianity.

Although the European revival of interest in Greek culture is usually reckoned to have begun with the Renaissance, it is only in the last two hundred years that researchers have begun to understand the rich and complex tapestry of interwoven strands that make up its mythology. Much was considered to be completely fictional until Heinrich Schliemann, using Homer's Iliad, discovered Mycenaean Troy in 1868 and demonstrated that civilisation in Greece went back deep into the Bronze Age.

An agrarian culture had been established in the southern Balkans by around 2800 BCE. It was a continuation of preceding Neolithic culture. Exposure to a more aggressive, herding culture from the northern Balkans brought change, although this cultural shift was slow and not universal; the Mycenaeans, for example, only practised limited animal husbandry. It has been argued, by Joseph Campbell and others that the earlier culture may have been a matriarchal, Goddess culture which was over-run by the more aggressive, patriarchal, warrior people. There are strong indications in the mythology to support this.

Perhaps the most striking aspect of Greek mythology is the sheer size of the pantheon. Unlike the relatively simple ones of Sumer and Egypt, in Greece there are hundreds of deities. Many of these are clearly cognate to others in the simpler cultures, where there is only one. For example, the Sumerian Inanna is cognate to a bevy of Greek goddesses including Hera, Aphrodite, Cytherea and many others. Why did this extreme proliferation occur?

Sumer and Egypt are alluvial plains crossed by major rivers that, except in time of flood, were safe and efficient means of communication. While individual cities did develop their own variations on an original mythological theme, there was so much cultural exchange that these were relatively minor.

Greece could hardly be more different. The mainland, the Peloponnesus, is a harsh and impenetrable country of high mountains intersected by narrow valleys with few passes. In winter, the mountains are snowbound, and even these passes are closed while, in summer, they are baking hot, arid and unforgiving. In ancient times, these were crossed by narrow trails that could only be followed by a single column. There are no major rivers to serve as navigation routes.

Greece is not just the Peloponnesus, however; it is also a great archipelago scattered across the Aegean Sea, which has an invidious reputation for treachery. In winter, storms that last for days can blow up in hours and the sea is full of deadly lee shores and rocks waiting to catch the unwary mariner. Even today, few small boats go out at all between the months of November and March. In summer, flat calms can last for weeks while a pitiless sun burns down from a cloudless sky, and Greek ships often had to rely on oars for propulsion. Even then, sudden storms and violent winds can appear from nowhere. Nonetheless, until recently the only means of communication between the islands was by venturing out onto this dangerous sea.

It should come as no surprise, then, that in this land where contact between populations was so difficult, different versions of culture and myth proliferated.

We have no independent record of the first oral traditions, although the earliest written records reference much older myths. Throughout history, the scribes who recorded myths changed them to suit their political ends, and Greece was no different.[199]

## Creation Mythology

The earliest known collection of Greek mythology was written by Hesiod, circa 700 BCE. It is called the Theogony, or 'genealogy of the gods'. In it, Creation begins with Chaos, which is an empty void. In its limitless nothingness, the Earth, Gaia, took form, along with cer-

---

199 Gilbert Cuthbertson, referencing a range of epic mythology, shows how myths and epics are written and modified to support political and social agendas. His view is now mainstream. (Cuthbertson, G. *Political Myth and Epic*. Michigan State University Press. 1975)

tain other primary beings, all of which are transcendent: Eros, Love; Tartarus, the Abyss; and Erebus, Darkness.

The goddess Gaia, without the aid of a partner, gave birth to the sky, Uranus, who then fertilised her. The similarity between this and the Sumerian myth of Nammu and An is obvious. From this initial union, the Titans were born. There were six males, Coeus, Crius, Cronus, Hyperion, Iapetus, and Oceanus, and six females, Mnemosyne, Phoebe, Rhea, Theia, Themis, and Tethys.

After Cronus' birth, Gaia and Uranus decided that no more Titans would be born. Instead, Gaia gave birth to the one-eyed Cyclopes and the Hundred-Handed Ones, or Hetaconchires. Uranus threw all of these into Tartarus, which enraged Gaia. She persuaded Cronus, her youngest and most wily son, to castrate Uranus in revenge, which he did with a sickle she provided.[200] Taking his sister Rhea as consort, he became ruler of the Titans.

Because Cronus had betrayed his father, he feared that his offspring might do the same, so every time Rhea gave birth, he swallowed the baby. After several such cycles, Rhea tricked Cronus by removing the child Zeus from his blanket and putting a stone there instead. Cronus was duped and swallowed the stone. Zeus grew up and drugged his father, causing him to vomit up all Rhea's other offspring, as well as the stone. With his siblings and the help of the Cyclopes, whom he had already rescued, Zeus challenged his father directly. He won, and Cronus and the Titans were thrown into Tartarus. Zeus then set himself up as king of the gods.

The meme of father-son conflict is then repeated as Zeus, also suspecting his children would attempt to overthrow him, swallows his first wife, Metis. However, she was already pregnant with Athena, who later burst forth from Zeus' head, in full battle armour and ready for war.

Both of these accounts are important because they appropriate the female power of creation through birth and give it to a male. Although the act caused his demise, the children Cronus had eaten were reborn through being vomited up. Furthermore, while Rhea was the instigator, the direct provocation for this came from another

---

200 Notice the symbolism – a sickle, given by the goddess, is used to cut down the god. The sickle is symbolic both of the Goddess and of agriculture.

male, Zeus, who administered the drug, which may be seen as a metaphor for male semen, to his father, causing him to give birth. The same meme is repeated in the way that Zeus ate his first wife yet gave birth to their daughter, from his head.[201]

One of the greatest of her powers, the ability to give birth, is here being stripped away from the Goddess and given to male deities. This strongly suggests a socio-political situation in which a Goddess culture was being overthrown by a patriarchal one.

Zeus set up his palace at the top of Mount Olympus, and the rest of Rhea's children formed his court. Later, he took as consort Hera, who symbolised the year and represented the Goddess' power to control time, and thus all cycles of life and death; she is the Great Goddess herself. By marrying the Goddess, Zeus gained ownership and authority over her: this is a meme with which the reader will by now be familiar.[202]

The Greeks also had a seasonal myth that is reminiscent of the familiar Dumuzi/Tammuz/Osiris stories, but with significant changes. In Greek mythology, dominion over the Underworld and the Earth is in the hands of a male deity, Hades/Pluto. As we have seen, chthonic male deities are the patriarchal usurpers of original Goddess power.[203] The seasonal dying and rising is done by a female goddess, Persephone.

Persephone's mother is Demeter, one of the most ancient deities in the Greek pantheon. She is responsible for the harvest, through the fertility of the Earth. She is also the law-giver, who is seen as representing the organised structure of settled agrarian life, and it is telling that we see a woman in this seminal role, which may hark back to an original matriarchy.

Demeter's name is made up of two parts, the suffix 'meter', which is derived from the Indo-European word for 'mother', and the prefix 'De'. There are divided academic views about this element, some ar-

---

201 Zeus gave birth to several deities, from different parts of his body, including his thigh. This is clearly an attempt to appropriate the power of giving birth to men.

202 Hera is not one of Rhea's offspring but comes from a different, older tradition. Since the 19th century, she has been identified by scholars, e.g. Johann Jakob Bachofen (1815–1887) as the Great Goddess, and likely the Supreme deity of a pre-existing matriarchal culture. Her subjection to Zeus probably mythologises the overwhelming of this matriarchal culture by a patriarchal one.

203 'Chthonic' means 'of or relating to the Underworld'.

guing that it comes from the Indo-European 'Da' meaning 'Earth', so Demeter is 'Earth-Mother'. Others suggest it may derive from the Cretan word for barley, making her 'Harvest-Mother' or, less literally, 'Mother of Life'. From our point of view, however, fascinating though these different interpretations are, they all signify that Demeter and the Great Goddess are identical.

Persephone is kidnapped by Hades and dragged down into the Underworld to be his bride. This is a metaphor for the annual autumn sowing of seed. In the city of Eleusis, this always took place at a full moon, another stamp of the Goddess. The seed of life, Persephone, is put into the soil, the Underworld, a form of death and burial. However, the seed and the Goddess rise when the new year warms, bringing life back to Earth.

In the Eleusian Mysteries, this was celebrated as a cycle of three phases. In the first, Persephone and Pluto went into the Underworld at the sowing time. This was the 'descent'. Then followed 'the searching', the months of winter when Demeter searches for her daughter and nothing grows. There is an echo here of Isis' desperate search for Osiris or Ishtar's for Tammuz. In spring came the 'ascent' when the new crops came forth and, metaphorically, Persephone rose from the Underworld to be reunited with Demeter.

We saw that in the earlier mythologies, the power of death and resurrection of life was in the hands of the Goddess. She regulated this cycle without the consent of a male, and through it controlled time itself. Persephone, who is both the dying back in autumn and the bursting forth of life in spring, is now controlled by a male deity. This is another illustration of how Goddess power was removed and again serves as evidence of a pre-existing matriarchal phase of settled culture, established before the patriarchy.

We have seen again and again how myths reflect the cultures that invent them. Examining a few well-known Greek legends will be sufficient to spot the symbolic messages contained within them.

## Oedipus

Oedipus, whose name means 'swollen foot' was the son of King Laius and Queen Jocasta of Thebes. Because of a prophecy that his son would kill him and marry Jocasta, Laius fastened the baby boy's feet together with a pin and left him on a mountainside to die.

The baby was found by shepherds and taken to Corinth, where he was adopted by King Polybus and Queen Merope, who raised him as their son. When he was grown, Oedipus learned of the prophecy that he would kill his father and marry his mother. Aghast and believing Polybus and Merope to be his natural parents, Oedipus fled the city, hoping to thwart the prophecy.

Oedipus decided to go to Thebes, which he did not know was his original home. On the way, he met an older man on a chariot, who refused to give way on the road. A fight ensued, and the older man was killed. Oedipus did not realise this at the time, but he had killed Laius.

On arriving in Thebes, Oedipus learned that the king had died, but still did not associate this with his own adventure. Thebes was under threat by a monster that guarded its entrance, the Sphinx. This beast asked a riddle of those who wished to pass, and Oedipus answered correctly; the monster fell from its perch and died. This heroic act won for Oedipus the crown of Thebes and also the hand of Jocasta in marriage; thus the prophecy that Laius had tried to prevent was fulfilled. The couple had two sons and two daughters.

Because of Laius' assassination, the gods made Thebes victim of a plague. Oedipus decided to identify the murderer and put him to death, in order to end the people's suffering. Eventually, he discovered that he himself was guilty. Jocasta realised that she had married her son and hanged herself. Oedipus took two pins from her dress and blinded himself with them. The people of Thebes, horrified, drove Oedipus into exile, accompanied by his daughters Antigone and Ismene. After many years of wandering they arrived in Athens, where Oedipus was given refuge in a grove of trees called Colonus. Civil war had broken out in Thebes between Jocasta's brother, Creon, who had seized the throne and Oedipus's son, Polyneices. The people called for Oedipus' return to restore peace; but too late. He died in Colonus, where his grave was thought to bring luck to Athens.

In Thebes, Creon killed Polyneices but refused to allow his burial. Antigone, who had returned, disobeyed and secretly buried her brother, for which Creon executed her.[204]

Although this story has been represented as an allegory of a boy-child's sexual desire for his mother, especially by Freud, this is at best a biased reading. In fact, the Ancient Greeks were not at all coy about sex; their mythology is full of it, their plays brimmed with sexual innuendo and ribald language, and their comedic theatre contained such elements as male actors with fake phalloi hanging out of short tunics.

In fact, the tale is about obedience. Firstly this is to the will of the gods. Prophecies in Greece and elsewhere were held to reveal the intentions of the gods, so any attempt to prevent one from being fulfilled was an act of defiance, of blasphemy. Secondly, it is about obedience to the father, and serves to promote the idea of filial loyalty. It warns of the punishment for patricide – exile, loss of throne, blindness and death. In this era, it was common for sons of kings to rise against their fathers to claim the throne, and Greek mythology repeats this theme again and again. The story supports social conservatism, issuing dire warnings about what might happen if the existing order were challenged.

Women are once again revealed as property. Oedipus, by outwitting the Sphinx, wins both the city and the hand of Jocasta. She was an object, a highly desirable, fertile and sexual trophy which was simply handed over to Oedipus as a reward. She had no choice in this.

---

204 This is a very much abbreviated version of one of the greatest of tragic tales.

# Perseus

Perseus' journey is one of the greatest epics in all literature. This famous myth has been the subject of many interpretations. In the following brief description we set out ours, but the reader should investigate the original texts.

Acrisius, king of Argos, had a daughter called Danae. The Oracle of Delphi prophesied that Danae's son would one day kill Acrisius. To prevent her from ever meeting a man and becoming pregnant, Acresius walled Danae up in a dark, miserable tower with one tiny window. One day, a shower of gold came through the window impregnating Danae and turning the cell into a paradise almost as beautiful as the Elysian Fields, where the gods walked.

When Acrisius saw light coming from the cell, he ordered his men to break down the wall. He found Danae with a baby boy, the child Perseus, on her lap. Acrisius had both mother and child locked in a chest and cast adrift at sea. The chest drifted to the island of Seriphus, where a fisherman named Dictys caught it in his net and pulled it ashore. Dictys gave shelter to Danae and her baby and, having no children of his own, raised Perseus as his son.

The king of Seriphus, Polydectes, learned of Danae's great beauty and wanted to marry her, but she rejected him.[205] Polydectes would have taken her by force, but by this time Perseus was a strong young man who could defend her.[206]

Polydectes devised a scheme to claim Danae. He arranged a false marriage to the daughter of a friend and commanded that everyone must come to the ceremony, including Perseus, but not Danae. Because Perseus was very poor, he brought no present, as Polydectes had foreseen. The king castigated Perseus, who replied that he would procure any present in the world that the king desired. The sly Polydectes asked him to fetch the head of the Gorgon, Medusa, believing this a suicidal venture. The Gorgons were three female monsters with serpents for hair and bronze hands of incredible strength. One look

---

205 Marriage, in this context, once again means 'sexual possession': Danae is an object.
206 In some versions, Dictys is Polydectes' brother.

at their faces would turn a living being to stone.

Hermes, the messenger of the gods, and his sister Athena visited Perseus. They told him that the god who had visited Danae in the tower was Zeus himself. Hermes gave the young man his winged sandals, which allowed him to fly, and the sickle Cronus had used to castrate Uranus. Athena gave him her polished bronze shield and told him to look at the image reflected in it, rather than directly at the Gorgon.

Perseus was instructed to find the Graeae, and make them tell him how to find the Hesperides, the three daughters of Hesperus, who had two other weapons he required: the Helm of Darkness, which made the wearer invisible, and a supernatural bag which could contain the severed head. The Hesperides would also tell Perseus how to find the Gorgon's lair.

The Graeae were three old women who shared one eye, which they fought over constantly. They were sisters of the Gorgons. Perseus hid nearby and when one passed the eye to another, and all three were blind, he grabbed the eye from them. He threatened that he would keep it unless they told him how to find the Hesperides. When he had the information, he returned the eye and flew off.

The Hesperides, who were kindly, gave Perseus the Helm and the bag, and he set off for the Gorgon's lair. There he put on the Helm and became invisible. As instructed, he looked only at the reflection of Medusa in the shield and severed her head with Cronus' sickle. Then he put the head in his magic bag and set off for home.

On his way back to Seriphus, after many other adventures, he found a young woman, Andromeda, chained to a rock by the sea. She explained that she had been sentenced to death by Poseidon, as a sacrifice to the sea monster Cetus, because her mother had boasted of Andromeda's beauty. When Perseus showed the sea dragon the head of Medusa, it turned to stone and crumbled. Perseus freed Andromeda, and she became his wife.

The couple visited Larisa so that Perseus could compete in the games there. Perseus threw his discus badly, and it struck and killed an old man in the stands. The old man turned out to be Acrisius. The prophecy had come true despite all efforts to evade it.

When they arrived at Seriphus, the couple met Dictys, who explained that Polydectes' wedding had been faked in order to get rid of Perseus. When Danae refused to marry Polydectes, he had forced her to be his concubine. Furious, Perseus left Andromeda with Dictys and went to the palace. He burst in, crying 'Let all who are my friends shield their eyes!' He held up Medusa's head, and Polydectes and his courtiers were turned to stone.

Perseus and Andromeda lived long and had many children, including Heracles, the strongest man in the world.[207] Perseus was the legendary founder of Mycenae and was eventually killed by Dionysius.

The story is replete with Goddess philosophy and symbolism. There are three Gorgons, three Graeae and three Hesperides. All are women, and their triple aspects tell us at once that they are the Goddess.

The Graeae are the Crone, who represents both death and the route to rebirth. Perseus' encounter with them is symbolic of the deadly nature of his quest and suggests that by ingenuity, a man can outwit his death.

The Hesperides are the Maid. These were nymphs who tended the Garden of Hera, in the West, a place of beauty, calm, and happiness. It is a parallel to the Sumerian island of Dilmun, where Ki/Ninhursag resided, confirming the link between Hera and Ki/Ninhursag.

The Gorgons were once the most beautiful women on Earth, but became hideously ugly, with serpents for hair. They represent the Great Mother. There is also a parallel with Tiamat, the Akkadian Great Goddess, who turned into the Serpent of Chaos and was killed by Marduk.

Later in Perseus' tale, he finds Andromeda, who had been condemned to death by Poseidon, the Greek sea god. In Sumer, the Sea is the Goddess Nammu, and this is an example of a male deity adopting a role of the Goddess. Cetus, the monster that is to devour Andromeda, is, like the Gorgon and Tiamat, the Serpent of Chaos, a manifestation of the Great Mother; Perseus kills it.

There is a parallel between Gilgamesh's delivery of Inanna from the bothersome monsters that haunt the Huluppu Tree and Perseus'

---

207 Heracles was known as Hercules in Rome.

rescue of Andromeda. Once again, the Goddess has to rely on a male hero, and subsequently marries him, which is to say, gives him her power and accepts his dominion over her.

Almost in passing, Perseus fulfils the prophecy that Acrisius had sought to deny, by killing him. Prophecies may not be thwarted, and within the mindset of the creators of this myth, there was no such thing as accident; humans merely played out their fate. The will of a deity is inviolable, and the priestly interpreters, the oracles and seers, are themselves infallible. This message is repeated time and again throughout the myths of Greece and the near east. Prophesying was a lucrative business, and its credibility had to be maintained.

Notice the weapons used to kill the two serpentine versions of the Great Goddess. The first is the sickle Cronus used to castrate Uranus. Since he did this at the behest of Gaia, the sickle is a metaphor for the Goddess' power to emasculate the gods. Then, when Perseus kills Cetus, he again uses the Goddess' power, this time directly, employing the head of Medusa to turn the monster to stone. These suggest that, in this stage of Greek mythology, the power of the Goddess may be wielded by a man. On his return to Seriphus, Perseus is given another set-piece to demonstrate his ability to deploy the Goddess' power, and he kills Polydectes and his court using it. This is an injunction against rape. Once again it is the power of Goddess that provides redress, but it is wielded by a man. Danae is released into the care of her saviour.[208]

Perseus can use the power of the Goddess because he is not an ordinary mortal but the son of a god, Zeus. This is a powerful parallel to the later myth of Jesus, also the son of a union between a mortal woman and a god, who preaches Goddess thealogy and uses her power, through healing and resurrection.[209] The warrior-hero's adventure is similar to the *Epic of Gilgamesh* and is probably derived directly from it.[210] The epic adventure-journey in search of the greatest prize on Earth, the power of the Goddess, is a format that will be repeated hundreds of times in the literature of cultures all over the

---

208 The tale of Perseus exists in many forms, of which only the simplest is discussed here.
209 Even the Christian apologist Justin Martyr recognised this parallel when he wrote that 'we propound nothing new or different from what you believe regarding those whom you call the sons of Jupiter (Greek Zeus.)' (Justin Martyr, *First Apology*.)
210 Burkert 1998.

world.

## Orpheus and Eurydice

The basic version of this story is well known and has been the foundation of many great works of art and literature. However, it is a deeply enigmatic tale.

Orpheus was a singer, player of the lyre and a prophet, whose ability as a musician could charm the gods themselves. He was one of the Argonauts, who accompanied Jason in his quest for the Golden Fleece, selected specifically to overcome the Sirens with his beautiful music. Eurydice was his bride, but on the eve of their wedding she was attacked by a satyr, who intended to rape her. Fleeing, she put her foot into a nest of vipers and was fatally bitten.

Orpheus, distraught, asked the deities what he should do. They advised him to descend into the Underworld, where his music would charm Hades and Persephone and cause them to release Eurydice. This he did, and Eurydice was indeed set free, but Orpheus had been warned that he must leave the Underworld before her and not look back until both had ascended into the World. Orpheus forgot this and as soon as he ascended into life he looked back. Eurydice was still in the Underworld and immediately vanished, to die forever.

When European cultures first rediscovered ancient Greek literature, during the Renaissance, no-one had any idea that Egyptian or Sumerian culture had even existed, and so for centuries this was the definitive tale of death and rebirth. Now, however, we can see the strong parallels between this myth and those of Inanna and Dumuzi, Ishtar and Tammuz and Aset/Isis and Osiris alongside many others. These other myths pre-date Orpheus by thousands of years.

All of these stories either have a common origin somewhere in a prior oral tradition that mythologised the seasons or they are directly descended from one another. The similarities between so many different tales from different regions and cultures make any other interpretation highly improbable. Because we can now place the appearance of these tales on a timeline, beginning in Sumer, we can see the differences among them as an evolution of the myth in response to changing socio-political conditions.[211]

Eurydice represents the Goddess. She is to be married, which is already established as a way to transfer her powers to a man. She is attacked by a satyr, a supernatural being, half man and half goat. It symbolised unrestrained sexuality and phallic power. The satyr may have its roots in animist cults of the hunt, but in this case it represents the power of male sexuality – expressed through the phallus – to overthrow the Goddess. It is rape personified.

A snake then bites Eurydice. Snakes can represent the Goddess, but the phallic shape of the snake is also frequently used to represent the male element. The context here suggests the latter interpretation. Thus, Eurydice is brought down three different ways: by marriage, which takes her powers, by rape, which degrades her, and by the snake, which kills her.

Eurydice is now helpless, imprisoned in the Underworld. Only Orpheus, a man, may help her. But Orpheus is not just any man, though neither is he a warrior in the conventional sense. He is a musician, a bard and a prophet. In other words, he is a priest. So this tale is saying that male priests may help the Goddess. She has lost all her powers, including that to control her descent and ascent and instead these have been transferred to a male. But here, the male is not another deity, but a human priest. The story may be interpreted, therefore, as a literary defence for a male priesthood not only taking to itself the powers of the Goddess, but also usurping and casting down the female priesthood which had previously served her.

This is a much darker interpretation of the myth than is often presented, but it fits neatly into the timeline of the development of the patriarchy. The details of this story can give us a guide to the nature of the culture that told it, and where that culture sits on the timeline as society moved from a matriarchy to a patriarchy. Compare this to the earlier myth of Inanna's descent. Eurydice is completely powerless to help herself, unlike Inanna, who had the whole thing planned in advance and remained in control throughout; this is a remarkable and telling shift.

---

211 This process is known to mythologists as 'syncretisation'.

Enki was the Sumerian god of wisdom and craft, and it is reasonable to suggest that he always represented a class of priests, initiated into their mysterious knowledge. Orpheus is clearly in the same role, able to use his special powers of music to charm the deities to do his will. In this sense, priests are shown as being more than mere interlocutors with the deities, but able to influence them. Orpheus, therefore, is Enki, or at least a later version of him. In Inanna's tale, the cycle is originally completely under the Goddess' control and then an element is introduced which references a new requirement for male aid. In Orpheus' tale this has gone much further, with the Goddess being completely powerless and totally dependent upon a man.

Why then does Orpheus fail while Enki succeeded? Partly, because Orpheus is human whereas Enki is a god. He may go far, and his powers may be great but the supernatural, the world of the deities, is more powerful. A mortal man may not stand against the hand of destiny, no matter how powerful a wizard he may be; only a deity may do that, and not always with impunity. More important, however, is the intent of the authors. In the Sumerian myth, the object was to see the goddess Inanna – the principal deity of the culture – restored, while in the Greek it was to see the Goddess cast down.

The importance of Greek mythology in helping to understand Western cultural development is immense. From Saul of Tarsus, later Paul the Apostle, onwards, the development of early Christianity was firmly under the guidance of people who had been brought up in Greek culture, with Greek myths. If it had not been made attractive to these Hellenised peoples, Christianity would probably have remained a little-known cult of the Eastern Mediterranean. The foundation of Greek culture in Goddess thealogy, albeit seen through patriarchal eyes, was imported into Christianity in order to maximise its popular appeal.

# The Celts

Northern and western Europe were colonised by *Homo sapiens nean-derthalensis* and *H. heidelbergensis* before modern humans. The first *H. sapiens sapiens* arrived around 40,000 years ago. The new arrivals remained and their DNA can still be found, notably in populations like the Basques of southwest France and northern Spain. These people hung on to their hunter-gatherer lifestyle, and it now appears that agriculture was spread to Europe by people from Anatolia, who migrated into Europe and brought their technology and culture with them.[212]

The early population of Europe left behind evidence that it was a Goddess culture. The Red Lady of Pavilland, the discovery of the remains of women shamans and the wealth of archaeological finds make this clear. The arriving agriculturalists brought with them a different conception of the Goddess, who now existed within a broad pantheon. This probably explains the similarities between the later European pantheons of the Germanic, Norse and Celtic peoples and those of the Mesopotamians. The two populations co-existed for many years, but in the end, the early Europeans adopted the new lifestyle and culture.

By the first millennium BCE, the new, settled agrarian lifestyle was widespread and well-established, along with the religious beliefs that went with it. One of the most significant of the cultures in this milieu was that of the Celts.[213]

Celtic culture originated in Central Europe and spread across the continent. For many years, scholars believed that the Celts were a distinct ethnic group that physically migrated out of central Europe to dominate the west by force of arms. However, extensive DNA sampling shows that this did not happen. Celtic culture spread and was adopted by the indigenous people, voluntarily. Celtic culture was welcomed, not imposed. It was a migration of ideas and technology rather

---

212 Pinhasi, Fort & Ammerman, *Tracing the Origin and Spread of Agriculture in Europe, Public Library of Science, 2005* (http://journals.plos.org/plosbiology/article?id=10.1371/journal.pbio.003041)

213 'Celt' is pronounced with a hard 'C'. This is because the name comes from the Greeks, who called them 'Keltoi'.

than of large numbers of people.

While the arriving agriculturalists had brought farming, the Celts had another, ground-breaking technological innovation: metallurgy. This advance spread like wildfire, replacing the old Neolithic stone technology. Celtic culture spread across Europe in two waves, the first at the end of the second millennium BCE, with its distinctive metallurgy being bronze and the second, five hundred years later, with iron.[214]

The Celts are a mysterious people in many ways. Unfortunately, because they did not write down important knowledge, much of what we know about them comes either from contemporary Roman historians or later Christian ones, who were often unsympathetic. As a result, the Celts were, until recently, often overlooked by historians. In recent decades, Celtic culture has been much more thoroughly researched, using both traditional methods and new tools such as DNA analysis, which has helped fill in many gaps. As a result, our understanding of their lives has evolved greatly.

The Celts deliberately did not write down important information and instead it was learned by heart as a way of preserving and protecting it. Nevertheless, and while only Druids would have been educated to this level, the Celts did know how to read and write. The Druids were the intelligentsia of Celtic society, of whom Caesar wrote:

> 'They are said there to learn by heart a great number of verses; accordingly some remain in the course of training twenty years. Nor do they regard it lawful to commit these to writing, though in almost all other matters, in their public and private transactions, they use Greek characters.'[215]

Druids are often represented as priests, but this is a caricature. In the first place, Druids were as likely to have been women as men.[216] Secondly, while their role did have an important religious element,

---

214 The Celts were not the first to adopt bronze metallurgy; it first appeared in Sumer around 2800 BCE. However they did spread it through central and west Europe, which at the time was completely Neolithic.
215 Caesar, Caius Julius. *Commentaries: The War in Gaul. Book VI*
216 Green, Miranda. *Exploring the World of the Druids.* Thames & Hudson. 1997.

this was only part of it. They were the educated class of society. They were doctors, lawyers, oracles, historians, political advisors, musicians, singers, scientists and astronomers, poets and educators. They were also artists and technicians, smiths and jewellers, and they wove a distinctive chequered pattern of cloth, which is still known today in Scottish tartans and plaids.[217]

The druidic life began at around the age of five, when a child was selected, either because of her ability or because of her family, for special education. Training probably began in her home village at the hands of the local Druid, alongside the other children. The chosen ones would then go on to one of the druidic colleges for further training. There were hundreds of such colleges across the Celtic lands, which, by the time they were Christianised, extended from the Alps to the Atlantic, as far south as Spain and north as Scotland.

A Druid was fully trained after nineteen years of education. This is equivalent to the length of time required for a young person, beginning at primary school, to achieve a Master's Degree today. The level of sophistication of this class should not be underestimated.

Druidic learning, however, was secret. Druids were only permitted to pass a little of their knowledge on to non-druids. Knowledge made the Druids indispensable in a culture that did not write, and the Druids encouraged this, decrying written knowledge as corrupt and not truly learned. There is an analogy here with music, where a piece is not considered 'learned' until it can be played without reference to notation. It means that the piece and all its nuances have been fully internalised. This is how Druids saw learning and their nineteen years of study was devoted to learning by heart the ancient lore transmitted to them, in small groups or individually, by qualified druids. Almost certainly this knowledge was preserved in the form of songs and repetitive chants.

Druids were encouraged to travel after their formal education was over, a tradition that persists even now in the successor cultures. Today in Europe, a craftsperson completing her or his apprenticeship has to undertake a tour, where she or he can work on active projects. These are the most qualified and respected of European craftspeople and the tradition has been recorded since the time of the medieval

---

217 Strabo. *Geography.*

Guilds, which themselves had their roots in druidic education.

It is probably as a result of this travelling that Celtic culture was so widely and so quickly spread. Druid teachers, doctors and craftspeople would have travelled out of the Celticised heartland, taking their culture and, most significantly, their knowledge and craft skills, with them. As educated people, they would soon have become very important to the communities they visited and even settled in, which in turn would have absorbed their learning and culture.

Even after the Romanisation of the Celtic lands of Gaul and southern Britain, it seems that the Druids did not disappear. The so-called 'Deal Warrior' was buried between 200-150 BCE.[218] He has been described as 'slight' in build, and attention has been drawn to his unusual headdress, which is very light, made of bronze (though this is an Iron Age burial) and has no padding to protect the skull.[219] Indeed, the British Museum website notes:

> 'The metal was worn directly on the head and not padded or strengthened with leather; when found impressions of human hair were left in the corrosion on the inner surface.'[220]

This suggests that the head-dress was not a war helmet but ceremonial or indicative of the wearer's status, and perhaps the Deal Warrior was a Druid.

Supporting this, Neil Oliver has shown that the headdress bears a striking similarity to items known to have been worn by priests hundreds of years later, in Roman Britain. This would suggest that the Druids were able to maintain their position in society despite the changes that must have taken place after the Roman conquest. It seems likely, then, that they would also have been able to do this in Gaul and other territories. In political terms, the Romans may have found it expedient not only to tolerate the Druids, but also to treat with them, since they held such an important role in Celtic society.

---

218 British Museum: http://www.britishmuseum.org/explore/highlights/highlight_objects/peprb/s/skullcrownofdealwarrior.aspx
219 Oliver, Neil. *A History of Celtic Britain, Part One: Age of Warriors.* BBC Broadcast. 2011
220 British Museum.

Indeed Miranda Green has described them as being more important than the chiefs and monarchs.[221]

If the Druid culture could withstand the catharsis of imperial domination, it is certainly possible that it could have adapted to Christianisation, especially in the Roman form with the Mother Goddess, Mary, ensconced at the centre. Further evidence for this is that the Druids, of Ireland in particular, wore a tonsure, which is to say they shaved part of their heads.[222] This practice became common amongst Christian clergy. These parallels suggest that the badges of priestly office may have been carried forward to Christian times and that the first Christian priests in these lands were actually Druids.

The Celts were not city-dwellers; their huge, hill-top fortresses were refuges into which they retreated in times of warfare and the depths of winter. Paradoxically, the hilltops are the warmest places in winter, because the cold air falls to the valley floors, and the sun is not obstructed. In the other seasons, the Celts lived in simple wooden huts on the land they worked, tending their herds and crops. Therefore, they challenge the accepted definition of the term 'civilised', which means, to historians, 'living in cities'. Because of a relentless tendency for scholars to see history through the filter of classicism, the Celts were not considered civilised by many academics, at least until the last quarter century. Their art and the richness of their culture makes such an assessment untenable, except in the strictest technical definition of the word.

## Celts and the Goddess

Celtic culture had many distinct expressions, myth cycles and deities. There was never one homogeneous Celtic religion but a multiplicity of different, related forms. This was probably a consequence of the fact that there was no one Celtic people, and all those who be-

---

221 Green, Miranda, quoted in Oliver 2011.
222 Von Pflugk-Harttung, Julius. *The Druids of Ireland. Transactions of the Royal Historical Society (New Series), 7,* 1893, pp 55-75 (on-line resource: http://journals.cambridge.org/action/displayAbstract?fromPage=online&aid=3428760)

came Celtic brought with them their prior beliefs. These were broadly consistent, but had distinctive nuances. Then, the mythology was only partially written down, across widely separated territories, with hundreds of years between the versions. Since it was often recorded by people who were not Celts, the story of the Celtic Goddess is confused and confusing and following the thread of Celtic belief is no simple matter. However, there are many similarities with other goddess-cycles, especially those originating in Sumer.

Celtic belief comprised an array of nature-spirits, many of them local gods and spirits of place, and an overarching pantheon with the sky-god Dagda at its centre. By far the most revered deity was the Great Goddess.

Male deities fall into two categories. These are the gods of the hunt and the gods of the sky. Although sometimes male gods appear as chthonic deities, in every case they have been co-opted into this role, to supplant an earlier goddess, usually from the pantheon of sky-deities.[223]

The best-known Celtic god of the hunt was Cernunnos, who was part man, part deer, and had a horned head. He represents a parallel to the Sumerian Enkidu, the wild man who sleeps and mates with the beasts. Enkidu is clearly a derivative of the hunter pantheon and is tamed, not by Gilgamesh directly, but by a priestess, Shamhat. Also cognate is the Greek god Pan, a deity of forests and shepherds. The parallels between Cernunnos, Enkidu, Pan and other Greek deities like Phanes/Protogonos, Dionysus and Eros all point to a common origin. Many scholars believe that this prototypical deity comes from an early Indo-European source though it may be even older. In other words, this deity probably has its origin in the pre-agrarian, hunter-gatherer phase.

These beast/man deities are strongly associated with the Goddess, and Cernunnos is no exception. He is not her consort but may be her son. This again suggests an origin in male hunter culture before the beginnings of the patriarchy because, in the era before marriage, patriliny and the patriarchy, men were known by who their mothers were. These hunter-gods do not possess women, though

---

223 A fine example of this is Lucifer, the Bringer of Light, who was an angel, or minor sky-god in the Hebrew texts, who was cast down for disobedience and insurrection, and became syncretised into Satan, the evil god of the Underworld.

they often represent unbridled sexual passion. We have also seen this in the Greek mythological creature, the Satyr; half man, half goat, constantly in pursuit of sex with beautiful nymphs. These deities have been part of the popular model for the Christian devil, who represents a link between sexual desire and evil.

The Celtic male sky gods follow the pattern established in Sumer with Dagda, a sky father; Lugh, the sun god; Taranis, the god of thunder and lightning and many others. These are all cognate to deities we have already seen in earlier pantheons. This strongly suggests either a common origin for all of these mythologies or direct borrowing.

In most cases, through time all the elements of the pantheon, including the Great Mother, come to be placed under the control of the sky father, and in the monotheisms only he remains. The Celts do not appear to have done this. Instead, they kept the gods of the hunt alongside their local deities and a sky pantheon and retained the Goddess at the top of the hierarchy. This may not be unique, but it is unusual. It provides a fascinating contrast to the situation in city-based cultures in which the Goddess was progressively stripped of powers.

The most ancient deity on Celtic record was called Dana. She is found in the Irish *Lebor Gabala*, dated to about 1000 CE. Dana appears to have been identical with a number of similarly-named deities, such as Danaan, Danu, Anann, Dan, Don and Anu.[224] These variations probably reflect the disparate nature of Celtic culture. Dana was the Earth Mother and the goddess of wisdom. She suckled the other deities and, in the Irish tradition, was their mother. These other deities were known as the Tuatha de Danaan, the people of Dana. Dana did not need the intervention of a male to create them, so her position in the pantheon is reminiscent of Nammu's.[225]

Dana is the maiden aspect of a triple goddess, along with Badb, the mother, and Macha, the crone. In this, Dana is cognate with Morrigan. In some traditions she has a husband, Bile, but again this is not consistent between the various sources. As Morrigan, she is

---

224 Not to be confused with the Sumerian god of the same name.

225 This interpretation is supported by the appearance of the Hindu Goddess Danu in the Vedic story *The Churning of the Oceans*, where she is the goddess of the primordial waters of creation, exactly as Nammu is.

one of the three wives of Dagda the Celtic sky father, who was cognate to An, El, Zeus *et al.* In this role she sleeps with Dagda during the festival of Samhain, in early November, to assure the return of fertility in spring; this has parallels both to the Mesopotamian Sacred Marriage and to Persephone's symbolic marriage to Hades in the Eleusian Mysteries. However, Dana was also both the mother of the Dagda and his daughter.[226]

The Celts prized craft skill and especially that of the smith. One of the Dagda's daughters was Brigid (Brighid), goddess of smithing, among other things. Swords and jewellery were highly valued markers of both the social status of individuals and the standing of the culture. It is interesting that, along with clear evidence of human sacrifice in water, we find caches of the finest artefacts. It has long been held that these were sacrifices to Dana.

Dana was always associated with water, frequently rivers. Her name is given to the Danube in Europe and the many Don rivers from Russia to Scotland. Sacrifices to her were often made in bogs, pits, lakes and rivers. Water represents the Goddess' amniotic fluid, in which life grows and which is the medium that surrounds us when we are born.[227]

Archaeologists have identified Celtic drowning pits. Execution in this way seems to have been restricted to kings and other high-status individuals. For example, in 734 CE, Talorgan mac Congussa, the king of the Scots, who had been fighting the Picts, was betrayed by his brother and captured.[228] The Picts drowned him.[229] Five years later, another Talorgan, son of Drostan, was also captured and drowned. Drowning, in the context of a culture that venerated the Goddess,

---

226 The genealogies of these Celtic deities have been described as 'chaotic'. We concur.

227 Wells, like all sources of water, were sacred to Celts as symbols of the Goddess, and in France, many cathedrals and churches are built on the sites of Gaulish holy wells. An excellent example of this is the magnificent Romanesque cathedral at Tournus. Here, in the crypt, directly under the altar, is one such well, sitting inside a Gallo-Roman temple basilica with four rows of columns. The cathedral was built on top of this structure, which denotes the huge importance it had, even to the Christians. This suggests a powerful link between the Goddess and early Christianity. The thealogy that was a deeply-rooted part of Gaulish, and all Celtic life, was merged into the Marianist form of Catholicism that became dominant for centuries.

228 Anderson, Alan Orr. *Early Sources of Scottish History AD 500 to 1286, Volume One.* Reprinted, with corrections by Marjorie O. Anderson. Paul Watkins. 1990.

229 *Ibid.*

may have been a sign of respect. It may have represented a passage back into the Goddess' womb, to await rebirth. Perhaps this was seen as speeding the passage of the prisoner from this life to the next.

As well as water, Dana is associated with the land and the Earth. She is also associated with light, the day and life, and this makes her a parallel to Inanna. In Irish mythology, her children, the Tuatha de Danaan, on arriving in Erin, first have to defeat the evil Fomorians, the children of the dark goddess Domnu, who is cognate to Eresh-kigal as goddess of the Underworld. This interpretation makes Dana symbolic of order and Domnu of chaos.

Most likely, the Celts saw the expression of order as the techno-logical advances the culture had made. Like the city-based cultures of the middle and near east, the Celts mastered nature through ag-riculture. However, instead of building mighty cities they retained a semi-sedentary lifestyle. This should not be taken to mean that they lacked the skills to build in stone; their achievements in jewellery and smithing make it clear that this was a very creative and techno-logically competent culture. Indeed, Pliny the Younger noted seeing combine harvesters pushed by oxen being used to harvest wheat in Gaul. The Gauls and other Celts knew perfectly well what cities were, for they had sacked Rome in 390 BCE under the charismatic leader Brennus.[230] Furthermore, once they adopted monumental building, they quickly became amongst the most skilled masons in Europe.

So why did they not follow the common path of city-based civi-lisation? It may be because city culture depends on the notion of per-sonal property. This was extended to cover women and slaves, who were regarded as property just as much as cattle or land. What we know of the Celts suggests that they never took this step. Although it is sometimes claimed that the Celts had slaves, in the main they did not. They did have a system of hostages, usually young men, who had been taken in formalised 'battles' between neighbouring clans, and who had to reside for five years with the victors. They were well-treat-ed and often married into the host clan, forming peaceful bonds be-tween them. They appear much more like envoys taken partly to en-sure peace than slaves, as a Roman would have understood the word.

---

230 This was the famous incident in which the Gauls agreed to leave the defeated city on payment of a ransom of 1000 pounds of gold ( Livius, Titus. (Livy.) c. 59 BCE - 17CE. *History, Book 5*).

Furthermore, the Celts do not appear to have regarded women as property, anywhere. Some Celtic populations remained matrilineal, and it is likely that they all had been at one time.

## The Picts

The Picts were a Celtic people who lived in what is now Scotland. Once again, this was a non-literate culture. It is not even clear what they called themselves; the name 'pictii' was given to them by the Romans because they had designs and images on their bodies. We are not sure whether these were painted or tattooed. The Picts had seven kingdoms in Scotland. One of the kings acted as 'first amongst equals' in decisions concerning the outside world, which largely concerned how to repel invaders and raiders, including the Romans, the Scots, Saxons from Northumbria and the Vikings. Despite being politically governed by both queens and kings, the Picts were matrilineal.

The Celts' notion of property is at odds with the patriarchal model. Celts understood and used money, and did have personal property in the forms of jewellery, artefacts, weapons and livestock.[231] Horses were especially prized. Both women and men wore much jewellery and patterned cloth and dressed their hair. On the other hand, land was not seen as heritable property that could be 'owned' by an individual; in Scotland until the eighteenth century, land in the Highlands was held by the clan chief in the name of all the people. The chief was 'first amongst equals' and the land belonged to everyone. The Celts appear to have retained many of the practices, like communal living in extended families, that characterise hunter-gatherers and the people we have seen at Çatal Hoyuk and Ain Ghazal.

Celtic women had exactly the same rights as men and were often leaders. Women could be Druids, the highest caste in the society. Women, not men, gave their names to their children.

Fighting amongst the Celts – rather than between them and outsiders – seems to have had an almost playful air. Women joined in the 'battles', to the horror of Roman historians who witnessed this, and who misinterpreted what they saw. Men often fought stark naked, which also perplexed historians, who have sometimes attributed this to an intense spirituality. While the Celts were certainly spiritual,

---

231 They were said even to lend money on the promise of repayment in the Afterlife!

there is another explanation for this behaviour. These battles might have been a form of field sport akin to the American Indian 'counting coup'. It is possible that the aim was not to kill but, in the case of men, to draw first blood, and of women, to take a lock of the opponent's hair.

The Picts cast an interesting light on the disadvantage that matriliny has when confronted by the patriarchy, which may in part explain how the patriarchy came to be dominant. Many theories have been proposed concerning how it happened that Kenneth mac Alpin, a prince of the Scottii, came to rule over Pictland, from victory in battle to subterfuge. However, the most likely answer is that he married a princess of the Picts, and arranged for the Crown Princess in each of the Kingdoms to marry another prince of the Scottii. Since kingship in Pictland was conferred by the mother and in Scotland by the father, this neatly ensured that the male offspring of these liaisons would inherit the throne from both sides.[232] This suggests that the creation of male property rights over women through marriage allowed the patriarchy to marry the matriarchy out of existence.

---

232 The union seems to have been arranged rather than forced. The Picts had been worn out fighting the Vikings in the north and east, and needed both reinforcements and to be sure that their western frontiers were secure, while it satisfied the Scottish desire for a unitary state, probably also for reasons of security.

## The Gauls and their Legacy

The Gauls were the Celtic people who lived in what is now France. Like other Celts they did not write down their beliefs. However, they left thousands of artefacts, many representing the Mother. Miranda Green has shown that there were even factories dedicated to the production of figurines of the deity just as similar ones produce countless figurines of Madonna and Child today.[233] The Gauls' allegiance to the Goddess was profound.

Until Vatican II, which began in 1962, the Roman Catholic Mass was always celebrated in Latin, and not in the local language of the congregation.[234] The tradition of celebrating Mass in Latin reaches back to the earliest days of Roman Christianity. The survival of both p-Celtic (Welsh, Breton, Manx etc.) and the older q-Celtic (Irish and Scottish Gaelic) tongues makes it quite clear that the populations did not generally become Latin-speaking, and so would not have been able to understand the liturgy.[235] To whom would they have turned for explanation of the new rituals? The Druids. The ordinary people of Romano-Celtic Europe would have been advised that their beloved Goddess was the Mother of this new Roman god, and that the Druids themselves would be there to protect and nurture their faith in her. How easy it must have been to slip into Christianity, especially for a people of whom Caesar noted, 'All the Gauls are very superstitious.'[236] Amongst the most devout of Christian lands would be Celtic ones like France, Ireland, Scotland, Spain and Portugal. The pre-existing Goddess worship in these areas greatly contributed to the phenomenon known as 'Marianist Catholicism', in which Mother Mary is the hub around which the pantheon revolves.

---

233 Green, Miranda. *Celtic Goddesses.* British Museum. 1997.

234 On-line resource: http://mb-soft.com/believe/txs/secondvc.htm

235 The Celtic tongues are classified into two groups, Goidelic and Brythonic: 'The Goidelic languages are often referred to as "Q-Celtic" because they use a "Q" sound, usually represented by a C or K, where the Brythonic or "P-Celtic" languages use P. For instance, Irish and Scottish Gaelic for "head" is ceann, or sometimes kin. Brythonic languages, P-Celtic Welsh and Cornish, use pen.' (http://www.digitalmedievalist.com/opinionated-celtic-faqs/celtic-languages/ Retrieved 10/07/2014)

236 Caesar, Gaius Julius. *De Bello Gallico.*

Medieval artists and masons, and the trade and craft guilds they belonged to, inherited the artisanal traditions that existed amongst the Gauls. These derived from the druidic system of learning and persisted after their Romanisation, and drew together the pre-existing Goddess belief with the new order, Christianity. Alongside the priestly successors to the Druids, these masons and artists ensured that the Goddess would remain at the heart of European Christianity.

# SECTION NINE:

## Patriarchal Monotheism

We are accustomed, in the West, to the idea of strictly enforced, written laws, of which the first known complete set comes from the Semitic king Hammurabi of Akkadia, around 1800 BCE. Hammurabi probably adapted his code, which he had carved onto a stone and set up in public, from an earlier Sumerian one known as *The Instructions of Šuruppag*.[237]

The Bible and the Qur'an borrow a great deal from the *Code of Hammurabi* via the later Assyrian *Code of the Assura*. These are not the source of human morality, but an attempt to define it in patriarchal terms. They codify the ownership of property. More significantly, they are preoccupied with controlling the fertility of women through marriage and the sexuality of both women and men through restricting with whom and how they are permitted to have sex. All of the codes go into great detail specifying the relative worth of women and men and what behaviour is acceptable. Most importantly, they define women as the property of men, in much the same way as they do sheep, goats or cattle; women become livestock that may be exchanged for other forms of material wealth.

To understand this development in Western culture, we need to look at early Judah.

## Ba'al's Challenge

Contemporary research of the archaeological sites in Judah and Israel has revealed that the people who became the Jews were originally Canaanite hill-people who worshipped a standard pantheon derived

---

237    http://etcsl.orinst.ox.ac.uk/cgi-bin/etcsl.cgi?text=t.5.6.1&display=Crit&charenc=g-circ&lineid=t561.p12#t561.p12 Retrieved 24/05/2014.

from the Assyrian tradition, a descendant of the Sumerian and Akkadian.[238] The principal male gods in this pantheon were El, who is cognate with the Sumerian Sky-god, An, and Ba'al, who is cognate with Enlil. Both El and Ba'al had female consort deities, Asherah and Astarte, thus forming a tetrad.[239]

Asherah's sacred symbol was a tall wooden statue which was set in a post-hole. These votives took her name and were themselves called asherahs.[240] Asherah-poles were often arranged on either side of an altar but sometimes in the form of a circle or grove. Discovery of the remains of a set of post-holes for such a grove within the confines of the Old Temple in Jerusalem confirms Asherah's importance. Judahite society was not religiously homogeneous; older deities continued to be worshipped.

One of the central themes of Canaanite mythology is the struggle for power between El and Ba'al. Their names mean 'God' and 'Lord' respectively, and they are father and son. In this tradition, these are very masculine, warrior gods. In the end, Ba'al eclipses El, who retires into obscurity.

The idea of younger deities struggling against and eventually overwhelming their elders is a recurrent theme of the ancient mythology of the Near and Middle East. This probably expresses the internal upheavals within very conservative cultures when confronted with new technological and social ideas. These cultures were extremely rigid, and it would be surprising if change and reaction to it were not reflected in their mythologies.

The great set-piece scenes in Hebrew Scripture such as, for example, when Moses comes down the mountain and is enraged to find the people raising altars to Ba'al, indicate that the writers were followers of El, resisting the challenge by his son Ba'al. This suggests

---

238 Finkelstein and Silberman 2002.

239 Some sources see Asherah as directly cognate with Astarte: once again, in an oral tradition as rich and diversified as existed in the Middle East, there were many versions of the same deities, and it is not now clear whether these were directly related to each other or were derived from an older common ancestor that informed them both.

240 We will use the convention of describing the votive object in lower case but capitalising the name when it refers to the goddess Asherah herself. Unfortunately there has been a great deal of conflation of the terms, which has led to confusion, both in Biblical times and now, and we should make it clear: we do not believe that the people saw these votives as incarnations of the goddess, but as representations of her.

a conservative, inward-looking and cautious society, which fits with what we know of Judahite culture at the time.

At every turn Hebrew Scripture rails against pluralism, polytheism and what it sees as the excesses of the more advanced and powerful cultures in the region.[241] This reflects the struggle between the culture of the poor, conservative, hill-farming people of Judah, and that of the more liberal, inclusive, urbanised Israel. The thrust of the Scripture is profoundly conservative despite a number of contradictory redactions that were introduced by priestly scribes influenced by the relatively liberal Israelite tradition.

In one myth, Ba'al and Astarte are allowed to rule over Canaan in El's name. There is a possibility that the adoption of El as Jahweh, the 'only god' of the Judahites, was a conservative reaction to this, a rejection of the new gods in favour of the old. The repeated injunctions in Hebrew Scripture to destroy the 'high places' dedicated to Ba'al support this. The whole narrative of the text may derive from it being one side in a socio-political debate, the other side of which is now lost. The Judahite tradition persisted, not because the culture triumphed, but because the more liberal, progressive and economically successful Israelite one was repeatedly destroyed by invaders!

For many years, scholars thought it possible that the Judahite monotheism was derived from the earlier monotheism of the Egyptian Pharaoh Akhenaten; indeed there are many tempting similarities.[242] These ideas have been challenged by archaeological evidence showing that the exile into Egypt as described in Hebrew Scripture simply did not happen. It is an invention, probably intended as a metaphor for the real Babylonian exile, during which the story was actually written. Similarly, while the Zoroastrian monotheist ideas were

---

241 We will use the term 'Hebrew Scripture' to refer to the body of religious texts written by the Judahites and adopted as the Christian canon of the Old Testament.

242 Akhenaten's cult might have been known about even in a place so fundamentally conservative and inward-looking as Judah in the 9th century BCE. This knowledge might have been transmitted through the Hyksos, who ruled in Egypt from around 1750 to 1530 BCE. They were slowly restricted to the north and the Nile Delta, and later fled to Gaza. (Gertoux, *Gérard. Dating the Wars of the Hyksos.* http://www.chronosynchro.net/wordpress/wp-content/uploads/Dating-War-of-Hyksos.pdf. Retrieved 09/12/2014.) Although it has often been postulated, notably by Josephus and later Christian apologists, that the Hyksos and the Biblical Hebrews were identical, this has been debunked by modern scholars (Finkelstein and Silberman 2002.) Nevertheless the possibility remains that some folk memory may have been passed by them to the Canaanites.

influential upon revisions of Hebrew Scripture carried out during the Babylonian Exile, there is, as we shall see, a prior and more compelling reason for the development of monotheism in this culture.

## Obedience and Redemption

Redemption, intimately familiar to anyone raised in a Christian cultural tradition, has a very particular meaning in Hebrew Scripture. Judaism is concerned principally with life on Earth.[243] Redemption in Judaism is the return of the people to the Promised Land, Israel, and the banishment of their oppressors. It has the same sense as 'to redeem' a slave – to buy that person's freedom. Redemption, put simply, is not a matter for the afterlife, but something to be striven for in this life, and that redemption was seen as a free Jewish people in a sovereign Israel.

In the earliest traditions, the Creatrix is the Goddess, but in the Bible's creation story this role is assumed by Jahweh. While no fault or blame is suggested in the earlier creation stories, the Hebrew tale contains the idea of 'original sin', and that sin is disobedience.[244] Disobedience is addressed in multiple symbolic ways in the creation myth found in the book of Genesis.

In the first version of the creation story, Genesis 1:26-28, Jahweh created a couple, Adam and his wife, but this first wife disappears in unexplained circumstances. In a non-Biblical Jewish tradition, she was called Lilith. This tale first developed in the Babylonian Talmud but was expanded in Jewish folklore. Lilith refused to obey Adam,

---

243 It is possible that the very indifference Judaism shows towards Resurrection, that other great pillar of Christianity, is because this is so intrinsically associated with the Goddess.

244 The Scriptural text is quite clear on this point. Many people think that the original sin was sex, but this derives from a very skewed interpretation by Saint Augustine, of whom Seán Fagan wrote: 'St. Augustine, one of the most distinguished theologians in the history of the Church... had no real understanding of marriage but only his own guilt-ridden experience of long years of sinful fornication. John Noonan describes him as holding that there was nothing rational, spiritual or sacramental in the act of intercourse. He saw it as intimately linked to original sin,' (http://www.churchauthority.org/resources1/fagan5. asp).

claiming that, having been made of the same clay at the same time, she was not subservient to him.[245] She was banished from the Garden of Eden, and she became a demon.

There is a link between Lilith and the lilitu demon who infests Inanna's Huluppu Tree. This is supported by the fact that the tradition first appears during the Babylonian Captivity, when the scribes were exposed to Mesopotamian culture. Lilith, after her banishment, was believed to procreate demonic offspring endlessly and spread chaos whenever she could, causing wine to turn into vinegar, men to be impotent, women to be barren and babies to die.[246]

In the second version of the creation story, Genesis 2: 21-23, Eve is created from one of Adam's ribs, thus removing any idea that they are equals. As far as this version is concerned, it is clear that Eve was created for the pleasure of Adam, since after his first wife disappeared, his 'companions' had been wild beasts. This implies a parallel with Mesopotamian literature, in the *Epic of Gilgamesh*. Gilgamesh sends a priestess of Inanna, Shamhat, to tame the wild man Enkidu, who lives and mates with the wild beasts in Eden, which was the Sumerian name for the uncultivated grassland.

Shamhat teaches Enkidu how to be a civilised man, in everything from how to eat, how to behave, what clothes to wear and how to have sex with a woman. Shamhat represents the Goddess, and one of the great symbols of Goddess-power is the Fruit of the Tree of Knowledge.

The Fruit is a powerful Goddess object, which is confirmed by its shape, that of the womb, and its contents, the seed from which life springs. Thus, the fruit is a metaphor for not just the womb, but the Goddess and the power of creation. A symbol of regeneration, it also confers the knowledge of good and evil, the power to govern fairly and administer justice wisely. This is what Aset gave to Osiris to allow him to be a good king. But in the Jahwist view, the power to rule resides with Jahweh, not the Goddess. So the story insists that people must deny the Fruit, in order to remain loyal to Jahweh: in other words, the Goddess must be denied in favour of a male God.

Eating the Fruit of the Tree of Knowledge might have inspired

---

245 This is a reference to the way the lesser Sumerian deities created humanity from the clay of the land, in order to do the work.

246 Schwartz, Howard. *Lilith's Cave: Jewish tales of the supernatural*. Harper & Row. 1988.

Adam to eat the Fruit of the Tree of Life, and become immortal. Expulsion from the Garden denies Adam the opportunity to do this and so become divine and set himself up in opposition to Jahweh. So it may again reflect the theological tension between El and Ba'al which is at the heart of the Hebrew Scripture. Jahweh was incensed that Adam had eaten the Fruit of the Tree of Knowledge because he feared he might use this knowledge to make himself an immortal god, and challenge his creator.[247]

The scribes writing Hebrew Scripture were social conservatives who had taken the side of El against the insurrection led by his son, Ba'al. Obedience of sons to their fathers is perhaps the most important underlying thread in the whole of Hebrew Scripture, so it was necessary for Jahweh to punish any filial disobedience; because of this, Adam is banished from Eden.[248] This is itself a metaphor, since the Garden of Eden can be read as the Promised Land, Israel, which the Judahite clergy and kings so coveted. So it is saying that only kings who are true to Jahweh may rule, and those who transgress will lose everything.

Satan is a complex character in Hebrew Scripture, because it is a syncretisation of Mesopotamian, Egyptian, Persian and other sources. However, in this example, Satan, as the serpent who gives Eve the Fruit, is derived directly from the Sumerian Enki. Enki was known to appear as a snake and throughout western mythology he and his successors have been the closest of all male deities to the Goddess. Enki gave the Mes, the gifts of civilisation, to Inanna, and these are equivalent to the Fruit of the Tree of Knowledge.

The Garden of Eden is a metaphor for Israel, and Adam and Eve the Judahite people; they are thrown out for disobeying Jahweh.

---

247 Genesis 3:22-23. 'And the Lord God said, Behold, the man is become as one of us, to know good and evil: and now, lest he put forth his hand, and take also of the tree of life, and eat, and live for ever: therefore the Lord God sent him forth from the garden of Eden.' (KJV)

248 Hebrew Scripture is firm on the point of filial obedience: 'If a man have a stubborn and rebellious son, which will not obey the voice of his father, or the voice of his mother, and that, when they have chastened him, will not hearken unto them: Then shall his father and his mother lay hold on him, and bring him out unto the elders of his city, and unto the gate of his place; And they shall say unto the elders of his city, This our son is stubborn and rebellious, he will not obey our voice; he is a glutton, and a drunkard. And all the men of his city shall stone him with stones, that he die: so shalt thou put evil away from among you; and all Israel shall hear, and fear.' Deuteronomy 21:18-21 (KJV)

Redemption, therefore, in Hebrew Scripture, is the possession of the land of Israel, and the freedom to live there in peace. It can only be achieved by absolute obedience to the word of El/Jahweh, as expressed in Scripture – in other words, obedience to the priests who wrote it.

Like the Adam and Eve story, the Egyptian Exile narrative serves to emphasise that obedience to Jahweh and his laws will be rewarded by return to the Promised Land, and disobedience by banishment. The fact that the Biblical Exile in Egypt is a myth does not mean that all the exiles also were. The Exile to Babylon, when the Hebrew Scriptures were heavily redacted and rewritten, was real. It only affected a relatively small percentage of the population, but these were the educated and skilled, the wealthy elite, including the scribes who were doing the writing.[249]

# Josiah

The ideas that crystallised into Judaism originated in the 7th century BCE, during the reign of King Josiah of Judah. Josiah ordered the renovation of the First Temple, and during this a set of scrolls was 'discovered' by the High Priest Hilkiah. The scrolls are believed to have been most of the book of Deuteronomy. They contained a legal code that was the foundation of a patriarchal state. Scholars now recognise that Hilkiah most likely arranged the writing of the scrolls, either adapting an older text or inventing a new one or both.[250] The multiple references to the glory of Joshua, Josiah's namesake, and the delivery to him of the Promised Land, make it clear that, as well as a constitutional framework of laws, the document was commendation and praise in favour of King Josiah and his policy of militarily asserting control over Israel in the name of Jahweh.

This elegant construction was the conclusion of a bargain between throne and priesthood. Josiah would give all religious power

---

249 Finkelstein and Silberman 2002.
250 *Ibid.*

and influence to the male priests of Jahweh, represented by Hilkiah, and suppress the priestesses of Asherah as well as the cults of Ba'al and Astarte. In return, Jahweh would deliver to Josiah the Promised Land, Israel, a far wealthier and more fertile kingdom than Judah. Josiah's father had died in a palace coup, probably fomented by the Hilkian faction of priests, while the young heir was still a child. He may have been brought up under the tutelage of the priesthood in order to ensure that he had the 'right' ideas. In any case, Josiah, either brainwashed or perhaps just through ambition to seize Israel, pledged allegiance to the social conservatism of the Jahwists.

The priests destroyed the political power structure of the priestesses, who had represented women and the Goddess and in the tradition of social conservatives before and since, they persecuted anyone who dared to disagree with them. And, for a time, the bargain was fulfilled. Josiah did indeed succeed in capturing the land of Israel for the crown of Judah, although this was largely due to the collapse of Assyrian power rather than his own efforts,.

It was a short-lived triumph. In 609 BCE war broke out between the two great regional super-powers: Egypt and Assyria. In order to join battle with the enemy, the Egyptian king Necho needed to lead his army across Judah, since it was the best route north. Josiah refused and led his army against the Egyptians. They met at the Battle of Megiddo, where the Judahites were utterly crushed by a vastly superior military force. Josiah died, either at the battle or by execution shortly after at the instruction of Necho. His land and people were effectively annexed by Egypt.[251]

For hundreds of years, whenever there were more progressive kings, Judah's condition ameliorated. Yet when conservative kings – the very ones described as 'good' in Hebrew Scripture – came to power, disaster upon calumny befell the land as these kings, egged on by a rabid priesthood, offended far more powerful sovereigns and were punished for it.

In 605 BCE, Necho was defeated by the Assyrian king Nebuchadnezzar. Judah, already annexed by Egypt, became a client state of Assyria and Jehoiakim, Josiah's successor, began paying trib-

---

251 Were it not for the fact that the syncretisation of Hebrew mythology into the canon we now know began during his reign, Josiah would likely be forgotten.

ute. After Egypt's defeat of Assyria in 601 BCE, Jehoiakim rebelled against Assyria. In 598 BCE Nebuchadnezzar laid siege to Jerusalem. During this, Jehoiakim was killed and replaced by Jehoiachin, his son. After three months of siege, Assyrian forces entered the city and pillaged it, destroying the Temple. The noble, wealthy and intellectual people of Judah were taken into captivity and sent to Babylon.


The religion of Judah had been a 'temple' religion. All authority came from the power of the temple priests to intercede with Jahweh, in that holy place, on behalf of the people. Once in exile and without a temple, the priests could no longer orchestrate the highly profitable sacrifices and other rituals that they used to supplicate the deity. To retain control, they had to turn the focus of the religion to the law and the scriptures, which only they were empowered to interpret. The captive priests edited and redacted these scriptures to suit their objectives.

In 537 BCE, the Persian king Cyrus the Great invaded and conquered Babylon. One of his first acts was to release the Judahites from captivity, and they returned to Judah. They declared the new version of the Hebrew Scripture, which the exiled priests had spent decades rewriting, to be the only authorised text. The Exiles reclaimed Jerusalem and built a new Temple.

The result of the differences in religion between those who had stayed and the Exiles was that Judahite society split along class lines. Those who had remained behind and adhered to the religious ideas current before the Exile were later known as Samaritans. They were vilified by the returning Exiles, who adopted the role of urban ruling elite and sought to impose their new version of Judaism on the entire population. From this point on, the socio-political and religious divisions between Jerusalem and rural Judah became important.

Judah and Israel remained under the heel of occupying powers for centuries during the Biblical period. By the end of the first century BCE, the land was under the control of the most powerful Empire yet seen in the West, Rome. The establishment's reaction was to cleave to tradition and social conservatism.[252]

---

252 This reflex is by no means restricted to ancient Judah; in the modern United States

The Judahites were originally simple peasant farmers who wanted security of tenure of their land and to get on with life. One does have to sympathise with a people so put upon – largely due to the strategic importance of their lands – by vastly more powerful and sophisticated cultures all around them, which did not hesitate to use ruthless military force again and again. Jews never evangelise; it is difficult to become a Jew even if one marries into the culture and the only land they want is a postage-stamp of desert with practically no resources. Nothing could be further from the core philosophy of Judaism than a desire for world domination, making it one of only a very few religions not so afflicted.

Nevertheless, this was one of the most grimly patriarchal religions in the world. While this is no longer the case for most of Judaism today, some ultra-conservative sects remain profoundly misogynist.[253] By the first millennium BCE, women's lot through much of the region was abysmal, and Judah was no exception. Men had legal power of life and death over women who had, effectively, ceased to be considered people. The male priesthood that served El (Jahweh) was socially conservative, determined to resist change, and committed to having absolute control.

Power in Goddess-culture flows from the Goddess, through the hands of a woman, to the king, and for the Jahwists to achieve the influence they desired, that link had to be broken. So, although in the Canaanite mythology that they had adopted, El (Jahweh) has a wife, the Goddess in the form of Asherah, it behoved the male priesthood to remove this powerful goddess and her priestesses, lest they demand access to the king's councils. The Goddess had to be airbrushed out and her supporters – women – cast down.

In the Judahite support of El over Ba'al, the father over the son, the writers had invoked a contract; if the Judahites would be faithful only to El, then El would not fail them. The First Commandment, 'You shall have no other gods before me', implies that there *are* oth-

---

for example, a culture of paranoia is maintained which serves the ends of right-wing conservatives and patriarchal Christians. Very much the same happened in Nazi Germany and the Soviet Union, and the principle was well described by the writer George Orwell.

253 Modern, enlightened Judaism is far more inclusive and egalitarian but traditions such as the Hassidic, which is a reaction to modernisation and even worse the Lev Tabor tradition, which has actually been thrown out of Israel, show how deep the roots of misogyny are.

er gods. The Judahites were told to put these other gods aside and pledge allegiance to El, who would deliver them the Promised Land – the more fertile and rich lands of Israel to the north. This faithfulness to 'one god' was not originally a monotheism, however. Other gods and goddesses still had cadres of priests and priestesses seeking influence over the temporal ruler. What more natural next step could there be than to remove all of the pantheon but one male god and give him all the divine powers? Over time, as we shall see, the replacement of all deities with a single, male god was the result.[254]

# Resurrection

Resurrection, that core philosophy of Goddess worship, is less important in Judaism; some Jews believe in it, and others do not. It is not a mandatory belief, nor is it central.[255] It confirms the persistence of an immortal human soul, which will be raised from the dead and clothed once again the flesh of a human body. Resurrection in this sense has a very long history. The Natufians buried their dead and then dug up the skulls and sculpted portraits onto them and Inanna, having died and her corpse rotted, was born again in a new body, out of herself. The concept of resurrection represents a cyclical comprehension of life and as such is intrinsic, indeed, quintessential, to the understanding of the Goddess as creatix and re-creatix of all life.

As part of their determination to excise all deities but one, the Jahwists had written out the Goddess, leaving only Jahweh and his reward of a material redemption: the Promised Land. This left a hard and cold comfort and, down the centuries, repeated efforts have been made to reintroduce aspects of the Goddess to the belief. In the Me-

254 This was not unique. In many cultures in the Near and Middle East at the time, there was a general tendency towards monotheism founded on the worship of a single male god. In every case the central deity was syncretised from previous deities, normally the king or chief of the pantheon of sky-gods and goddesses. This appears to have been the result of both political and religious change.

255 Since so much of Judaism is concerned with how one lives, it is possible to consider oneself both Jewish and atheist. This again sets it apart from many other religions.

dieval period, the Kabbalists, doubtless at least to some extent influenced by the powerful Goddess-cult of Marianist Christianity that surrounded them, re-introduced the Goddess as the shekinah, the breath or fire of Jahweh. Even in the Biblical era, the idea of resurrection, that core element of Goddess-culture, had been adopted by the Pharisees, one of the principal politico-religious groups in Judea and Galilee. It is interesting, in this context, to note that Jesus has an association with Nicodemus the Pharisee, since Jesus was a preacher of Goddess philosophy and of Resurrection.[256], [257]

We should not imagine that Judaism was any more homogeneous in the Biblical period than any major religious cult then or since, and the dichotomy between the Pharisees, who believed in Resurrection, and the Sadducees, who did not, is one clear confirmation of this.[258] We should, therefore, see surviving Hebrew Scripture as representing only one version – albeit the dominant one – of the religion of the Judahites. It may well be that many other versions were current but were simply never written down or were lost or destroyed.

Although Babylon had long since become a patriarchal society, its roots were in the Goddess-culture of Sumer. At the time of the Exile, it was still polytheistic, and representations of the Goddess were everywhere. In particular, Ishtar, who was the direct descendent of Inanna, had become the principal military deity of the Babylonians. She was the standard of the very army that had swept the Hebrews into decades-long exile. It would be surprising if the Hebrew scribes had not excised from their own scriptures every favourable reference to the Goddess they could find.

Just because the educated elite believed a certain set of ideas and tried to promulgate them, does not mean there were no opposing points of view. Women, in particular, must have resisted the suppression of the Goddess, and the rural poor, especially those who had been left behind in Judah during the Babylonian Exile, must have

---

256 John 3, 7, 19.

257 John Dominic Crossan argues that James the Just was Jesus' older brother or half-brother. He may also have been a Pharisee. (Crossan, John Dominic. *A Revolutionary Biography*. HarperCollins. 1995.)

258 There were four recognised politico-religious groups active in Judah, later Judea. These were the Sadducees, the Pharisees, the Essenes and the Zealots. The former were the establishment parties and the two latter outside it.

retained other, older beliefs and practices that were not modified by exposure to far-off Babylon. However, history is not only written by the winners, but by the literate. At the end of the Exile, when the Hebrew elite returned to Judah, those who had remained behind were looked down upon by the former exiles as heretics who worshipped a false version of Hebrew Scripture.

Raphael Patai and, more recently, Francesca Stavrakopoulou and others, confirm that in the earliest versions of the Judahite religion, Jahweh/ El did indeed have a female consort, Asherah.[259] It is also clear from the many references to it in the Biblical texts, usually surrounded by sulphurous fulminations, that the worship of Ba'al and his consort, Astarte, remained widespread, especially in the rural areas.

Astarte is the sister-wife of Ba'al. In Hebrew Scripture, Astarte is referred to as 'Ashteroth', but the suffix 'oth' is pejorative, and the name means 'the abomination Astarte'. This is in line with what we would expect of the followers of one politico-religious camp struggling against another. It supports the premise that Judahite culture was by no means monolithic, but full of contradictory beliefs.

As consorts of El and Ba'al, Asherah and Astarte are the representations of the female principle, the matron goddesses of women, the goddesses of love and sex, and the Mother. Most of all they represent Resurrection through the love and forgiveness of the Goddess. They are the antithesis to the Jahweh of the patriarchal scribes and clerics. Their message is that rebirth comes from the Goddess, that hope for another chance at life, therefore, comes from her too, and that the reward for a good life is release from the clammy gloom of the Underworld to be reborn.

The writers of Hebrew Scripture wrote out the ideas of rebirth and instead saw hope in materialistic terms.

---

259 Patai, 1990.

# The Resurrection cycle: descent and ascent

Despite the fact that resurrection is played down in Hebrew Scripture, there is one obvious example of it. In Genesis, Abraham the patriarch and his nephew, Lot, decide to part company and Abraham gives Lot the choice of territory. Lot picks the best, 'well watered everywhere...even as the garden of the Lord' and 'pitches his tent' towards Sodom.[260] Although Lot is just and 'righteous' and troubled by the way the local people lived, he settles there, becomes a citizen, and eventually the mayor.[261] He is treated with respect because he is related to Abraham, who had saved Sodom from an Elamite invasion. He marries a local woman and by her he has two daughters, whom he permits to be married to local men.

Jahweh decides to destroy Sodom, but is persuaded by Abraham to refrain, on condition that 'ten righteous men' could be found there.[262] Only Lot can be found, so Jahweh sends two angels to warn him and tell him to flee.[263] This story is a parallel to that of Noah, in which one 'righteous' man was given a warning of the impending destruction. That story itself is a parallel to, or may have been directly derived from, the Sumerian tale of Atrahasis, who was warned by Enki that the deities intended to destroy humanity.

The angels are welcomed into Lot's house overnight, at which point a gang of men appear and demand that the angels be handed over to them. Lot, bound by the rules of hospitality that oblige him to protect his guests, refuses, instead offering his virgin daughters.[264]

---

260 Genesis 13:10.

261 2 Peter 2:7-9.

262 This is one of the examples of Jahweh in anthropomorphic form, where he can be reasoned with by mortals; also note that only men are to be counted. The patriarchy was well established here.

263 Genesis 19:1-3.

264 Two injunctions are made clear in this story. The first is against breaking the law of hospitality, which had grown out of the harsh desert conditions of that region. Strangers were to be made particularly welcome (Lev. 19:34). The second illustrates the patriarchy's hostility towards sexual acts between men. Anal sex was expressly forbidden in this conservative culture. As in most patriarchal cultures, only the male/female binary model was accepted. Sodom is portrayed as a vile, evil place, and the idea that the men of Sodom would come to Lot and ask him to hand over his guests for such sex was an affront to both

In the morning the family members are so reluctant to leave that they have to be bundled out of the city by force. They are given an injunction not to look back as volcanic fire and sulphur obliterate the city, but Lot's wife, who was walking behind her husband, does so and is turned into a pillar of salt.[265]

This story bears unmistakable similarity to the Greek myth of Orpheus and Eurydice in its references to 'looking back' and to the woman being behind the man. We have already seen how the Orpheus and Eurydice myth is a patriarchal development of similar descent and ascent myths from all over the region, and how they fit into a timeline. These myths all derive from the Sumerian Inanna's Descent into the Underworld, or perhaps a precursor to it. The story of Lot is a further development of this, but not substantively different.

Sodom and Gomorrah are a metaphor for the Underworld. To live there is to die before Jahweh, to be estranged from him. Therefore, when Lot leaves the city and returns to the land of Jahweh, he is being reborn. Here the metaphor is subtly reworked. This myth is saying that the condition of being 'unrighteous' is equivalent to being dead and because Lot's wife, who is not named, has the pleasures of the city in her heart she is not righteous and must die.

The tale celebrates the simple rural life and condemns that of the cities, a theme oft-repeated in Hebrew Scripture as cities are cast down, their walls destroyed and their populations slaughtered. It is the voice of a poor people, living in a barren, infertile land, who were profoundly jealous of the great civilisations around them. The writers of Hebrew Scripture, who so coveted yet condemned the

---

the law of hospitality and the idea of decency. The shock value of this outrage has led the English-speaking world to invent the term 'sodomite' to describe, in a pejorative manner, any who participate in acts of anal penetration.

265 Note that Lot's wife was walking behind him; this is common in cultures where the most aggressive forms of patriarchy exist. In Genesis 19:8 the men of Sodom gather around Lot's house, threatening his guests. Lot offers the mob his two virgin daughters, saying 'I have two daughters which have not known man; let me, I pray you, bring them out unto you, and do ye to them as is good in your eyes.' Lot is still considered worthy of being saved from the destruction of the city in spite of offering his daughters for gang rape because of the low status of women; Hebrew Scripture sees nothing immoral about rape providing the woman's legal owner – in this case her father – sanctions it. In a later passage, the daughters seduce their father in order to get pregnant and ensure the continuation of patriliny. Even incest is permissible in the name of the patriarchy.

richness and luxury of city life, sought to destroy them, if not in truth then at least in fiction.[266]

# Winners and Losers

In the long struggle between priests and priestesses there were temporal winners and losers. Men gained everything: religious and political power, wealth and control, and the subservience of women. The Judahites were not at all unique in their misogyny, but there was a significant difference between them and others, such as the Athenians or the Assyrians. These latter, though they too reduced their women to the status of chattels, never took away their access to the Goddess, their light in the darkness of male oppression. In Judah, the monotheist priests of El effaced his consort and did everything they could to eradicate the Goddess and destroy her power. It needs little imagination to see how this, by extension, was also perpetrated on women, who had every vestige of equality stripped from them, always in the name of greater devotion to Jahweh.

The cumulative effect of this was shocking. Women were literal possessions of men, for all of their lives. They were not even counted as people in the official censuses, a system of enumeration that began in Greece, continued throughout the Middle East and spread across the Roman Empire. No census ever counted a woman – since she was merely the property of a man. In Judah, especially after the return of the Babylonian Exiles, the oppression of women was suffocating. Men could beat or even kill the women they possessed and, in some cultures, they could have many wives. Of course, women were forbidden to have sex with any but their husbands, on pain of horrific death, and had to obey their commands. A woman had to be a virgin when she married. She could not speak to a man who was not her husband, brother, father or son. A woman could not speak to any

---

266 Finkelstein and Silberman have demonstrated that the many destructions of cities claimed in Hebrew Scripture simply never happened; they were all invented as part of a greater story. (Finkelstein and Silberman 2002.)

man, no matter his relation to her, during her monthly flow, and then she had to hide away from society and neither cook food nor otherwise attend to her family. Women could not eat at the same table as men. They could not inhabit the same space as men and instead lived in a closed compartment of their husband's tent, or in a separate room in his house. They could not walk beside their husbands, but had to remain several paces behind. They could not show themselves in public, nor hold political office or property in their own names. Even citizenship was denied them.[267]

> 'They had become second-class Jews, excluded from the worship and teaching of God, with status scarcely above that of slaves.'[268]

This was an oppressed and oppressive culture, and ripe for new ideas.

# Birth of Christianity

When the Jahwists rewrote their scriptures to excise the Goddess, they did something that would have far-reaching consequences, for their monotheism was adopted by two following, and numerically much greater, faiths. One of these was Christianity and the other was Islam. While the political focus of Judaism was the recovery of a fairly unimportant parcel of land, both Christianity and Islam had a different objective, the domination of the world; one through becoming the state religion of Rome, and the other through violent challenge to Rome and its successors.

---

267 The imposition of the veil upon women was not originated by Muslims, it is just continuing as part of Islam. 'If the wives of a man, or the daughters of a man go out into the street, their heads are to be veiled.' *The Code of Assura.* c. 1075 BCE, Assyria. (http://www.world-mysteries.com/awr_laws3.htm Retrieved 01/09/2014.)

268 Metzger B.M. & Coogan M.D., *The Oxford Companion to the Bible*, Oxford University Press. 1993. Cited at http://www.religioustolerance.org/ofe_bibl.htm Retrieved 14/10/2014.

The harmonious balance implicit in the polytheisms and expressed in the tetrads was upset by removing the feminine and leaving only the masculine. In particular, the focus of the religion changed from love, procreation, sharing, protection, forgiveness, fertility and above all resurrection, to possession, status, warfare, law (to be ruthlessly and pitilessly applied in all its force), the desire for property and material wealth, and the subservience of women to men and the family to the father.

By the beginning of the first century CE, the lot of women in Judah was execrable. Their only hope, the Goddess, had been outlawed, and both she and women were blamed for the political disasters that befell the state. Even the great King Solomon was regarded by the Jahwists as a 'bad' king because he 'set up high places' to the Goddess. The only parameter that qualified a ruler as 'good' in Hebrew Scripture was unquestioning obedience to Jahweh – and the Jahwist priests.

The cyclical conception of life, derived from the phases of the Moon, the waxing and waning of the tides, women's periodic cycles, the burgeoning and withering of the agricultural year, and the associated annual cycle of the sun, had been replaced with a linear understanding of one life leading to everlasting bliss or torture in the afterlife. The focus changed from fertility and the making of life to death and preparation for it. The cycle of resurrection was suppressed, to be replaced by terror of an angry, judgemental god. What remained was a death cult that was intolerant of any challenge to its doctrine.

Christianity is simultaneously a preservation of Goddess culture, through rehabilitating its central themes of resurrection and forgiveness, and a suppression of the Goddess by putting these themes under the control of a man. Throughout prior history the clerics of the Goddess had been the priestesses who served her, either as shamans in the earliest times or, later, in her temples. To deliver the message of the Goddess through the medium of a man speaks to the social condition of women in the society at large.

We have no real idea who Jesus was, despite the Gospel writers' repeated attempts to contextualise him as a first-century Jew; indeed we have no solid evidence that he actually lived at all. Yet, paradoxically perhaps, whatever the reality or otherwise of Jesus' life, it is the message spread in his name – of the Goddess – that is pertinent here.

By the time that Jesus is said to have lived, patriarchal Judaism was not only stifling but had failed completely in its promise. The lands of the Jews were occupied by idolaters; their Jahweh publicly mocked and completely ineffectual. The last resort of a cleric who is unable to deliver the promises he has made in the name of his god is to denounce the people for their lack of piety. Women and the rural poor especially felt the opprobrium of a fanatical priesthood, as they were blamed for causing Jahweh to turn away from his people and allow the occupation of their land by infidels.

This was a culture ripe for revolution, especially after a whole dynasty of Kings, the Herods, became the agents of the Roman State, with priestly connivance.

## Isolation and Invasion

The kind of deeply conservative, rule-bound culture that existed in Judah depends on something that is not always within the power of its controllers to ensure: isolation. No matter where the extremes of religious conservatism flourish, their greatest enemy is contact with the outside world. This is true in extremist Islamic states today; it is true in the pulpit-thumping darkness of America's 'Bible Belt' as well.

Isolation is the one thing that Judah could not have. It straddles the only viable route from the Near East into Egypt, an important strategic position both in military and trading terms. It was inevitable that the great powers, keen to protect their interests in the region, would want to ensure that it was pacified or brought to heel. Assyrians, Egyptians, Babylonians and Greeks had all taken their turn, and by the end of the first century BCE the Romans were in control.

The Romans were polytheists with many gods and goddesses. Their women, though by no means unaffected by the general suppression of women throughout the warrior patriarchy, were nevertheless seen in public, could own property and were treated with respect. Roman slaves were better treated, by and large, than Jewish women of the era. If slaves became free, they could set up businesses in their own right and their children, born free, would be full citizens. All in all, Roman life must have appeared extremely desirable to the average Jewish woman of the day.

Rome was a melting-pot, a magpie that assimilated ideas from every culture it touched, even if those cultures were crushed under its military boot. All the deities of the Greek pantheon, with suitably Romanised names, were present, alongside a host of others from North Africa, Phrygia, Germania and Gaul. Roman religion was replete with aspects of the Goddess.

For the Jews, the fanatical and exclusive worship of one god, Jahweh, was the only route to redemption. In return for such devotion, Jahweh would not only reward them with the return of the Promised Land and the right to live there in peace and freedom, but also destroy all those who did not accept him as the only god – the polytheists, in other words.

But manifest polytheism had not led to Rome's downfall at the hand of a raging desert monster; rather the opposite. Rome was in robust health and in control of Judah, where it showed little respect for Jewish customs. Pontius Pilate even had statues of Roman deities placed in the Temple, to the outrage of the Jews. Despite all the slights and blasphemies, no divine retribution was taken.

As might be expected, the priesthood was appalled by the presence of 'false gods' amongst them. They had railed against the Babylonian deities but as exiles they had little choice. The Romans were in their land, demanding taxes of them and using that money in the furtherance of idolatry and polytheism, as was evident from the temples they built to what the Jahwists considered 'abominations'. The frustration was intense.

Patriarchal social conservatism, then as now, is not a level playing field. At its heart is discrimination. It strongly favours the hereditary elite against the most disadvantaged in society. In first century Judea, the two most obviously disadvantaged classes were the rural poor and women. The version of Judaism then promulgated had little succour for them. Jahweh was a bitter, angry, vengeful god whose only interest was in being worshipped. His cult had no conception of forgiveness; the slightest lapse in observance of the Deuteronomic Laws would be punished by temporal disaster. 'Abide by the letter of the law or be punished, and if you are being punished it is because you did not abide by the law.' People had to obey laws drawn up in the name of an appalling god because they were browbeaten into terror by a class of priests who reaped the temporal rewards as their influence grew.

And yet, before the people's very eyes were others who did not fear Jahweh and mocked him with impunity. The Romans were successful, wealthy, had good lives and held the keys to the Promised Land. This had a profound effect.

## Hellenistic influence

Alexander the Great and his successors, the Ptolemies of Egypt and the Seleucids of Damascus, had long since begun the process of Hellenising the eastern Mediterranean hinterlands. They had established Greek cities at Alexandria, Antioch, Tarsus and elsewhere, and imported their culture to many more. The Romans took this insertion of Hellenistic culture into the region even further. They adopted the entire Greek pantheon as their own and employed Greeks – or enslaved them – as clerks, business managers and scribes. Everywhere the Romans went, one might say, the Greeks were sure to go, and Judah was no exception.

The Hellenes were the product of a successful and rich culture. Hellenistic ideas became the basis of philosophy throughout the Roman Empire and beyond. The Hellenes, not all of whom were Greek but who shared their culture, were open-minded and receptive to new ideas. They were also profoundly superstitious. As a result of these factors, Hellenistic culture had become a hotbed of competing religious cults, and many of these were very wealthy and powerful.[269]

---

269 'Hellenistic' refers to Greek culture after 323 BCE. It is generally confident, flamboyant, celebrates the individual and is given to spectacle and grandeur. The earlier phase of Greek culture is called 'Hellenic' and was more reserved, formalised, and stylistically simple. This is the culture of Homer that was once generally known as 'Classical'. 'Hellenes'

Whatever the reality of Jesus' life, the mythology surrounding him is of two sorts. One is an appeal to the conservative Jewish people by arranging to have the hero fulfil Hebrew Scriptural prophecies, and the other is an appeal to Hellenised people, whose gods and religious ideals were very different. Since the Gospels – Matthew, Mark, Luke and John – are heavily laden with fulfilments of Hebrew prophecies and Hellenistic miracles, we can see that conservative Jews, as well as more secular Jews and Hellenised Gentiles, were being targeted by the writers.

In the patriarchy, the qualities and powers of the Goddess were appropriated and given to male god-figures and Jesus is an extension of that process. Judaism had no trace left, at this time, of the Goddess. It was a religion based on fear, but fear can only hold people's hearts and minds when they believe there is no escape.

For Hellenised people living in the region, Jahweh must have seemed an uncouth and violent brute, quite unworthy of devotion. Zeus may have been fickle, tricky, unfaithful, vengeful and prone to bouts of temper, but Jahweh was far more harsh. While Zeus' wife Hera was subordinate, she often rebuked him for his excesses and was a powerful counterbalance. Hellenistic culture, though by that time thoroughly patriarchal, was based in Goddess culture; the Hellenes had kept many goddesses, and they were not about to do away with concepts like forgiveness and love. The stark, bitter, jealous and angry Jahweh may have come from the same source as Zeus via El and An, but without a female consort to temper his harshness, all that was left was grim, stony judgementalism, condemning and repeatedly punishing the only people loyal to him.

Since the Jewish religion is not evangelist and it does not proselytise, there was never any need for the Jahwists to soften the harshness of Judaism to attract more followers. It is arguable that the opposite is true, that Judaism was kept as rigid as it was in order to ensure its uniqueness and the unsullied bloodlines of the Jews. The result was that Judaism was a non-runner in the evangelical race that was taking place all over the Hellenised world, where religions and cults were springing up everywhere.

---

refers to people who were part of Hellenistic culture but who may not themselves have been Greek. 'To Hellenise' describes the process by which the culture spread. Generally, peoples were Hellenised not by coercion but because of the attractiveness of the culture.

Christianity, from its inception, was a religion that one joined. Adherence was a matter of choice and in this Christianity was like many other cults that appeared in the Hellenised world around the same time. Since joining these cults was voluntary, people had to be persuaded. Their leaders had to evangelise, and this is one reason why we see so many parallels between the stories of Jesus and other god-men, most of whom were preaching a very similar message.[270]

The territories that had been Judah and Israel were no longer the sole property of the Jews, if they ever had been. The influx of peoples from different cultural backgrounds had been ongoing for many hundreds of years, which stiffened up the already rigid cult of Judaism. The Jews were not even prepared to accept those who had been left behind in Judah during the Babylonian Exile as Jews.[271] They detested the Romans and their idolatrous ways, and resented the fact that the Romans held dominion over the Temple. The Herodian Dynasty of client kings of Rome who ruled in Galilee was also hated, but at least it was Jewish; it was against the Romans that hard-liners railed the most.

## Insurrection

During the first century CE there were repeated rebellions in Judea, aimed at throwing out the Romans. The leaders of these popular movements were both political and religious. It could not have been otherwise since religion and politics were indivisible. Anyone able to mobilise and organise resistance to Roman rule in a temporal sense must have based his power in religion.

Regardless of the feelings of the general population about the Romans, the establishment – the religious leaders of the Temple and the Herods and associated aristocracy – were fervent appeasers of Rome in order to maintain their position. They carried out its will in

---

270 These included the cults of Mithras, Dionysus, Simon Magus and others.

271 It is more likely that the exiled Jews had changed than those who stayed, but as it was the exiles who were writing and redacting the Hebrew Scripture, their opinion persists.

all matters temporal. At the same time, they preached that if the Jews strictly observed the religious code of the Bible, then Jahweh, one day, would reward them by destroying the Romans. The evidence of the many insurrections of the period tells us that the establishment view was not universally popular and that, amongst the ordinary people, anger against the occupation frequently boiled over into violence.

To be against both occupiers and a supine political class is one thing, but to whom could a revolutionary activist movement appeal, and how? There were two potential constituencies: the rural poor and women. Both of these groups were disenfranchised under the established Judaism of the time. Polytheism repeatedly appeared amongst these groups and this maintained the establishment's anger.[272] The polytheism that they would have returned to was probably the reforming cult of Ba'al and Astarte, since this is so often, and so bitterly, attacked in the Bible. On the other hand, women's allegiance to Asherah, El/Jahweh's consort, had been almost impossible for the establishment to eradicate or suppress, especially outside Jerusalem. The increasing pressure of misogyny, instead of killing off Asherah and women's loyalty to her for good, appears to have had the opposite effect and women clung to their Goddess, as they had been doing since the dawn of human culture.

By the time Jesus is said to have lived, these two constituencies were ripe fruits for the plucking by a creative and imaginative religious leader who challenged the authorities, which is exactly what the Gospels say Jesus did.

In the Gospels, Jesus repeatedly breaks Jewish law by talking to and indeed helping women to whom he is not related. One of these is a Samaritan, a group shunned by the Jewish establishment.[273] He is surrounded by women but never marries – in other words he never becomes the possessor of a female slave, to which it was tantamount. When he is anointed with oil – the name 'Christ' just means 'Anointed One' – *it is by a woman*.[274] In Matthew and Mark, this happens

---

272 Patai 1990.

273 John 4:4-26.

274 In each story, the woman appears to be an independent woman who has the means to purchase expensive perfumed oil and ignores the indignation of the surrounding men. The fact that the women are, in some cases, described as 'sinful' probably only means they are unmarried. This will be elaborated in a later chapter.

at the home of Simon the Leper, in Luke it happens at the home of a Pharisee named Simon, and in John it happens in the house of Lazarus before Jesus' triumphal entrance into Jerusalem.[275] Although the details differ, the powerful scene in each case symbolically confers upon Jesus the right to rule in the name of the Goddess. It is exactly as we have seen in Sumer and Egypt: the right and power to reign flows from the Goddess but is administered by a man.

The rural poor living in Judea and Galilee were largely the descendants of the Judahites who had been left behind during the Babylonian Exile. Shepherds, who metaphorically represent the rural poor, are celebrated all over the Gospels, and Jesus himself is identified as a 'good shepherd'. In the same way and for the same reasons, he is identified as a carpenter and a fisherman. On the other hand, the Jewish elite – the Pharisees and the Sadducees and the priesthood itself, as well as the rich and powerful – could not be painted in a worse light. The overall strategy is clear; the writers of the Gospels were appealing to marginalised and disaffected groups in the region.

Whoever wrote the stories was targeting these groups, and it doesn't matter whether it was Jesus himself or his real followers or even if Jesus was a literary invention. In any of these cases, the result would have been the same.

Jesus' message was aimed at those who had been most victimised by the ruthless social conservatism of established Judaism. He was a reaction to centuries of such oppression, an explosion of despair that was at the same time a cry of hope.[276]

So what was the message? It is clear: love, forgiveness and resurrection. These core messages of the Goddess are at the heart of the Christian faith. They are what distinguish it from the harsh, punitive excess of Hebrew Scripture. Jesus preached forgiveness, the helping of those who are not of your faith or nation, the healing of the sick, the succour of the poor, the celebration of women, the rising again after death, the pardoning of sins.

At the core of the Gospels' message we have the Goddess.

---

275 Matthew 26:6-13, Mark 14:3-9, Luke 7:36-50, John 12:1-8.

276 While the authors hold differing opinions about the historicity of Jesus, we are in complete agreement that it does not matter. The facts need not be historical for the metaphor to be true. Knowing this helps us understand the appeal of all mythologies.

## Two Testaments: two views

At every step along the path of human cultural development since the beginnings of the patriarchy, we see the Goddess' powers progressively stripped from her to be given to a male god, just as, in the society at large, women's status and rights were stripped away and given to the men who legally possessed them.

Female deities have their powers given to male deities in order to justify the ongoing suppression of real women in the real world. Nephthys is cognate with Ereshkigal, but while Ereshkigal is absolute ruler of the Underworld, that power is given to Set in the Egyptian version. In Sumer, Inanna condemns her husband Dumuzi to death for sitting in her throne while she was absent – in other words, demonstrating that she is in charge. It was her throne, just as the throne of the Underworld was Ereshkigal's. Aset/Isis' relationship to Osiris is what we expect in later, more patriarchal yet still Goddess culture: political power flows from her to Osiris as king. The Goddess remains the source of power, but the man wields it in her name; he sits on the throne, but she stands behind him. We see something similar in the relationship of Asherah to El and Astarte to Ba'al.

It should be no surprise that such a deeply misogynistic cult as first-century Judaism should be associated with two things: the absolute condemnation of the Goddess as 'an abomination' and the reduction of women to virtual and practical slavery. In a culture so determinedly patriarchal it is inevitable that women must seek something more, so that their spiritual needs may be met.[277]

While Jesus may or may not have been a real man, he most certainly is a real myth, which persists to this day, and so obeys the rules of mythology. The Goddess' message of forgiveness and resurrection and the cyclical understanding of life which is encapsulated inside it remain deeply appealing to both women and men. Although the

---

277 That the iron fist of patriarchy can never destroy the spirit of women – which is the Goddess – is shown today by the 'My Stealthy Freedom' movement in Iran, in which women take pictures of themselves unveiled and post them to social media. The apoplectic reaction of the misogynist mullahs shows how effective such a seemingly simple protest can be: the patriarchy can tolerate no sign of rebellion.

hard-line successors to Hilkiah had excised the Goddess, she could not be killed and to think so was pure conceit.

The male gods of the patriarchy reward those most successful in its terms, the materialist aggressors, and they condemn those who do not measure up. Men are judged solely on their behaviour in the one life that the patriarchy permits and by how well they perform under the abstract rules of the patriarchy. We all make mistakes and we all crave forgiveness, yet within the cult of first-century Judaism there was no forgiveness or resurrection, no cyclical foundation, none of the Goddess. All that was left was a harsh, barren code of male 'honour', misogyny, obedience to bizarre and arbitrary codes of conduct, and judgement.

The Jewish culture of the time was heavily predicated on the primacy of cities, principally Jerusalem, over the countryside. Success in the culture was to become a wealthy, powerful, city-dwelling man. Failure, therefore, was to be a poor country person, particularly one who clung to the old ways.[278]

In such a resolutely misogynist culture, women had no significance except in terms of the men they served with sons. All they were left with was the expectation that they would wear the yoke of enslavement to men, either their fathers or their husbands, or even their brothers, without protest or breach of the patriarchy's many rules controlling their sexuality. By far the most important of these is that they bear male children who are known to be their fathers' sons, so that patriliny, the basis of the patriarchy, may be ensured. Within the patriarchy, just *being women* made them failures.[279] To be judged solely on the basis of how well one plays the meek, dutiful and obedient wife of a powerful and rich man, is a condemnation for women.

In a very real sense, Jesus, whether he lived or not, was indeed a saviour. He saved many people, starting with the rural poor and

---

278 As seen in the pejorative terms 'pagan' and 'heathen' which originally meant 'from the countryside' (Latin '*paganes*') and 'from the heath'.

279 A morning prayer, originating in the Babylonian Talmud, that is still in use, says:
'Blessed are you, Hashem, King of the Universe, for not having made me a Gentile.
Blessed are you, Hashem, King of the Universe, for not having made me a slave.
Blessed are you, Hashem, King of the Universe, for not having made me a woman.'
(http://originaljewish.com/static/posts/35)

women, from suppression under the most rigid and divisive version of the patriarchy that had till then existed. This salvation was not by virtue of his being the 'son of god' or whatever other fiction about his divinity had to be concocted, but by his message. Forgive those who sin against you; love your neighbour; share with the poor; through me everyone is born again. The Gospels are filled with notions and ideals that come directly from Goddess culture. At every turn, Jesus sympathises with the rural poor and women, and rails against the establishment, its patriarchal hierarchy, and the men who serve it. Despite the fact that the texts were chosen to fit within a patriarchal framework, the Gospels are deeply subversive works.

# SECTION TEN:

# Roman Christianity

Judaism was the product, like all religions, of the society that invented it. In this case the society was small, insular, isolated, poor, weak, extremely socially conservative and constantly threatened by vastly more powerful and acquisitive cultures all around it. It would be difficult to think of a greater contrast with Rome in the early centuries CE, which was expansionist, cultured, cosmopolitan, confident and the most economically and militarily powerful civilisation for thousands of miles. Judea suffered from fear and weakness, which made it put all its faith in one warrior god. Romans were highly religious and superstitious, but Rome was far from powerless, and its culture was built on the exploits and examples of god-like warrior kings like Alexander, and more recently the Caesars.

The initial success of Christianity was due largely to the popular appeal that is integral to the faith because of its roots in Goddess culture. Within the extreme form of the patriarchy that existed in the first century CE, its message fell on fertile ground. Paul the Apostle brought the new religion into the Hellenistic milieu of the eastern Mediterranean, and here it took firm root. However, in practical terms, Christianity became the dominating world religion that it did for another, much more pragmatic, reason altogether.

The Roman Empire was fuelled by expansion. It needed to conquer new lands and peoples, for the spoils were what kept the Roman people happy, so conquest was never far from an emperor's thoughts. It was the Empire's custom to reward loyal soldiers with land, but since Roman Law protected land within the Empire, new territories had to be added continually. This is not a sustainable practice, and by the end of the third century CE, two problems had begun to appear.

The first was the inevitable result of expansion: lines of communication and supply became longer and more tenuous. Armies marched for hundreds of miles to reach their destinations and on the way they consumed vast amounts of food. While Roman armies could, and did, simply help themselves to supplies from the peoples they were conquering, they could not do this within the Empire. Food and replacement clothing, animals and things as mundane as boots had to be transported to them and paid for. Even though Roman commanders were able to make strategic decisions without reference to political control, as demonstrated by Julius Caesar during his war in Gaul, the greatly extended lines of communication rendered the Empire vulnerable.

The second problem, which made the first worse, was that the Romans began to encounter other acquisitive cultures, which in turn invaded Rome for plunder or to take territory. The Empire promised protection to those whom it had conquered, and this meant that responsive measures had to be taken, and quickly, to defend Imperial assets far from Rome.

Roman expansion halted, and the Empire began to contract. At the same time, internal stresses began to appear. These erupted in the Crisis of the Third Century, during which the Roman Empire split into competing states: the Gallic Empire in the far West, centred on Gaul and Roman Britain, the Roman Empire proper, and the Palmyrene Empire in the east.

While this was a short-lived arrangement that was ended militarily by Aurelian, it had lasting consequences. In 284 CE, Diocletian consolidated the fractured Empire into two, the Western Empire, which was initially ruled from Rome and the Eastern, ruled from Byzantium, modern Istanbul. However, the volatility of Gaul and the Celtic west had been demonstrated and could not be ignored. Gaul was the breadbasket of the Western Empire, and its allegiance was vital.

After such recent violent schism, there was a call for a state religion that could unite the Empire politically, spiritually and morally. Rome had, for hundreds of years, incorporated deities and cults from all over its conquered territories to add to a basic Hellenistic pantheon. After the consolidation of the Empire into West and East, Romans began to search for unity in religion.

The cult of Sol Invictus was made the official Imperial religion by Aurelian in 274 CE.[280] Although it was the state religion, it was not

---

280 Watson, Alaric. *Aurelian and the Third Century*. Routledge. 2003.

compulsory, and many Romans continued to worship older deities. Despite this, we must wonder why Sol Invictus was replaced. After all, had it not been, it is likely that billions of people across the globe would now be following it and worshipping the sun.

We have no records of Constantine's deliberations before he adopted Christianity and replaced Sol Invictus with it, although the circumstances he was in are well known. The Empire was fading and menaced by adversaries, and had recently split in a cathartic schism that had only been resolved by diverting military resources that were badly needed elsewhere. At the heart of that schism had been Gaul, along with Britain and Spain. This was the world of the Celts – the Goddess-worshippers.

Gaul was indispensable; its rich, broad farmlands were incredibly productive and vital to the Western Empire. The Gauls had been hard to conquer and doing so had entrained decades of civil war in Rome. They had re-asserted their independence during the brief Gallic Empire, and this must have weighed on Constantine's mind. Strategically, Gaul was a corridor made up of the Rhine and Rhone valleys, through which invading armies, having crossed the German plain, could reach the Mediterranean and threaten Rome itself. Constantine could not afford to lose Gaul; its protection and retention at the heart of the empire were essential. The Gauls and the other Celtic peoples had to remain bound into the family of Rome.

Adopting a new religion that satisfied the Gauls would be one way to assure this. In doing so, in offering an olive branch of appeasement and showing them how important they were to the Empire, Constantine would have followed well-established tradition. Gaius Julius Caesar had made Gaulish nobles senators of Rome, much to the outrage of many Patricians, and his heir, Augustus, carried out programmes of public works in Gaul, notably at the new city of Augustodonum.[281]

Finding a religion that would fulfil Constantine's aims had a major obstacle. The Celts were resolute in their devotion to the Goddess. Any attempt to remove her would have provoked outrage, political turmoil and possibly insurrection, threatening not only the essential supplies of grain but also the integrity of the Empire. On the other

---

281 Modern Autun in France.

hand, imposing the Goddess on the other, more patriarchal peoples would have been equally divisive, and might have been rejected. In short, Constantine needed a patriarchal cult centred on a male deity, which retained a core of Goddess thealogy, a widespread popular appeal and a hierarchical structure that would match Rome's.

Christianity had all of these elements. Its structure had been established by Saul of Tarsus, later known as Paul the Apostle, who used the hierarchy of the Empire as his model. Paul was a Hellenised Jew, a tax collector for Rome, so he was intimately familiar with its pyramidal command structure. Paul's quasi-militaristic hierarchy, with priests, bishops, and archbishops, each level with increasing authority and responsibility, meant that the Catholic Church dovetailed seamlessly with the Empire's military and civil structures. The religious authorities could be slipstreamed into the temporal bureaucracy. Christianity was a patriarchal religion, but it was built around a core of Goddess thealogy. It would require little alteration to accommodate the Gauls.

# The Goddess in Christianity

Constantine became Western Roman Emperor in 312 CE after routing his predecessor, Maxentius, at the battle of Mulvian Bridge. A year later, he and the Eastern Emperor Licinius co-authored the Edict of Milan, legalising Christian worship and bringing to an end the 'Age of Martyrs'. By 324 CE, Constantine had become ruler of both Empires and had made his capital in Byzantium, which he renamed Constantinople. He continued to promote the Christian faith, and convened the Council of Nicea in 325, where the basic tenets of Christianity, the Nicene Creed, were established. The Eastern Emperor Theodosius and his western counterpart Gratian made Nicene Christianity the official religion of the Empire in 380.

Rome was a patriarchy, but one with the Goddess at its heart. She was everywhere, in myriad forms. The Goddess was deeply loved, and a part of everyone's life: for her not to appear centre-stage in the new Roman state cult would have been unthinkable. It would have immediately led to the rejection of that cult by some of the most important peoples of the Empire – not least the Romans themselves!

The overtly Goddess-worshipping cultures within the Empire, as well as Romans, would require the Goddess to be represented materially, rather than just within the terms of Christ's message. In other words, there would have to be an actual goddess character in the mythology.

There was only one possible candidate, and that was Mary. As the mother of Jesus, she was the Mother of God, so she assumed the role that went with that, Queen of Heaven. Like Isis, she remained a perpetual virgin. Within Catholic dogma, hers was an 'immaculate conception', without 'original sin', which is similar to the way Ki/Ninhursag was born thousands of years before. She appears in the Bible in the three key roles of the Goddess – the virgin, the mother, and the crone who grieves over the dead god at the foot of the cross. The god is resurrected from a tomb, from within the Earth itself, which is also cognate with the Goddess. The name 'Mary' appears in triplicate at the crucifixion of Jesus, again at his tomb, and three times as the daughters of St Anne, who was the mother of the Virgin Mary. These symbolic references suggest that the gospel writers intended the followers of the new religion to recognise Mary as the Goddess, and the Catholic Church simply developed this in terms of ceremonial practice.

In order to establish the structure and dogma of the new state religion, the Romans organised a series of formal councils. The First Council of Ephesus, in what is now Turkey, in 431 CE, established Mary, the mother of Jesus, as Theotokos or 'Mother of God'.[282] This step put the Goddess at the centre of the new state religion, to make it attractive to those imperial subjects who were devoted to her.[283] At a stroke, the Church Fathers had transformed Christianity, making the central role of Mary, the Goddess incarnate, not only implicit in the faith but also explicitly at the centre of it. The so-called 'Marianist' tradition had been made the dominant strain of Catholicism and, since Catholicism was by definition 'the universal church', the

282   *Encyclopaedia   Britannica.*   http://www.britannica.com/facts/5/281254/Council-of-Chalcedon-as-discussed-in-Theotokos-Eastern-Orthodoxy
283 http://www.newadvent.org/cathen/05491a.htm

Goddess was placed at the head of Christianity.

This move is sometimes referred to as Mary's 'promotion' but it can only be seen this way from a particular point of view. The Gospels themselves identify Mary as the Goddess, the Mother of God. Her acceptance as such, and the title 'Queen of Heaven' that went with it, was a natural progression. This role was to become, as Dr. Francesca Stavrokopoulou has noted, possibly the most commanding that the Mother Goddess has ever had.[284]

The Goddess-worshipping Celts had been granted their Goddess, in a position of supreme authority at the heart of the church. It is little wonder, then, that Christianity was so readily adopted by the Celtic peoples and that they should become some of the most devout Catholics in Europe. The political ends of the Empire were well served by the Council of Ephesus and, while the temporal Empire's decline was not prevented, the spiritual authority of Rome was assured and would persist.

## Public Religion

The Romans had long known that entertaining the people through staggeringly extravagant spectacles, holidays and feast-days, was an effective way of maintaining civil order and the loyalty of the people. The object of the new religion was to include everyone and unite them. While the final canon, the 'official' collection of writings to be included in the New Testament of the Bible, had already been determined, this did not impede the adoption of procedures and practices which went beyond what was written.[285]

Since only the priestly hierarchy had access to the collected canon, and only they were allowed to interpret it, a completely new base of knowledge grew up: dogma. This was a means to apply the interpretations of the holy texts, arrived at by committees of priests and

---

284 Stavrokopoulou, Dr. Francesca. *The Bible's Buried Secrets.* BBC Television Broadcast. 2011.

285 Although the canon would not be officially rubber-stamped for another thousand years!

prelates, to a whole raft of very different cultures, in many languages, across the Empire. The people would know of the Bible only that which the priesthood told them. Thus, the new religion had enormous flexibility, and its appeal was very broad; and of course, should that have failed to persuade, there was always the ruthless power of the State to back it up.

With this system in place, there was no difficulty in modifying the essential core of Christian practice to accommodate local requirements. This was a masterful stroke, since it allowed Christianity to spread virtually unopposed throughout the Empire and far beyond, simply by assimilating local belief and practice as it went along.

Part of this process was to dress up the new religion with all the spectacle and entertainment that the Roman populace demanded. Festivals and feast days were imported from other cultures, and none were more important than those of the Goddess. Every major calendar event in Goddess culture was adopted directly into Catholicism.

The midwinter festival, already widely celebrated, became the official birthday of Christ, even though examination of the Biblical texts clearly shows that they claim he was born at Passover – as was appropriate for a Jewish Messiah. Easter, which is named in English after the Saxon derivative of Ishtar, is the day of Jesus' resurrection – the day of the Sacred Marriage, when the Goddess, radiant in her blaze of divine light, brings the resurrected god to her bed to 'plough her furrow'.

All Saints Day, on November 1, was equally celebrated as a feast of the Goddess, the time when her consort, the harvest god, perished, to be born again on December 25 when the sun could be seen to rise in the sky once more.

There were, by Roman times, so many variants of Goddess culture that the celebrations proliferated. The night before All Saints Day, All Hallows E'en, or Halloween, is derived from Samhain, the night when it was believed by the Celts that the membrane between the Real and the Otherworld was so thin that the denizens of the Otherworld – the dead – would rise and walk amongst the living.[286] May Day, originally the same as Easter, became a separate fertility festival. Within the Roman Catholic calendar, every day has a patron

---

286 'Samhain' is pronounced 'SAOW-en', not 'Sam-hain'.

saint and to a large extent these were local deities adopted by the Roman Empire.[287]

Although many early Christians had been readers, most people in the Empire were illiterate. Only the educated patrician class could read, alongside scribes and other specialist slaves. Bibles, like all books, had to be hand-copied and were rare and precious. Books were of no use to most of the common people in the Empire. Others, like the Gauls, were suspicious of written culture. The new religion had to be spread not by books, but by priests who had studied the texts. This was not a problem. While the early Christians had decided to establish a fixed canon before Rome adopted the religion, it was never intended to be read by everyone. In fact, establishing a canon and outlawing the writing of competing texts was a way to keep biblical knowledge in the hands of the priests and prelates. Christian priests were already trained to interpret the Bible and contextualise it in terms that non-Christians would understand, in order to evangelise the faith.[288]

Revelation and interpretation were, as they remain, at the core of all religion. Oracles were consulted, auguries taken, and many other means of communing with the gods and spirits were employed, similar to those used by our early shamans entering the spirit-world of the Goddess. The biblical text was seen not only as a document of reference – by which the authorities could measure any piece of theology – but also as a document of inspiration. The priestly class took the texts of the New Testament and interpreted them for the faithful, as Christian preachers and priests still do.[289]

Of the Spanish conversion of the Philippines, over a thousand years later, Charles Derbyshire wrote, in the introduction to his translation of Noli me Tangere by the Filipino hero and muse José Rizal,

---

287 The Catholic Church has been replacing these with human saints for nearly a thousand years, but many of the originals are still in place – Saint Bridget, for example, the Celtic Goddess Brighid or Bride.

288 Justin Martyr, the Christian evangelist and apologist, often likened the stories in the Bible to Greek myths, in order to make them more widely acceptable.

289 The actual books of the Bible have always needed contextualisation, because they describe a time and place that is totally unfamiliar to the audience.

'no great persuasion was needed to turn a simple, imaginative, fatalistic people from a few vague animistic deities to the systematic iconology and the elaborate ritual of the Spanish Church. An obscure Bathala or a dim Malyari was easily superseded by or transformed into a clearly defined Diós, and in the case of any especially tenacious "demon," he could without much difficulty be merged into a Christian saint or devil.'[290]

Few more succinct descriptions of the process by which Christianity was proselytised, and still is today, have been set to paper.

On the other hand, the gentle words of missionaries and the preparedness to accept local belief into the nascent religion were only two of the methods used to promulgate Christianity. As ever with patriarchal monotheisms, behind the velvet voice of persuasion was the iron fist of coercion through violence. Charles Derbyshire, again, gives us an insight to the methods used by the Roman state on reluctant populations, as the same means were used in the Philippines by the Spanish:

'When any recalcitrants refused to accept the new order, or later showed an inclination to break away from it, the military forces, acting usually under secret directions from the padre, made raids in the disaffected parts with all the unpitying atrocity the Spanish soldiery were ever capable of displaying in their dealings with a weaker people. After sufficient punishment had been inflicted and a wholesome fear inspired, the padre very opportunely interfered in the natives' behalf, by which means they were convinced that peace and security lay in submission to the authorities, especially to the curate of their town or district.'[291]

---

290 Rizal, Dr José, tr. Derbyshire, C. *The Social Cancer: A Complete English Version of Noli Me Tangere*. Manila Philippine Education Company. 1909.
291 *Ibid*.

## Mary and the other Goddesses

All Christian sects use the Catholic canon of the New Testament with only minor textual differences. Within this, Mary is the Goddess. This is the reason the misogynists Luther, Calvin and Knox hated her. But the Romans did not invent Mary's identity with the Goddess, it was in the Gospels from the very beginning. God and Jesus are indivisible, as the Bible tells us, and since Jesus was born from her, Mary was the Mother of God.[292]

Mary's status as the mother of Jesus/Jahweh defines her not just as a goddess, but the Goddess. That Jesus is both God and the Son of God is made clear in John 14:10, when Jesus says 'Do you not believe that I am in the Father, and the Father in me? The words that I say to you I do not speak on my own authority; but the Father who dwells in me does his works.' Although in the Catholic tradition she has been forced to wear the robe of a chaste Roman matron, Mary is Asherah, Astarte, Isis, Ishtar, Inanna, Ki, Nammu and every other aspect of the Goddess that has ever existed.

From Isis, whose cult had spread throughout the Roman Empire, the early Christians imported the Madonna image of the nursing mother with the child-god on her lap and gave it to Mary. But Isis is no shrinking violet; she is the Goddess in all her glory. She outwitted and defeated the terrible power of evil, Set – the New Testament Devil – and gave birth to the resurrected god Horus. Once again, this fits the Roman conception of the ideal woman – the chaste but fiercely loyal wife and mother who will do everything for her husband and son. The patriarchal sentiments of Rome may have, as they had in Egypt and before, tempered the Goddess, made her subservient to men though her relationship to a male deity, but Mary remains the daughter of all the aspects of the Goddess that went before her.

Goddesses from all over the Empire were incorporated into

---

292 John 1:1 states that 'the Word was God.' John 1:14 states that 'And the Word was made flesh, and dwelt among us' This confirms that Jesus is God made flesh; he is an anthropomorphic version of himself, but the two are nevertheless one. This is precisely the relationship of Inanna to the Great Goddess – the anthropomorphic, humanly comprehensible form of a transcendent deity.

Christianity and given feast-days and the title 'saint'. Since most of the deities in the Empire were strongly anthropomorphic, living in their home regions, the Christian priests were able to evangelise the new religion just as a repackaging of the one the people already knew, with the familiar characters.[293] They only made one major change: all these gods and goddesses were subservient to one god, just as all the peoples, local kings and temporal leaders were subject to one Caesar. It was a brilliant stroke, and it was phenomenally successful: the disparate peoples of the Empire, seeing their deities integrated in this way, adopted the new religion with almost no resistance.

# Sex in Rome

Romans had contradictory ideas about how women should behave. Roman noblewomen – setting the standard for all free women – were expected to be chaste and faithful, and to produce noble children.[294]

While this was the ideal, the practice was very different. Prostitution and the possession of sex slaves were commonplace in the Empire. Roman women attended orgies and had sex with slaves for illicit pleasure because this did not carry the heavy sanction that adultery with another noble entailed.[295] Although the Romans were nominally monogamous, it was commonplace for a man to have several wives in succession, and the usual prerequisite that a bride should be a virgin only applied to her first marriage. It was common for a man to divorce his wife, and for her to marry again. This was even a matter of public policy; Augustus Caesar divorced his first wife Scribonia in order to marry Livia, who herself was married and had to

---

293 These were probably the very same priests as had been preaching to their people before. The Romans, being practical fellows, would have realised that the simplest way to convert the Empire would be to persuade the local priests to slightly modify their message, a spear in one hand, and a promise of reward in the other. This was, after all, the Roman way of doing things.

294 Like many Roman ideals, this one was rather more for public display than private reality. The moral superiority of Patricians over Plebs had to be demonstrated.

295 Very strict laws forbade adultery, which was punishable by death.

be divorced. Fortunately her first husband Nero, whose child she was carrying at the time, was a willing participant in this exchange – for which he was well recompensed by Augustus.[296]

For the ruling patriarchy, a model had to be found to inspire Roman women; one whose virginity was sacrosanct, whose sexual pleasure was totally under the control of her husband, and who saw herself as the loving mother of a new generation of Roman men. For many Romans, this ideal was symbolised by Atia of the Julii, who was matriarch of her household. In her personal history, mythologically at least, she was chaste and responsible; she deferred to her son, Caius Octavius, later Augustus Caesar, but was still a powerful figure. Augustus himself, according to legend, was not sired by a man, but by the god Apollo. This made Augustus the son of a god and moreover, he promoted himself as and was worshipped as such by the Romans. In her personal mythology at least, Atia was proud, of noble birth, chaste and supportive of and loyal to her menfolk.[297]

This cultural motif was much too strong to ignore, so Mary, at least in Roman times, was Atia, the ideal Roman woman, and the idealised role she played would remain the idealised role of women for hundreds of years. Mary is intended to represent the ideal of womanhood within the culture: chaste, devout, obedient, devoted.

This is a patriarchal vision of womanhood; it is a straitjacket, or perhaps a chastity-belt. It appropriates women's sexuality and fertility and makes these the property of a male – in Mary's case, Jahweh/Jesus. Fascinatingly, while the Catholic and Orthodox traditions insist that Mary had no other children, in order that she might remain a virgin all her life, the Gospels clearly state that Jesus had brothers and sisters.[298] This has nothing to do with mistranslations or differences in grammar because, in Catholic mythology, Mary is the bride of Jahweh/Jesus, not Joseph.[299] According to this tradition, Mary's

---

296 Roman women had no legal choice in this. As possessions of men, they could be exchanged at the will of men.

297 A mythology somewhat at odds with her personal history.

298 Three of the Gospels mention Jesus' brothers: Matthew 12:46, Luke 8:19, and Mark 3:31. The Gospel of Matthew gives their names: James, Joseph, Simon, and Judas (Matthew 13:55), and also states that Jesus had sisters (Matthew 13:56). This is not a translational issue, since the specific Greek words for 'brother' and 'sister' are used.

299 For Catholics, authority does not come from the Bible but from priestly (not individual) interpretation of it, or *dogma*. Where dogma and the Bible disagree, dogma is relied

marriage to Joseph was never consummated, making it invalid. Since adultery is completely condemned, at least for women, Mary, who as Jahweh's bride is the Goddess, must never have sex with anyone other than Jahweh. Mary's perpetual virginity is a part of the patriarchy's campaign to appropriate the sexuality and fertility of women. Since authority in Catholicism comes not from the specific words of the Bible but from the priestly interpretation of them, it sufficed simply not to mention the other children to support the doctrine of Mary's perpetual virginity.[300]

In Rome, a particular set of attitudes towards sex had become established, which inform Western attitudes today. Sex was seen as an act of status in which the penetrator dominated the penetrated.[301] A whole hierarchy of sexual behaviour was established around this, and culturally associated with a system of honour. Men (the penetrators) were dominant over women (the penetrated). Men, therefore, had more honour than women. All acts of penetration were seen as dominant and therefore honourable for a man. So a man who penetrated another man was not demeaning his own honour, but reinforcing it, since the important issue, for the Romans, was not with whom one had sex, but how. On the other hand, a man allowing himself to be penetrated had abandoned all male honour and was a laughing-stock.[302]

Other sexual acts too, were subject to this hierarchical model. Since fellatio involves oral penetration, the person performing it loses status. For man to perform cunnilingus on a woman was also seen as submissive and a betrayal of his male honour. In fact, all of the techniques used to give women sexual pleasure were seen as dishonourable, and a man who practised them reduced his status.

Even women's sexual pleasure itself became dishonourable. The patriarchy condemns women's sexual pleasure, and this is nowhere more starkly obvious than in the hideous practice of Female Genital

upon.

300 When they are mentioned at all, in response to a literate questioner, it is as children of Joseph by a previous marriage.

301 Skinner, Marilyn B. *Sexuality in Greek and Roman Culture*. Wiley-Blackwell. 2013.

302 This association between male homosexuality and male honour leads directly to the abuse of homosexual men, since by acting in a way that the patriarchy considers demeaning, they impinge on the 'honour' of all men, and defy the patriarchy; which no man may do with impunity.

Mutilation, which carves out a woman's clitoris, an organ that has no function other than providing pleasure.[303]

Women's honour in Rome derived from being good and loyal wives and mothers. Sex for a woman was about procreation and satisfying her husband, rather than her own pleasure. The chaste and loyal wife could ameliorate the debasement of honour that being penetrated entrained because she served a greater honour: the production of Roman sons who would carry their father's name. Women were not expected to take pleasure in sex; it was only for the purpose of reproduction, an idea that remains central to patriarchal belief today.

At the same time, however, Romans were extravagant libertines. Julius Caesar has been described as a 'pan-sexual playboy' and this was a commonplace lifestyle for patrician men. Although the public expression of sexual indulgence was at its height during the notorious reigns of Caligula and Nero, even the socially conservative Vespasian, who followed them, merely insisted on greater discretion and privacy; the practices continued apace.

Clearly there is a dichotomy here, and it needs to be explained: how could all the sex that we know was going on have been happening in this bizarre construct of sexual morality?

Nearly all the workers in the common brothels and bath-houses were slaves, and many Roman households kept slaves specifically to service the desires of the masters, and even, sometimes, the mistresses. A Roman man had power of life and death over everyone in his household. They were all his personal property, to do with as he wished, from the lowest scullion to his wife, and while his wife did enjoy limited legal protection, absolutely none was afforded to slaves. He could have sex with as many of them as he liked, in any way he liked. We know from Pompeii that patrician homes had special rooms designed as places where orgiastic acts of sex could be performed, with slaves.

Roman society was divided into four different strata, the Patrician or noble elite, the common people or Plebeians, 'Freed' men and women, who had once been slaves, and slaves themselves. All of these

---

303 This disgusting cruelty is still practised today within Islamic communities even in Europe, but also by other groups.

groups wore badges to identify their class; the toga was only worn by Patricians, for example, and Freed people wore a distinctive cap.

Being born free gave honour to the Patrician noble class and the Plebeian common people, but this honour could be lost – if, for example, they were sold into slavery. People from either of these classes could rise to the highest echelons of Roman society. Freed people could own businesses and gain respect and honour, but they could not take part in government, though their children, born in freedom, could.

Honour supported the patriarchy. Since honour flowed from men, it was hierarchical and could be won and lost in terms of how one behaved or was seen to behave. Rising through the ranks of the army by dint of his ability afforded the great general Pompey Magnus sufficient honour to become a Consul of Rome, even though he was a commoner. So the system did, to an extent, reward ability and merit, at least for men.

Slaves' absolute lack of honour meant that they could never dishonour anyone, no matter what they did or was done to them, any more than a horse could. This was the key to the double standard of Roman life, and nowhere more so than in matters sexual.[304]

After Augustus Caesar passed a law that required all prostitutes to be registered, this dichotomy took another twist. Prostitutes' names were entered in a register, and they were issued a licence. Once a name was on the register, it could never be removed and this was tantamount to the surrender of any honour the person might have had. To mark their distinction from 'honourable' women, female prostitutes were not allowed to wear their hair up, but had to leave it down. They were not allowed to wear matronly gowns, and they were forbidden to wear the colour purple. Even if the person were free and so possessed honour, entry on the register formally removed it, so that no matter how she or he might be used, it would have no consequences for the honour of the user. This conveniently removed the wild and libidinous sex that was an everyday part of Roman life from the rigid honour system.

Sex in a religious context was also excluded from the prohibitions, and in many temples, particularly those to Bacchus, orgies

---

304 Burton, Neel. *Hide and Seek: the psychology of self-deception*. Acheron Press. 2012

were organised several times per month. For a Roman wife to commit adultery with another noble would have been illegal, yet Roman women of good families attended such orgies, where all manner of sexual acts were performed. Nothing was taboo here.[305]

Roman culture associated particular sexual behaviours with honour, status and class. It made appearing to be sexually abstinent honourable, while turning a blind eye on what was actually going on. Romans thought very little more of having sex with a slave or a prostitute – of either sex – than with a modern sex toy. Slaves were possessions, their lives at the whim of their owners, and free prostitutes had adopted the same status.

This attitude toward sex and honour had two important consequences as Roman culture was crystallised into the nascent Christianity. The first was to associate women's sexual independence with prostitution, and prostitution with slavery – that is, to have no honour. Being a sexually independent woman became dishonourable, and being a prostitute was the abandonment of all honour. By implication, for a woman to seek sexual pleasure became dishonourable.

This is reflected in the Christian opposition to women enjoying sex for its own sake, and of course lesbian sex, which cannot be procreative.[306] The function of women in the patriarchy is to produce sons that bear their fathers' names; were they to enjoy sex, then they might take control of their own sexuality, and this the patriarchy cannot countenance.

# After Rome

The Roman Empire's decline and fall is not our subject here. Suffice to say that during the reign of Diocletian and the Tetrarchy in 285 CE it split into two Empires, with two bureaucracies and two capital

---

305 The patriarchy relies on lower-class, mostly female prostitutes to sexually satisfy high-status men and preserve the illusion of 'moral' rectitude. Limiting their freedom to own property or businesses or to be employed in other ways tends to ensure a ready supply.
306 This is one of the causes of the widespread fallacy of female sexual reticence, still promoted by patriarchal apologists, even when they are pretending to be scientists.

cities.[307] The Western empire was based initially in Rome and later Milan and Ravenna, and the Eastern in Constantinople, modern Istanbul. The Western Empire declined after successive waves of invasion and finally came to an end in 476 CE while the Eastern survived until it fell to the Ottomans in the 15th century CE.

This was not the end of Roman influence. The Roman Empire had long since begun to devolve power into the hands of local rulers – the Herodian Dynasty of Biblical Galilee had been one such – with the specific understanding that these rulers exercised power in the name of Rome. After 476 CE, the temporal power of Rome in the West collapsed, but its religious authority remained, through the Papal rights to legitimise monarchs and to arrange royal marriages.

The presence of the Goddess at the heart of Christianity was maintained as the Roman Empire fell away. As Mary Theotokos, she had been cemented into place during the period before Christianity's adoption as the formal religion of the Roman Empire. France became 'the first daughter of the Catholic Church', and Marianism was adopted enthusiastically; it persists today, despite the changes made at Vatican II. Many cathedrals in France are either built on older temples to the Goddess or have prominent badges of the Goddess in visible locations. Typical of these are the ceremonial entrances at Autun, Chartres and elsewhere, where Christ is depicted in front of a huge, encircling *mandorla*. This iconic shape is always representative of the Goddess.[308]

Medieval art contains a very sophisticated language of symbolism, which allows the viewer to interpret the narrative within any piece of art. While today such ability is restricted to those who have studied it, this language was understood by ordinary people at the time the art was being made. The vast majority of these people were illiterate, but they were sophisticated. Visual art was a lingua franca that everyone understood. It is unthinkable that Medieval artists, like Gislebertus at Autun, would have created these monumental images

---

307 And also, usually, two Emperors, though not always; Constantine, who adopted Christianity, was ruler of both Empires.

308 The mandorla, also known as the *vesica piscis* or *yoni* can also be seen in the fish shape common as bumper stickers on cars owned by Christians. It is even used as the official symbol of the Presbyterian Church of Scotland.

without fully understanding the message implicit within them.[309]

After the fall of the temporal Roman Empire, the Popes maintained their authority over European culture and politics. God had married Mary, the Goddess, so now she belonged to him, and he exercised her power; the male priestly hierarchy was the bureaucracy that administered it. They had the authority to crown kings and extend their property rights over other kingdoms through royal marriages, as well as to give all men power over women through the ceremony of marriage.

The Church became the single most important political organisation in the whole of Europe. In every royal or princely court within Catholic Europe there were senior clergymen, bishops, archbishops and cardinals, whose function was to ensure that the Pope's will be done. For over a thousand years, the Papacy wove a web of influence that bound Europe together, driven by its power to sanction monarchs and their marriages.

Catholic Christianity, now distinct from the Orthodox form that had evolved in the Eastern Empire, was spread by these European monarchs to the Americas, Asia and elsewhere, and in turn these territories came under the control of the Papacy.[310] As the church spread over the planet, it took the Goddess and set her up in high places everywhere. Without the core message of Goddess thealogy – Resurrection – there simply is no Christianity.

Today, Christianity accounts for over a third of the world's population, and even where secularism has begun to chip away at ancient faith, the cultural consequences of millennia of Goddess thealogy remain powerful. From our earliest awareness as wandering hunter-gatherers to our domination, as a species, of the planet today, the Goddess has always been, and remains, with us.

---

309 Although it is generally true that between the fall of Rome and the Renaissance the names of individual European artists are unknown, Gislebertus is a remarkable exception.
310 As was exemplified when Pope Alexander (the Borgia Pope) gave all the Americas to the King of Spain.

## The Reformation

The Protestant Reformation was essentially materialistic rather than spiritual. Its origin was partly in reaction to the continued political power of the Papacy and the corruption that accompanies such absolute power, such as the practice of selling 'indulgences'.[311] As argument for their ideas, the founders of Protestantism could indeed point to many inconsistencies between Catholic doctrine and the actual words of the Bible. Furthermore, ordinary people, or at least the wealthy and literate, could now see for themselves. The development of water-powered paper mills in the late 14th century CE, and Gutenberg's invention of letterpress printing half a century later, meant that for the first time, Bibles could be made available cheaply enough for people outside the clergy to have access to them. These factors aided the spread of the new sects.

Despite translation into vernacular language, as for example in King James the VI of Scotland's seminal version, the codex of the Protestant New Testament was the same as had been decided upon by the founders of the Catholic Church a thousand years before. In doctrinal terms, Protestantism is just Catholicism with a few details changed.[312] This is most markedly seen in the Anglican Church, which maintains the bureaucratic structure of priest, bishop and archbishop that it inherited from the Catholic Church. In parallel fashion, it confers the power to reign – the gift of the Goddess – from the hands of the Archbishop of Canterbury to the monarch of England.

The most important single cause of the Reformation was not liturgical, technological or economic, however, but bubonic plague which, as the Black Death, started in Crimea in 1346 and spread

---

311 An indulgence was the remission of punishment due to sin by forgiving the sin, a sort of 'get out of Purgatory free' card.

312 The Catholic, Orthodox and Protestant New Testaments are identical. The Catholic Old Testament includes Tobit, Judith, Wisdom of Solomon, Ecclesiasticus, Baruch, I and II Maccabees, and additions to Daniel and Esther. Because these were not in the Jewish biblical canon, Protestant leaders placed them into a group called the 'Apocrypha' though they remained part of the Protestant Bible until the 19th century.

across Europe, carried by fleas on ship rats.[313] By the end of the century it had killed perhaps 200 million people, in waves of horror interspersed with periods of respite when societies struggled to recover and come to terms with the disaster that had befallen them.

After the Piora Oscillation that afflicted Sumer in the late 4th millennium BCE, the culture changed. Inanna was obliged to accept Gilgamesh, on his terms, not hers. This transformation of the society and its beliefs happened because Inanna had treated her faithful so badly, ignoring their pleas for an end to their suffering for centuries. In exactly the same way, the Black Death caused people to question the Catholic Church, which could provide no relief.

When decades of misery endure despite all the praying and offerings, the inevitable result is that people begin to lose faith in their religion. They begin to look for other answers. During the scourge of the Black Death, people turned to their beloved Goddess, through the Catholic Church, for help, but their pleas were ignored. Furthermore, the church had become immensely wealthy, while the European economies collapsed and a new horror was visited upon an already-devastated people – poverty and starvation.

Revolutions do not happen without extreme social tension. Politics and religion are deeply entwined, and religious revolution is, if anything, harder to provoke than the secular form. People cling to the gods and religions they know and love and only powerful and widespread anger will make them change.

So it was with the Protestant Reformation. All the books and printing presses in the world could not have turned people away from the Catholic Church unless they were already fulminating with anger and resentment and seeking change. In pre-Christian Rome, there had been many gods and goddesses, and one could always try another. But in monotheistic Christian Europe this was not available so people began to interpret the Christian message in unorthodox ways. Examples include the Cathars and the Albigenses, and the Church, in the main, tolerated them for decades. It was only when the clerical hierarchy began to feel threatened that they took viciously extreme action and established the Holy Office of the Inquisition to combat heresy.

---

313 *Rattus rattus;* also known as black rats.

The re-interpretation of Christianity by the Protestant reformers was one of many such 'heresies'. The Protestant Reformation was a political, theological and popular reaction against broken promises of relief from suffering made by the increasingly distant and egregiously wealthy religious elite to a people who were dying in the most appalling manner.

The existence of large numbers of mass-produced Bibles, albeit written in Latin, was a resource of immeasurable advantage to the Reformists, and without cheap paper and Gutenberg's press, the spread of the new cult would have been slower. The Cathar heresy had been spread by word of mouth, by individual priests communicating to one another their theology and then going out into the world and preaching it, exactly as new religious cults had been promulgated for thousands of years. Now, only Bibles had to travel, not people, and anyone who could read Latin – which was any educated person – had access to the revelatory book, the foundation of Catholicism which had been agreed upon and codified by the Catholic Church itself.

The essential core of Protestant belief was that everything Catholic had to be presented as wrong, without actually rejecting Christianity. The reformers held that anything which was not written in the Bible was not Christian, and it was up to everyone – essentially, every man – to read it for himself and shape his life around it, rather than simply accepting the word of the Catholic Church. The reformers had an easy target. The public mood was ripe for revolution, and technology had given them the means to challenge the huge and omnipresent Catholic Church, not just on a local scale, but across Europe.

The reformers provoked a new mindset that was to become an important feature of their cults: an absolute insistence on the literal truth of every word of the Bible. In the early stages of the Reformation, the first converts were educated people who made up their own minds about what they read. But as Protestantism spread into the less educated strata of society the emphasis became increasingly placed on the acceptance of every word as true. This would lead, in the late 19th and early 20th centuries, to American 'Bible Belt' fundamentalism, comprising some of the most intolerant Christian cults known today.

Catholicism, based on revelation and interpretation by the priest-ly class, has never suffered this literalism, and has been able to adapt to changes in society, at least over time. The modern Catholic Church fully accepts the fact of Evolution and the scientifically established age of the Earth. For centuries it has been able to, albeit reluctantly, accommodate advances in science without abandoning its core, be-cause the Bible is to be interpreted in the light of the world we live in, rather than taken as literally true in every word.

Extreme Protestantism cannot allow this and ultimately, cen-turies later, would confront its followers with a choice: make the world conform to the Bible's literal words or abandon Christianity altogether. This, perhaps paradoxically, has played badly for Protes-tants, since the evidence of science makes it clear that the literal word of the Bible cannot be true. This literalism has provoked the absurd hysteria of modern 'Evangelicals' and Bible fundamentalists and sci-ence-deniers. It has also catalysed the increasing secularism of large numbers of nominal Protestants, who find such denial of reality at best embarrassing.[314]

Catholicism in the early part of the second millennium CE was not as it is today; it was immersed in the Goddess. Today, in places where Marianist Catholicism remains firmly entrenched, such as the Philippines, South America and southern Europe, we can still see in-credible devotion to Mary as the Mother of God, the Queen of Heav-en and the Goddess incarnate. This vision of Mary was the perfect target for the Protestant reformers. They saw it as idolatrous worship of the Goddess, as anathema and fundamentally anti-Christian.

Christianity is based on Goddess thealogy, since it has at its heart the concept of resurrection, something which we have seen was a part of Goddess worship for 10,000 years at least. Jesus' message is the Goddess' message. But Mary's role as the Goddess had been expressed symbolically in the Gospels, implied rather than boldly stated, in order to avoid offending the deeply conservative and pa-triarchal Jewish authorities of Judea and Galilee where the cult of Christianity first appeared. This was an apparent discrepancy that the Protestant reformers could use as theological ammunition.

314 Compare the pragmatic and scholarly stance of Fr George Coyne, of the Catholic Ob-servatory in Rome, with the populist delusions of Ken Ham or Kent Hovind, both prom-inent 'creationists'.

The Catholic Church was primarily concerned with the New Testament, the actual Christian writings, and tended to give far less weight to the Old, the Hebrew writings. These two bodies of work are diametrically opposed. The Old is profoundly conservative, misogynist, understands redemption in a temporal way and has only a vague concept of Resurrection. It is judgemental and harsh. The New, on the other hand, is all about spiritual redemption and resurrection in a body incarnate. It is quintessentially forgiving, because it is based on the message of Goddess thealogy.

The two collections could not be more contradictory in their underlying messages, something the Catholic tradition had got around by essentially ignoring the Old Testament and basing its dogma on the New. Protestant reformers like Luther and Calvin, and the latter's follower, Knox, latched onto this. They set out to attack Catholicism and to spread misogyny by basing their core beliefs in the Old Testament instead; which we have previously described as the Reference Manual of Western Patriarchy.[315]

It is impossible to equally believe in the Old and New Testaments, because they are directly contradictory. Christians have to promote one set of values over the other. The Catholic tradition is fundamentally that of the New Testament: they wrote it and they decided on its canon. The Protestant tradition, being reactive against that, had to lean far more heavily on the Old Testament.

What Luther, Calvin, and Knox created was a cult every bit as harsh, dry and judgemental as first-century Judaism had been, but which had at its centre a god-hero preaching the Goddess thealogy of love, forgiveness and resurrection. One may occasionally spare a moment of wry sympathy for those still trying to resolve this conundrum.[316]

---

315 The extent of Knox's venomous misogyny was recorded by Mary Queen of Scots; her description of him is telling. (Fraser, Antonia. *Mary Queen of Scots*. Phoenix. 2009.)
316 But only a moment; *schadenfreude* is far too compelling to let it last.

# SECTION ELEVEN:

# Turning the Tide

## The Legacy

The first centuries of Christianity offered women new opportunities, and many became leaders within the young religion. The Empress Flavia Iulia Helena Augusta, beatified as Saint Helen,(c. 250 to 330 CE) was one such. Helen was the consort of the emperor Constantius Chlorus and more importantly the mother of Constantine the Great. There is little doubt that her powerful religious influence was instrumental in Constantine's decision to adopt Christianity as the official Roman religion.[317]

Awareness of the influence of such women has been suppressed for centuries by patriarchal clerics as well as academics. However, today, women are researching neglected and ignored texts. This has led to a new, more representative interpretation. Karen L. King notes that, according to scripture, women such as Mary Magdalene, Joanna and Susanna accompanied Jesus during his ministry and supported him and the other apostles out of their private means.[318], [319] Mary Magdalene was a prominent disciple and a leader of one wing of the new faith. The Gospels tell us that she was a visionary leader of the early movement.[320] At the time of his resurrection, Jesus gave her special teaching and instructed her to be an apostle to the apostles

---

317 Helena made a pilgrimage to Palestine during which she claimed to have found the remains of the cross on which Jesus was executed. She is still venerated in the Catholic, Orthodox and Coptic traditions.

318 Karen L. King is Professor of New Testament Studies and the History of Ancient Christianity at Harvard University, in the Divinity School and has published widely in the areas of Gnosticism, ancient Christianity, and Women's Studies.

319 Luke 8:1-3

320 Mark 16:1-9; Matthew 28:1-10; Luke24:1-10; John 20:1, 11-18; (Canonical) Gospel of Peter, Gospel of Philip (non-Canonical)

and tell them the good news. Nonetheless, once the patriarchy took over, her role was diminished and rewritten as that of a prostitute.[321]

The Gospels also tell us that Jesus met and taught women, and shared meals with them, even though this would have been forbidden within the strictly patriarchal Judaism of the era. The inclusion of these stories, whether or not the actual events occurred, shows that women were significant in early Christianity. Within the other parts of the New Testament scripture, women held leadership positions and had significant influence on the growth of the movement. King elaborates:

> 'Paul tells of women who were the leaders of such house churches (Apphia in *Philemon 2*; Prisca in *I Corinthians 16:19*). This practice is confirmed by other texts that also mention women who headed churches in their homes, such as Lydia of Thyatira *(Acts 16:15)* and Nympha of Laodicea *(Colossians 4:15)*. Women held offices and played significant roles in group worship. Paul, for example, greets a deacon named Phoebe *(Romans 16:1)* and assumes that women are praying and prophesying during worship *(I Corinthians 11)*. As prophets, women's roles would have included not only ecstatic public speech, but preaching, teaching, leading prayer, and perhaps even performing the Eucharist meal.'[322]

However, once the prospect that women might regain power and influence became realistic, the patriarchy took action, as it had done in preceding cultures, to suppress them and put men in absolute control of the new religion. Women again slid into invisibility; they were admonished to 'keep silent in church' and were not even allowed to enter the holiest areas lest they accidentally befoul them with their menses. They were not allowed to worship during their periods or for some time after giving birth.

In North America and Western Europe, especially after the Ref-

---

321 The Romans saw women in two categories. They could be the chaste, obedient and humble property of men, or they could be independent, which was considered equal to being without honour, lascivious and threatening, a prostitute.

322 http://www.pbs.org/wgbh/pages/frontline/shows/religion/first/women.html

ormation, women's lot was hardly better than it had been in Assyria or Judah. In Catholic cultures, the presence of Mary at the centre of the cult had signalled some relief for women, but this was fought against by Catholic clerics as early as Tertullian, who latched onto the Hebrew condemnation of women, saying:

> 'Each of you women is Eve...You are the Gate of Hell, you are the temptress of the forbidden tree; you are the first deserter of the divine law.'[323]

The reliance of the Protestant Reformers on the Old Testament, the Hebrew writings, only reinforced this. To distance themselves from Catholicism they suppressed Mary, especially in her roles as Queen of Heaven and Mother of God, and posited the Tertullian view of women as the descendants of Eve and the inheritors of her sin. For the next two thousand years, women remained second-class citizens. Women had few rights or privileges, and their 'honour' was found only in the service of the men who had property rights over them. Women who were not married were castigated.

By the time of the Plague, the start of the Inquisition and the Reformation, this level of abuse grew to such an extent that women who did not have significant defenders could be named as witches and burned at the stake. First they were tortured to extract a 'confession', had to pay the costs of their imprisonment and torture, and after they were killed whatever they owned became the property of the church and state. Men who were considered 'heretics' were similarly abused, but the victims were overwhelmingly women, particularly widows with property.[324] After the end of the witch burnings, the

---

323 Tertullian (c. 160-225 CE) was one of the most important and prolific early Christian writers, though he was never canonised by the Catholic Church. This was probably because he was a member of the Montanists, a sect within Christianity regarded by the Church as heretical. Nevertheless, many of his teachings were adopted into Catholicism after his death. Amongst other things, Montanists required unmarried women to wear the veil.

324 Totalitarian regimes that depend on terror for their power do not need to exterminate large proportions of populations to maintain control. As examples in South America and elsewhere in the twentieth century demonstrate, the murders of a few thousands or tens of thousands are sufficient to keep millions subservient.

terror subsided, but women's rights did not improve.

Religious laws and social taboos continued to restrict women's freedom. While they no longer had to wear head coverings or remain indoors, they did have to wear cumbersome clothing that restricted movement.[325] Laws regarding inheritance, property ownership, employment and outcomes of divorce conspired to keep women from seeking independence. Marital abuses, including domestic rape and violence were not considered crimes and men had the legal right to 'discipline' their wives. Poverty ensured there were always women available to provide sexual services for a price. As in Roman times, using the services of such women did not dishonour the men and did not constitute adultery, although the women could be arrested for indecency.

# The Enlightenment and Literate Women

The circumstances that led to the Protestant Reformation, particularly the questioning of authority and the dissemination of information through the printed media, were as huge a catharsis to the development of our culture as the arrival of the first monumental cities. They led to cultural initiatives that changed the world completely.

The speedy communication of ideas that printing allowed led directly to the Renaissance and the Enlightenment, the burgeoning of Science and the Industrial Revolution. Questioning became widespread, and Reason became, increasingly, the philosophical foundation of a broader intellectual culture, one that challenged the monolithic social structure imposed by church and state, and upon which their authority depended. Indeed, Martin Luther had predicted this and fulminated against reason in several treatises in an effort to maintain control.[326]

---

325 Deuteronomy 22:5: The woman shall not wear that which pertaineth unto a man, neither shall a man put on a woman's garment: for all that do so are abomination unto the LORD thy God.

326 Luther's aim was not that people should question all religion, only the ones he was opposed to.

The exclusion of women from political representation, the denial of their equal status with men, and their situation as literal possessions of their fathers and husbands continued in the West until the twentieth century. The concept of the 'ideal woman' had not changed much from the Roman vision of Atia and the 'humble vessel' straitjacket of the early Jahwists. They were expected to be silent, demure, and house-bound and were represented as weak and insipid, with delicate sensibilities that should not be troubled by the harsh realities of the outside world. Women took their husband's names when they married, and virtually disappeared as their former selves.

Nonetheless, education for women became widespread in the 19th century and so they were able to read. Both women and enlightened men were influenced by the ideals that developed from the Renaissance and the Enlightenment and led into such social movements as the French Revolution and rapid changes in medicine, astronomy, physics, philosophy and art. Both women and men re-examined the roles of women in light of these developments.

Suffragettes began to appear, protesting in public and arguing for inclusion of women in governance and improvement in their legal status. Finally, women were enfranchised under the law and were allowed to vote. In the US this happened with the 19th Amendment, in 1920 while, in Canada, it was 1929. In Europe, the timing ranged from Finland in 1907 to France in 1944, Italy in 1946 and Greece in 1952.

The change in legal status was helpful, but even that did not significantly change the everyday lives of most women. Married women stayed home to tend the children and the house, and unmarried women who had to find employment were restricted to jobs classed as 'women's work' such as domestic servants, factory workers, nurses or teachers. These were low-paying jobs, and the best way for a woman to find security in life continued to be to find a husband and give up her independence.[327]

---

327 Pair bonding in marriage can be a beautiful thing, but only if the partners are, in fact, partners and are in the union by choice. This will be discussed in more detail in later chapters.

# Capitalism: an Unlikely Ally.

Both Europe and United States had seen Industrial Revolutions and had growing middle classes made rich by imperialism. In Europe, imperialism was based on the classic model in which the master nation extracts cheap commodities from its overseas colonies and exports finished goods to them, along with a class of educated managers and technicians. American imperialism was based, initially at least, on colonising the territory where it existed. The country developed two different economic models, one in the North and the other in the South. Manufacturing finished goods made the industrial cities in the North rich and powerful and, just as in Europe, expanded the middle class. In the South, slave labour was used to produce cheap basic commodities such as cotton. These were then processed into finished goods by the factories in the North. Thus, the US economic model was parallel but not identical to the European imperialist model.

The South could only compete with producers in other parts of the world through the use of imported slave labour, whereas in the European model, the equivalents to slaves were the indigenous people of distant colonies. The North objected to the South's use of slaves because it challenged the northern interpretation of the Constitution; this, it was argued, was intended to apply equally to all men.[328]

As a result, the South seceded and in 1861, the American Civil War broke out. The war was cathartic and vicious, and would presage the bloody conflicts of the twentieth century. The Northern economy, fuelled by manufacturing capability, overwhelmed the South, which was obliged to import the materiel of war that it needed. The North blockaded Southern ports and gradually strangled it.

At the end of the war, in 1865, by which time the South was ready to capitulate, President Abraham Lincoln forced through the legislature the passage of the Thirteenth Amendment, which would permanently make slave-holding illegal. The South was defeated, and its economic base destroyed.

---

328 Gender indication deliberate.

The consequence of this was that the capitalist model in the US had to evolve. The Northern cities could no longer prosper by buying cheap, slave-produced, raw materials from the South and selling them back as finished goods and they had no overseas colonies to serve these functions.

This fuelled expansion into the Far West. Since these lands were already occupied, military action was needed to conquer them, which further benefited the industries that had helped defeat the South.[329] Once settlements were established, the Northern economy boomed as its factories produced the railways, engines and rolling stock, machinery, tools and household goods needed for this colonisation. Soon the US was attracting millions of immigrants from poor parts of Europe such as Ireland and Italy. Some of these went to work in the factories, some joined the Western expansion, and some became millionaire industrialists themselves.

This economic boom led to a new economic phase: consumer capitalism. Its underlying principle is that as many people as possible should buy manufactured goods. This in turn requires that they should have the money to do so, and to earn this they would work in the factories that produced them. As Karl Marx pointed out, ownership of the means of production, rather than of land, was the key to capitalism, and it remained so in this new phase, which depended upon increasingly large numbers of people buying relatively low-value goods.

Humans have a very limited need for manufactured goods. We evolved without them. But consumer capitalism depends on people having sufficient disposable income to buy things they don't need, but can be persuaded to want. The classic imperialist capitalism had depended on a disenfranchised urban proletariat earning only just enough to feed and clothe itself. Consumer capitalism requires that as many people as possible have enough not only to buy the essentials, but also to buy luxuries.

The end, implicit in consumer capitalism, is to create a vast middle class with varying levels of disposable income, and a tiny upper class whose billions are made by supplying manufactured goods to

---

329 The establishment of the United States, as throughout the Americas, was afforded by the complete disenfranchisement of indigenous people, their violent suppression and the theft of the land they lived on. The US is the successor to European imperialism.

be purchased with that income.[330] It is further enhanced by lending ordinary people money to buy higher-value luxury items; money which must then be repaid with interest. Thus, in consumer capitalism, the ownership of money eventually becomes the means by which the rich enslave the poor. As a consequence, the manufacturing base of Western economies has shrunk dramatically in recent decades while individual levels of personal debt have soared, and the businesses that enable borrowing have mushroomed.

Within this model, it makes no economic sense to have over half the population excluded! Consumer capitalism required the economic empowerment of women, in order that they might be exploited exactly as men had been. They too must be persuaded to buy things they do not need, and to borrow the money to do it. In order to do this, women's position had to change, from being the possessions of individual men and totally subject to their will, to having independent incomes and the liberty to choose how to spend them.

While the beginning of this change can be traced to the American Civil War, male reluctance impeded the transformation for decades. In the early part of the twentieth century, women's rights activists began to protest, and gained some publicity on both sides of the Atlantic. But the real boost came with the European War of 1914-1918, the First World War.

So many men were called up from all the warring nations that women had to be employed in the factories producing the necessary munitions and equipment. Women entered the workforce and tasted the benefit of having their own money to spend. When the war ended, they were reluctant to lose the ground they had gained, and the nascent women's movement expanded from a small number of educated, upper-middle-class activists to a much broader base. The wall of patriarchal domination had developed cracks.

The US entered the war late, not committing troops until 1917. It was in the US that the women's movement really took hold, but it had to wait until the outbreak of the Second World War, in 1939. This was a true World War; it was fought on or involved troops from almost every continent.

---

330 The politicians of the North fully understood this, and that was one reason for their hostility toward slavery. Slaves had no money and could not buy manufactured goods.

It was won, without question, by American industry. All of the combatants on the Allied side used weapons and equipment made in and shipped from the USA. All over the country but especially in the North and California, factories were booming. Unlike the 1914-18 war, American troops entered the conflict early and in huge numbers and again, women were called to work in the factories.

In post-war Europe and America, consumer capitalism, which had remained in the doldrums during the inter-war period, took off. Over the next twenty years, the European nations were divested of what remained of their empires and the consumer capitalist model took hold across the world.

Women were now workers and consumers too. Huge manufacturing sectors developed to help them spend the money they earned. These included the fashion industry, the cosmetics industry, the entertainment industry and manufacture of ever more ingenious devices that made housework (then still regarded as the preserve of women) less time-consuming. Soon even the motor industry was producing models specifically aimed at the women's market.

Along with having money and a vote, women wanted equal pay, representation in trade unions and much else. Pioneering women took the lead in raising their gender's profile. While these were often from a privileged background, this was not always the case, especially in the United States. Women began to see that they could challenge the patriarchal hegemony, and they established reputations in the arts, letters, politics, business and science. They studied and became graduates and added to the increasing call for the simplest yet most important of things – to be treated as equal to men.

It was, paradoxically, war, the invention of the patriarchy, that empowered this challenge to it.

# The Radical Sixties and Vietnam

By the 1960s, women in the USA had already begun to raise their profile in reforming politics. Billie Holiday, a black woman, had recorded *Strange Fruit* in 1939. This song protested the lynching of black people in the South, which had become commonplace. Holiday was a star and for her, in that era, to sing such an overtly political song was a ground-breaking statement.

During the war years and through the 1950s, dissent and protest were muted because the national focus in both the US and in Europe was on ensuring survival. War has always been a self-serving invention of the patriarchy; as long as there was a real military threat to bind people together, the patriarchy would not be challenged.[331]

After the end of the war and through the 1950s, Americans were revelling in their new-found financial strength, and the rest of the world was busy repairing itself. But the post-war baby boom meant that the population had increasing numbers of young people, characterised by their daring and their desire to push boundaries and to establish a cultural identity for themselves. Everything changed in the 1960s.

There were many causes. The oppression of black people in the South had continued unabated and had become a national disgrace. The black Civil Rights movement grew and became more effective in response. In 1960, four black students went into a branch of Woolworth's in Greensboro, Alabama. They sat at the counter marked 'whites only' and asked to be served. When they were refused, they remained seated till the store closed. The next day, they returned with twenty others and again stayed all day. The day after, hundreds took part. The 'sit-in' protest caught the public imagination and within weeks it had had spread to fifteen cities across the South. This galvanised other groups who saw how powerful it could be. Mark Kolinsky wrote:

> 'by the mid-1960s the movement...had thrilled the world with its imagination and the daring of its ideas, inspiring students as far away as Poland to stage sit-ins.'[332]

In 1964, the USA embroiled itself in the aftermath of a colonial war that France, the former master, had left behind: Vietnam. At

---

331 The patriarchy has never been slow to commit to war in order to bolster itself.
332 Kurlansky, M. *1968*. Random House. 2008. (ebook)

the time, the so-called 'domino theory' was widely accepted within American politics. It held that Communism would spread from country to country, as if by contagion. The Vietnamese Communists, led by Ho Chi Min, were supported by the USSR and it was widely believed that the USSR was a direct threat to the US. Preventing the expansion of its sphere of influence into Southeast Asia became a priority.

Unlike previous wars, however, the Vietnam war did not automatically bring with it increased support for the Government. Americans had fought hard in Europe and the Pacific with many casualties, and they had fought again in Korea. A naturally isolationist perspective, which has always been a part of this most self-sufficient nation's character, was provoked. Life was good, and everyone was doing well. Was there really support for American involvement in another war?

Then, in 1964, the *USS Maddox* was attacked by a few North Vietnamese torpedo boats in the Gulf of Tonkin, which it easily fought off.[333] These attacks gave President Lyndon Johnson an excuse to escalate the war.

Conscription was an immediate focus for dissent. In a House debate, Senator Ernest Gruening was forthright in his objection to:

> 'sending our American boys into combat in a war in which we have no business, which is not our war, into which we have been misguidedly drawn, which is being steadily escalated.'

Gruening was not alone, and as the death toll rose, the war was increasingly seen as a pointless political exercise. Far from unifying the US, the war tore it apart.

Incongruously perhaps, the interests of the black Civil Rights movement and anti-war protesters came together. A new atmosphere of radicalism appeared. Central to this was a creative, non-violent form of protest pioneered by the Civil Rights activists.[334] This reached

---

333 There were two alleged incidents, on the 2nd and 4th of August. The first appears to have actually happened, whereas the second may have been invented to bolster the case.

334 They took their lead from Mahatma Ghandi's non-violent protest that did so much to liberate India.

its zenith in 1968, when protest dominated the news across the US, Europe and Japan. Although they were not a united front and were protesting a wide range of injustices, all of the protestors across the world had one thing in common: they regarded the political status quo as having failed. They realised that it was dominated by vested interests. They had torn aside the mask of the patriarchy.

The women's movement was galvanised by the general mood of dissatisfaction and determination to organise and do something about it. Women were prepared to protest and to stand up against the violence of the authorities. Not only were women prominent in campaigns against the Vietnam War and institutionalised racism, now they were campaigning on their own behalf. The modern feminist movement was born in the radical crucible of the 1960s.

All of these popular movements had their roots in the same phenomenon: the financial empowerment of the people supporting them. There was now an educated black middle class and black students of both genders were involved in the Civil Rights movements. While the majority of those conscripted to Vietnam were young men with little education and low-status jobs, better-off women and men dominated the protests. Consumer capitalism had led to the direct challenge of the old, monolithic certainties of the patriarchal state and to the end, not just in the US but across the world, of the 'deference society'.

# Goddess and Spirituality Re-united

The earliest Goddess gave birth completely on her own, without the need for a consort. In matriarchal cultures, women decided if and when they would reproduce. When the patriarchy emerged, it took control over the sexuality and fertility of women. The most fundamental statement of a woman's rejection of patriarchal authority is for her to regain control over her sexual pleasure and reproduction, and that is the patriarchy's most visceral fear.

In 1960, the combined oral contraceptive pill, often referred to as the birth control pill or simply 'the Pill', was approved for use in the US. Suddenly women, the collective Goddess, regained control over their ability to create life. They could participate in sexual activities without the fear of a lifelong commitment to a child, or of cultural opprobrium if they became unwed mothers. They regained a type of freedom and empowerment they had not known in thousands of years – and they embraced it wholeheartedly.

In 1971, Erica Jong published *Fear of Flying* in which she celebrated the 'zipless fuck'.[335] This she defined as sex without strings or commitment, carried out for the pleasure of it. She wanted to experience sex exactly as a man might, as a physical event with no baggage of emotion or commitment. Needless to say, the book was met with condemnation from the patriarchal establishment. Irrespective of the reaction, Jong articulated a concept that terrifies men – women can be sexually free. Worse, women can have all the pleasure of sex and never have to share the product, their children, with a man, even the fathers of those children. All they have to do is not tell who got them pregnant. This caused a furore within the patriarchal mainstream.

The Goddess and women's rights are closely intertwined, and it should come as no surprise that during the 1970s the women's spirituality movement appeared. Realising the link between the patriarchal organised religions and their own suppression, many women turned to secularism, but others sought out alternative cults and religious ideas that could provide spiritual sustenance on their terms.

Books with titles like *When God was a Woman, The Once and Future Goddess, The Great Cosmic Mother, Goddesses in Everywoman,* and *The Women's Encyclopaedia of Myths and Secrets,* began appearing on bookstore shelves. Alongside these were 'How To' books, designed to help women create groups for the purpose of celebrating Women's Spirituality as an alternative to patriarchal religions. Other books led readers to investigate feminist, neo-pagan and Wiccan interpretations of deity. Women who had grown up not knowing there could ever have been a Goddess were soon able to name dozens of them.

A new cultural paradigm appeared alongside this. Until the 1960s, with few exceptions, women were rarely icons of popular cul-

---

335 Jong, Erica. *Fear of Flying.* Signet. 1971.

ture, and where they were, they usually represented a controlled female sexuality which reinforced the notions that women were not only available to but also to be governed by men.[336] The classic 1958 Western *Big Country*, starring Jean Simmons and Gregory Peck, is a stereotype in which the largely passive heroine's fertility (in the form of her availability for marriage) and that of the land she owns are identified with each other and then fought for and won by the hero. Many films made the connection between land and women, and the theme was so commonplace in film scripts of the era as to be almost unremarkable.[337] However, during the 1970s a sea-change in women's cultural status, partly predicated on their spending power, took place. Women in film became much more assertive and in control both of their destinies and their sexuality, as in *The Witches of Eastwick* (1987), *Thelma and Louise* (1991) and *Fried Green Tomatoes* (1991).

In music, from pioneers like Janis Joplin, Grace Slick and Joni Mitchell, a new breed of female musical artists arose. Far from being the puppets of patriarchal corporate business, these women were increasingly in control of their careers. From 1997 to 1999, Lilith Fair drew crowds of women who came to see all-female bands and artists, raising over ten million dollars for women's charities. Amongst its other achievements, Lilith Fair highlighted the prejudice in the booking practices of male-dominated concert tours and provided a platform that saw women move to the centre of the stage.[338] Cher and Tina Turner stepped out from behind their husbands and overshadowed them, and Madonna proved once and for all that female artists could control their own careers and become hugely successful business women in the music industry, paving the way for others to

---

336 Remember June Cleaver from the popular TV programme *Leave it to Beaver*, or Margaret Anderson from *Father Knows Best*?

337 There are so many variants on this theme that we could not list them here, but the reader is directed towards *Gone With The Wind* (1939) and *Forbidden Planet* (1956) for two more excellent examples.

338 Colombian Shakira Isobel Mebarak Ripoll is a striking example of today's women artists; highly intelligent, creative and multilingual, under her stage name Shakira she has become the centre of a huge entertainment business that spans the globe and which she personally directs. A passionate supporter of education for all, she established the *Fundacio Pies Descalzos* (Bare Feet Foundation). The charity builds and maintains schools in poor parts of Colombia.

follow.

Documentary films, such as *The Goddess Trilogy (Goddess Remembered; Burning Times; Full Circle)* by Donna Reid and the (Canadian) National Film Board, provided an understanding of the rise of the patriarchy and its deleterious effect on women. The concepts had become mainstream.

## The Patriarchy Strikes Back

Patriarchal retaliation against the many forms of protest challenging its assumed authority began quickly. In 1970, four students were shot and killed by National Guardsmen during a protest at Kent State University in Ohio. Nine others were injured. While the confused circumstances of the actual shootings were disputed, the consequences are not. This was the moment the Vietnam War 'came home' to America, and Robert Haldeman later wrote that it led directly to the Watergate scandal and the overthrow and disgrace of Richard Nixon.

Again, in 1972, British soldiers opened fire on a crowd of Civil Rights protestors in the Bogside area of Derry (Londonderry) in Northern Ireland. Twenty-six unarmed protestors were shot by paratroops and thirteen died either on the spot or soon after. Far from calming the situation, the shootings caused it to explode, as many in the province threw their support behind the Provisional IRA and the campaign of bombing it launched. In 2010, the Prime Minister of the UK was forced to apologise for the killings.[339]

The Lithuanian-American archaeologist Marija Gimbutas (1921-1993) had become Professor of European Archaeology and Indo-European Studies at UCLA in 1963. From the early stages of her career, Gimbutas had identified Goddess-culture in early European Societies, especially through the publication, in 1963, of her book *The Balts*. This was followed by several other titles expanding the theme,

---

339 After a twelve-year investigation, Lord Savile's report concluded in 2010 that the shootings were 'unjustified and unjustifiable'.

notably *The Goddesses and Gods of Old Europe* (1974), *The Language of the Goddess* (1989) and *The Civilisation of the Goddess* (1991).

Contrary to some sources, Gimbutas had no involvement in the nascent women's spirituality movement during the 1970s. Then, in 1982, The Gods and Goddesses of Old Europe was republished. In it, Gimbutas had concluded, from the evidence she discovered through many years of research, that Old Europe was a matrilineal society worshipping a female deity. She said in an interview in 1990:[340]

> 'Motherhood determined the social structure and religion because religion always reflects social structure. Old Europe was a matrilineal society where the queen was on the top and her brother next to her.'[341]

While others have misinterpreted the Mother Goddess as an icon only of love and nurture, Gimbutas knew that she was far more complex than this:

> 'She was not only the Mother Goddess who commands fertility, or the Lady of the Beasts who governs the fecundity of animals and all wild nature, or the frightening Mother Terrible, but a composite image with traits accumulated from both the pre-agricultural and agricultural eras. During the latter she became essentially a Goddess of Regeneration, i.e., a Moon Goddess, a product of a sedentary, matrilineal community, encompassing the archetypal unity and multiplicity of feminine nature. She was (the) giver of life...she promotes fertility, and at the same time she was the wielder of the destructive powers of nature. The feminine nature, like the moon is light as well as dark.'[342]

---

340 As a result of criticism by other academics, Gimbutas stopped using the term 'matriarchal.' However it is clear from this quote that she is referring to a matriarchy.
341 Gimbutas, M. *Interview with Kell Kearns. The Marija Gimbutas Collection (Box 101)* (Audio) Santa Barbara. OPUS Archives and Research Centre 1990. Quoted at http://WNW.springerreference.cam/ docs1edit/ chapterdbid/310423.html
342 Gimbutas 2007.

Until and throughout the 1960s, it was widely held in academia that Mother Goddess worship had once been widespread and that the matriarchy had most likely been a viable system of social organisation. Marija Gimbutas believed the evidence supported this, as did James Mellaart. They were accompanied by supporting voices from many other disciplines, including mythologists like Joseph Campbell and Robert Graves. However, in the 1980s a backlash took place. In essence, this was a patriarchal reaction to the idea that a matriarchy had ever existed, and its aim was to discredit the academic supporters of the idea. James Mellaart found his work being attacked by his student Ian Hodder, but the most virulent assault was against Gimbutas, led by her former colleague and friend Colin Renfrew.

The criticism against Gimbutas surrounded her interpretation of evidence. Gimbutas was an archaeologist but also a folklorist and a student of mythology. She had used the interpretative skills that her background gave her to look at the physical evidence and assess from it the type of culture that might have been its creator. It is true that interpretations of this kind must always to some extent remain subjective but the consequence of this can be reduced where the interpreter is thoroughly informed in other aspects of the culture, which Gimbutas certainly was.

Gimbutas, whose work had been globally celebrated, was attacked because she had used her interpretative skills to posit that, alongside the welter of other evidence, the many thousands of Goddess figurines that had been discovered in Europe, dating from as early as 35,000 BCE, suggested that a non-patriarchal society had been in place, which Gimbutas called matristic and matrilineal. A concerted effort was made to destroy Gimbutas' reputation in a feeding-frenzy of academic self-interest, which largely ignored her thorough and balanced assessment of the evidence.

The purpose of this was clear: the patriarchy would not tolerate any challenge. Women, as ever, must be brought under patriarchal control. Dale Spender says:

'These techniques [of control] work by initially discrediting a woman and helping to remove her from the mainstream; they work by becoming the basis for any future discussion about her; and they work by keeping future generations of women away from her.'[343]

Despite the flaws in the arguments against her and the clear difficulties some of her critics had with basic concepts of mythology and religion, Gimbutas' reputation was severely damaged by the attacks, which began when she was dying of cancer and reached fever-pitch after her death. Gimbutas herself said that she thought it would take thirty-five years before her ideas were once again accepted. Unfortunately, she died in 1993 and did not see the rise of a new generation of feminist academics and scientists or the success they have had.

Partly as a result of Gimbutas' work and her call for a broader approach which involved disciplines other than archaeology, a new discipline has appeared, called Archaeomythology. It is based on the holistic, inter-disciplinary approach taken by Gimbutas, Mellaart and Campbell, and which is normal in the natural sciences.[344] While still young, this new discipline is already challenging the orthodoxies promoted by Renfrew, Hodder *et al.*

Today, courses in Goddess culture are available in Western universities and senior academics like Bethany Hughes and Francesca Stavrakopoulou have written bestselling books and made television programmes in which they discuss the Goddess and the influence of Goddess culture. Despite the most strenuous efforts of the patriarchy, the pendulum appears to be swinging back.

---

343 Spender, Dale. *Women of Ideas and What Men Have Done to Them*. Routledge. 1982. Cited by Spretnak, C *Anatomy of a Backlash: Concerning the Work of Marija Gimbutas*. The Journal of Archaeomythology, Special Issue. 2011.

344 The holistic approach is not by any means new. It was the method of Darwin, was well expressed by William Emerson Ritter, and remains the basis of the natural sciences. The exclusivist views taken by some academics are a function of modern disciplinary restrictions and of the academy itself. These latter all contain the inherent flaw that their very narrowness may lead to the exclusion, sometimes deliberately, of contradictory evidence; Hodder's inability to correctly identify a matriarchy, from evidence that conclusively indicates the presence of one, is an example.

# The Return of the Earth Mother

The new progressive movements that were born in the 1960s were about social divides like race, gender and sexuality. They were about individuals and how they could protect their personal freedoms and their identities. They were founded by individuals and were about individuality. They depended upon individual ideas, individual leadership and most importantly, individual participation.[345] In the same cauldron of ideas that gave birth to the race and gender equality movements, others appeared.

The Earth movement had its roots in earlier times. Romanticism, the great artistic flowering of the 19th century, took various inspirations, but one of the most powerful was from nature. William Wordsworth, John Constable, Walt Whitman, Henry Thoreau and Ansel Adams amongst many other artists had blazed this trail. They were joined by scientists and philosophers like Charles Darwin, John Muir and Albert Einstein.

The veneration of the Earth that is implicit in their ideas, however, was not a focussed movement. The element that changed this and forged a popular movement out of these ideas was not artistic or philosophical but political. Alongside the developing feminist and black consciousnesses that were coalescing in the 1960s, was the anti-war movement. While one thrust of this protest was against the ongoing war in Vietnam, a clear and present danger, there was another target: the Cold War and the nuclear arms race.

Popular fear and hatred of nuclear weaponry consolidated into the Campaign for Nuclear Disarmament, which was formed in the United Kingdom in 1957. It became a focus for the nascent Peace Movement and rapidly spread across the West. While the United States initially lagged behind, after the Cuban Missile Crisis of 1962 and during the ongoing war in Vietnam American radicals and protesters eagerly joined this campaign too.

At the heart of this new form of the Peace Movement was the un-

---

345 The rise of the individualistic movements founded in the 1960s is the point that marked the beginning of the slow decline of conventional socialist class politics.

derstanding that through nuclear weapons, people had the power to destroy the world. This implied that humans could damage the world in other ways too. This notion was reinforced in the minds of many by the inspirational pictures of Earth, the Blue Planet, taken by the pioneer astronauts who first landed on the Moon in 1969. Suddenly, in a very graphical sense, the Earth was no longer vast, unlimited, so huge as to be impervious to anything we could do to it. Now it was a tiny, beautiful, precious space capsule, alone in the darkness of infinite space, incredibly vulnerable and, above all else, to be protected.

Because the other movements of the era proposed that individuals could change society through direct protest, the new Earth Movement held the same tenet – that protecting the planet was not the job of governments but of everyone. Once again, the political establishment was seen as having failed, and it was up to ordinary people to do something about it.

Ecology – hitherto a minor field – burst onto the popular stage and very quickly began to draw media attention and numerous followers. Greenpeace, perhaps the most famous campaigning ecological movement, was founded in 1971, and this led to the appearance of many other campaigning groups. Although these mostly adopted the principles of non-violent protest enshrined in the popular movements of the 1960s, they also, like the others, promoted and practised direct action by individuals in support of their causes.

## Reconciling Spirituality and Science

Just as the feminist movement needed Goddess thealogy, the Earth movements needed something similar, and as the damage humans are causing becomes both more evident and well-supported by science, such a spiritual element has appeared.[346]

The umbrella term for this is 'Pantheism' though, within it, there

---

346 As of 2014, 97% of climate scientists agree that not only is climate change happening, it is being provoked by human activity. A consensus as unanimous as this is rare in science; it is equivalent to the consensuses on Evolution, the Big Bang and Plate Tectonics. It may be regarded as fact.

are numerous expressions of similar concepts.[347] Pantheism expresses the idea that there is no deity apart from Nature.[348] Pantheism and Goddess thealogy are extremely closely related because at the heart of both is the Earth, the material form of the Goddess.

Pantheism contains a holistic world-view in line with James A. Lovelock's Gaian philosophy, which holds that the Earth is a self-regulating, autonomous organism that will respond to changes that occur to its environment. Pantheists range from those who have a very materialistic conception to the passionately spiritual, and they find resonances in many different religious ideas and philosophies from all over the globe and from all periods of human history. The essential concepts are: we are the products of the Earth; it is our only home and we must protect it; and only science can provide real answers about the nature of the physical universe.

Pantheists are open to the experience of awe and wonder and mystery and majesty that has informed many religions, but they eschew the idea of a supernatural deity. Thus, they may be described as 'spiritual but not religious'. Their philosophy is informed by science, in addition to the wisdom of a free and educated humanity. Some Pantheists anthropomorphise the planet as Gaia, while others are quite content to consider the Earth sacred just as it is, without any special names or designations.

The patriarchal Sky-Fathers were invented to control the Goddess when the new technology of agriculture began to control the Earth's fertility. At the same time women, the human form of the Goddess, were subjected to the control of men and the patriarchal structures they developed. The consequences of this have been extreme. Human women have for millennia been abused, vilified, denigrated, obliged to hide themselves, tortured, beaten and killed. And the planet has been brought to the point at which its ability to support human life may collapse, causing our species to be marginalised, if not worse.

The Fermi Paradox asks: Why, if life exists elsewhere in our Galaxy, have we not encountered it? One answer is that there are challeng-

---

347 Most Taoists, some Buddhists, deep ecologists, pagans, animists, followers of many native religions, and many Unitarian Universalists are also Pantheists.

348 The word comes from the Greek pan (meaning 'all') and theos (meaning 'God' or 'Divinity'). Pantheists see all of Nature (which can be taken to mean the Universe) as sacred, and do not believe in a distinct personal or anthropomorphic deity.

es intelligent life must survive in order to become advanced enough to travel outside its own immediate space. In other words, advanced civilisations may destroy themselves before they develop the technology required for interstellar travel. The question is, 'have humans passed this point or not'? It seems likely that the impending climatic catastrophe is such a challenge, and humanity, led by the patriarchy, appears determined to fail it.

Since the patriarchy and its religious, political and economic systems are now threatening the very planet they feed on, we should consider what alternatives are available. Women are the majority of the world's population and it is only through violence and the fear of it that men have established dominance over them. It is time to challenge that dominance in spiritual, cultural, sociological, political and economic terms. It is time to emasculate the patriarchy before it destroys us. It is time to rediscover the Goddess Earth and re-establish the matriarchy. Our future may depend on it.

# SECTION TWELVE:

## Redefining the Sacred

## Civilisation Without War

Were our ancestors savage, murderous brutes who lived in a society dominated by violent and sexually aggressive males? Or had they evolved cooperative, non-violent social structures that were overturned when the establishment of growth-based economies led to an explosion of warfare and violence? The debate between these two opposing views has always had one overwhelming problem: the lack of conclusive evidence.

For many years, it was suggested that humans gave up the scattered settlements they had established after abandoning the wandering lifestyle and built cities because of war. Those who argued this said that people had to defend themselves from attack and cities were easier to defend than villages, which is, of course, true. They said that the monumental architecture, which they held to be characteristic of early civilisation, required large numbers of workers and this implied a command structure, and this is also true. They pointed to the evidence of kingship and argued that this man was a warrior whose success in battle was his key to the throne, and this is a historically accurate profile of kings in many civilisations. And then there was the art. Everywhere there seemed to be images of warriors, depictions of battles and of death, and the existence of these works and their meaning is undeniable. The archaeological argument was backed up by Evolutionary Psychologists using flawed methodology, and by a raft of others for whom the idea of a matriarchy is frightening. In the end, lacking a preserved example of an original city, all of these arguments are based upon opinions, and these opinions were and remain, conditioned by the mindset of the observers.

For those on the other side of the argument, this theory was intrinsically repugnant. Many saw trade as the alternative to the 'war begets civilisation' theory. People lived where they could make a living. Settlement occurred in response to natural resource and the trading of the abundance that agriculture would bring. As they became wealthier and more numerous, they invested that wealth and their collective effort to create for themselves a city. Once cities became huge and beautiful and displayed their wealth, they became targets. Why waste years building up wealth when you could just put together a band of soldiers and steal someone else's? Perhaps it was not 'war begets civilisation' but 'civilisation begets war'.

The problem is that humans build their new cities on top of their old ones, often re-using the materials. In Inanna's city of Uruk, there are eighteen layers of building, one atop the other. We saw the same at Çatal Hoyuk and elsewhere. Getting back to that original city, the very first instance of civilisation, that pristine example that could provide the necessary insight, is difficult.

In many ways, there was already adequate evidence to support the theory of peaceful and cooperative societies. Çatal Hoyuk and Ain Ghazal in Anatolia, where there are no walls or weapons or signs of war, and the peaceable Goddess culture on Malta are examples. But the patriarchal apologists insisted that they would only accept as a city a settlement with characteristics such as monumental architecture, large public spaces and so on. Since these became typical of later, patriarchally-organised cities which did depend on warfare, the search became even harder. The earliest phases of a civilization were invariably buried under many layers of later ones, and had themselves, in many cases, been destroyed by war, even if that were not what caused them to be built. What was required was an original city that had been abandoned at the height of its life, neither destroyed by warfare nor built over; a time-capsule city.

That first city became known as the 'mother city' and the search was on to find one and settle the argument once and for all. If a city could be found that met all the requirements to define it as such, yet had no evidence of warfare or defence, then those who argued that civilisation evolved as a response to war would be faced with a serious challenge.

# Caral

In the late 1990s, a Peruvian archaeologist and anthropologist, Dr Ruth Shady, began investigating a forgotten city called Caral. Lying in a desert valley some twenty-five kilometres from the Peruvian coast, it had been discovered by Paul Kosok in 1948, but ignored because it appeared to lack the artefacts being sought at the time. Dr Shady had no idea how old it was so she began to dig. Soon she uncovered monumental architecture, built from stone blocks. Samples of rushes, used to make baskets to carry stones, were discovered trapped between foundation stones, showing that they must be contemporary with the buildings. It was a stroke of great good fortune, because it meant that the city could be accurately carbon-dated.

Caral was built in 2700 BCE, making it, by a thousand years, the oldest city in the Americas and the oldest unspoilt city in the world. The people of Caral left it just the way it was, they never rebuilt it. It was, at last, the long-sought mother city and it became the focus of international research.

Naturally, the experts on early civilisations immediately began to search for the signs of war and fortifications that they believed were essential. But there were none. Caral had massive pyramids that clearly took a huge, organised effort to build, large public spaces and monumental architecture. But there was no wall, no sign of fortification, nor any weapons or images of war. And the city was not hidden. This was a wealthy and prosperous city in plain view, yet it had no need of defence.

No defence equals no war. No war means something else caused Caral to be built. If the only genuine mother-city we have so far discovered was not based on war, then the 'war begets civilisation' theory was in deep trouble, not only here but everywhere. More than that, such a discovery would question the idea that only patriarchal, violent cultures that suppressed women could be called 'civilised'.

As a result, Dr Shady's discovery was doubted. Repeated tests of age were demanded. They all came to the same conclusion: the evidence was sound, and something other than war had caused this city to be built.

Evidence of trade began to emerge very early on. There were discoveries of a diet high in fish, which must have been imported from the coast, and other items that came from the rain forest, 250 kilometres further inland.

The people of Caral used to divert the water running down from the Andes to irrigate the broad, fertile valleys surrounding the city. They grew vegetables and grains for sustenance, but principally cotton for commerce. The cotton was used to make clothing and was exported to the coast to make fishing nets. The nets allowed the fishermen to catch more fish, and the cotton was bartered against the surplus. Caral was founded on agriculture and trade, not on war and defence. If agriculture and trade founded Caral, there is no reason at all to imagine that these did not found the other mother-cities, like Eridu and Uruk, the city of Inanna. The link between patriarchal violence and the beginnings of civilisation could no longer be considered intrinsic. Instead, it appears that early civilisations may have been matriarchal and only later were they corrupted by violence and warfare.

Caral shows that a period of peaceful development, with no warfare, may have persisted in the first mother-cities for centuries or even millennia after their birth. These towns and eventually cities were places of culture, markets, and trade, with comfortable permanent residences and shared public spaces. Their governance was probably under the direction of a council of elders. Viewed through our patriarchal glasses, this has historically been seen to mean 'of elder men', but there is no evidence to support this assumption. Why would women, in this early phase, not be at least equally represented in the decision-making bodies? Why, except for the patriarchal presumption that 'men are always in charge' would we think otherwise?

While Caral was isolated, with no other comparable settlement that could threaten it, the cities of Mesopotamia were not. At some point, their increasing wealth attracted the attention of brigands, perhaps from far away, or perhaps from a nearby town. Maybe this was provoked by outside factors, like climate change, or the migration of peoples, or simple covetousness. Whatever the cause, men gathered together weapons and armour, and all the tools of killing, and attacked the Mesopotamian towns and cities. At first this was probably trivial, amounting to little more than raids by landless nomads. In Sumer, some evidence of warrior culture appears in the fourth millennium BCE, but it is small in scale. There is no evidence of widespread war, professional soldiery or military action; these city 'warriors' were more like men-at-arms whose task was to repel low-level harassment.

The wars that raged in Sumer beginning in the early third millennium BCE were on a different scale altogether. After the drought caused by the Piora Oscillation, we see real war in all its horror, with large armies attacking and razing major cities. The cities had to defend or die. These wars were not fought according to any chivalrous code. The raiders killed almost everyone, probably raping the women, and those they did not kill they took as slaves.[349] A pattern of sociopathy and its political and philosophical justification was established at the very heart of the patriarchy and its version of 'civilisation'. We can find it in the Roman Empire, the Islamic Caliphate, the European colonisation of the Americas, the villainy of Hitler – and in the genocides they all carried out.

Caral is undeniably the product of an advanced culture, and it was both civilised and without war. The discoveries there are recent, and the academic debate as to their wider significance continues. Nonetheless, they prove that war is not a necessary pre-requisite for the development of a city, and therefore, that civilisation itself need not be based on the violent patriarchal model.

The discovery of Caral not only changes our understanding of what the first cities were like, it also challenges the mainstream understanding of what civilisation is. By depending on an absolutely patriarchal model of a militarily-organised culture being responsible for the development of the first cities, the mainstream view implicitly denied any possibility that there might be an alternative. It was saying that civilisation was a function of living in cities, and these

---

349 Rape is not a form of sexual pleasure but an expression of sexual dominance. Men rape in order to subdue their adversaries and establish their superiority, not just over women, but their sons and husbands. The well-documented atrocities carried out by the Red Army as it crossed Germany in 1945 are shocking testimony to this. Men who resented the authority of women in these cultures would be, therefore, more inclined to use rape as a weapon.

came about because of the patriarchy and its military command structures; therefore, to be civilised requires the supremacy of the patriarchy. It was saying, in other words, that civilisation was a result of war, chaos and destruction. Yet Caral shows that this is not necessarily true; large, organised cities can indeed evolve without any sign of the patriarchy; no defences, no images of war, and no evidence of militarism.

What the patriarchal apologists have been doing is the same sleight of hand as they used in the definition of the matriarchy. By using a definition that could only be achieved within the model they themselves proposed, they deliberately quashed any opposing voice, even when, as we have seen, there are myriad examples of the matriarchy operating successfully all over the world and in all periods of history. They were saying that for there to be civilisation, men must be in charge – and until Caral, they were able to get away with it. Now, however, they must reconsider their position, just as they have had to do regarding the matriarchy.

The gifts of civilisation, Inanna's Mes, are not, it turns out, an indivisible bundle of good and evil where the one must be taken with the other. Caral shows that the good, the peaceable, the refined, the cultured, the artistic, the protective of women and children, the loving of men, and the nurturing of family may exist without the bloody, the savage, the greedy, the cruel, the murderous, the raping, the misogynist and the brutal. These latter, it transpires, are inventions of the patriarchy. They are what happens when men are allowed to rule alone without the equal balance of women. The patriarchal pretence that there is no alternative to its anti-human machine is once again exposed for the flagrant lie that it is.

Civilisation does not need warfare, nor does the patriarchy define it. In that case, does civilisation need the patriarchy?

# Human Nature

European and American historians and anthropologists, conditioned by the overt and innate violence of their own cultures, have
for centuries been misinterpreting the nature of hunter-gatherer societies. The men have been described as warriors when, if they were,
they only became so to defend the women and children against violently acquisitive cultures like our own.[350]

Evolutionary Psychology proposes to discuss what the minds
and behaviour of people who have been dead for tens of thousands
of years were like, based on observations of the behaviours of other
species. Professor Jerry Coyne, of the University of Chicago Depart-
ment of Ecology and Evolution, who is an outspoken critic of pseudoscience, wrote of it:

> 'The latest deadweight dragging [evolutionary biology]
> closer to phrenology is evolutionary psychology, or the
> science formerly known as sociobiology. If evolutionary
> biology is a soft science, then evolutionary psychology is
> its flabby underbelly.'[351]

Evolutionary Psychology sets out to support the patriarchal dogma that humans are naturally violent, competitive and warlike and
that the only possible model for human society is one ruled by the
biggest, most competitive and aggressive men. To do this, it has had
to ignore the evidence from existing peaceful, hunter-gatherer societies, amongst much else.[352]

In 1986, the United Nations sponsored the International Year

---

350 The extent to which some will forsake academic and scientific principles in order to
forge a career is illustrated by the case of anthropologist Napoleon Chagnon, who wrote
*Yanomamö: The Fierce People.* He wilfully provoked the phenomena which he then
claimed to observe.

351 Coyne, J.A. *The fairy tales of evolutionary psychology: Of vice and men. The New Republic,* 3 April, 2000, pp. 27-34, cited at http://thelastbehaviorist.blogspot.fr/2012/12/de-
bunking-evolutionary-psychology.html Retrieved 27/07/2014.

352 An even-handed critique of the issues with this discipline has been written by Mike
Samsa for the *Last Behaviourist* blog. http://thelastbehaviorist.blogspot.fr

of Peace and as part of that, commissioned a study by a group of leading scientists. Their report, which became known as the Seville Statement, makes the following propositions:

1. It is scientifically incorrect to say that we have inherited a tendency to make war from our animal ancestors.

2. It is scientifically incorrect to say that war or any other violent behaviour is genetically programmed into our human nature.

3. It is scientifically incorrect to say that in the course of human evolution there has been a selection for aggressive behaviour more than for other kinds of behaviour.

4. It is scientifically incorrect to say that humans have a 'violent brain'.

5. It is scientifically incorrect to say that war is caused by 'instinct' or any single motivation.[353]

The Statement concludes:

'We are not condemned to war and violence because of our biology...*War was invented.*' (Our italics.)[354]

These assertions have been repeatedly confirmed by more recent research which supports the proposition that people are naturally co-operative and peaceful.

In 2012, Robert Cieri, along with colleagues at Duke University in North Carolina, measured 1,400 ancient and modern skulls to determine the amount of testosterone they had been exposed to during development.[355] He found that 50,000 years ago, just when modern humans were crossing the Red Sea to populate the planet, there was a marked reduction. His study suggests that living together and co-operating put a premium on agreeableness and lowered aggression. These traits would have been selected for in mating, and that, in turn, led to changed faces and more cultural exchange. Cieri said:

> 'Humans are uniquely able to communicate complex thoughts and cooperate even with strangers...research on fossilized Stone Age humans from Europe, Africa and the Near East suggests these traits are linked, developed around 50,000 years ago, and were a driving force behind the development of complex culture.

> 'Human fossils from after modern behaviour became common have more feminine faces, and differences between the younger and older fossils are similar to those between faces of people with higher and lower testosterone levels living today,'[356]

Higher testosterone levels are implicated in higher levels of violence in humans as well as chimps and bonobos. Cieri added:

> 'Reduced testosterone levels enabled increasingly social people to better learn from and cooperate with each other, allowing the acceleration of cultural and technological innovation that is the hallmark of modern human success.'[357]

Cieri's research may be a crucial in helping us to understand how human culture developed. It provides an explanation for the underlying cooperation among modern humans that led to the two-group social system we have explored, which in turn led to settlement, agri-

---

355 Published in the August 2014 issue of the journal *Modern Anthropology*. Cieri is currently at the University of Utah.

356 http://unews.utah.edu/news_releases/did-lower-testosterone-help-civilize-humanity/ accessed 13/08/2014

357 *Ibid.*

culture and civilisation. It fundamentally challenges, with evidence from actual humans, the patriarchal orthodoxy of Evolutionary Psychology.

Human numbers were reduced to perhaps only a few thousand after Toba, and recovery was very slow. The survivors were one related population, which then spread out, not only across Africa, but also, through the Gates of Grief, across the whole planet. We, the modern human descendants of those low-testosterone ancestors, are innately cooperative, mutually supportive, and friendly; we are altruistic and artistic. These things are not functions of civilisation, religion or law; they are just how we are. Being friendly and cooperative was the key to our success.

Anthropologist Robert Sapolsky has been studying baboons in Africa for over thirty years. The group he was researching showed typical baboon behaviour. It was dominated by violent, aggressive, competitive males, who bullied all the other males, denying them access to females and often injuring them. They also violently raped both males and females. Stress levels and routine violence were high. Then, the troop discovered a cache of raw beef that had been dumped in a pit on their territory by a nearby safari lodge. The meat was contaminated with bovine tuberculosis, which is invariably fatal in baboons. Because the aggressive males had eaten it, having prevented the others from doing so, they all died and left a reduced population of non-aggressive males and females. Astonishingly, the males did not fight amongst each other for dominance but remained friendly and cooperative. When a wandering aggressive male appeared and attempted to take control, the gentle males teamed up and killed him – and then went back to peaceful grooming. Ten years after the meat incident, Sapolsky's group was still friendly and peaceful. Social systems that favoured violence and competition had been removed and new ones that favoured cooperation and peacefulness learned. The baboons in this group live longer and show little stress.[358]

Cieri's work demonstrates that even if our earlier human ancestors were violent and aggressive, the group we are descended from, the survivors of Toba, were not. Instead, they were likeable and co-

358 Sapolsky, R M. and Share L J. *A Pacific Culture among Wild Baboons: Its Emergence and Transmission PLOS Biology*. April 2004. http://www.plosbiology.org/article/info%3A-doi%2F10.1371%2Fjournal.pbio.0020106 Retrieved 14/11/2014.

operative. It is probable that this key advantage ensured our survival when other human species died out. We didn't 'kill them off'. We just knew how to get along better, and that made us stronger.

Sapolsky's findings are damning for those who condemn us as irretrievable monsters whose violent urges can only be contained by more violence or the threat of it. No-one would pretend that baboons are nice. They are not. Most baboon societies are ridden with aggression, violence and stress. But Sapolsky shows that even baboons can learn not to be that way. They can learn to get along. So could we.

# Why Men Invented God

Our original deity was the Goddess, and we have seen how, little by little, she was supplanted. First she was given a male consort, to whom she had given birth. Then she was put under the control of that consort and had to rely on his approval. Later, she was married to him and became his legal possession. Moving on, she lost her powers to him – to the point where she disappeared altogether and her most basic and significant of all powers, creation, was given to a male god.

Women, once the centre of the culture, at least as high in status and power as men and able to regulate their own fertility, choose their own lovers and direct their own society, were similarly debased. First, the sisterhood of independent women and mothers was shattered, and women were made into objects to be possessed by men. No longer did they keep to their own group, their children around them knowing only their mothers. They were locked into their father's houses until they were sold in marriage to a man, who would then imprison them in his home, where they would bear and raise children to carry his name.

By the beginning of the first millennium BCE in Assyria and elsewhere, women's lot was execrable. Their sexuality and reproduction were totally controlled, and their only protection was as the property of individual men. Even to look at a woman was to defile the property of another man, so women had to hide themselves:

'If the wives of a man, or the daughters of a man go out into the street, their heads are to be veiled.'[359]

Even worse was to come. Not only were women oppressed to an unbearable level, their goddess had to be killed. Asherah, Astarte, those enfeebled descendants of the mercurial Inanna, who were women's only light in the darkness, were cast down, their altars removed from temples, their images broken. Women no longer even had the right to love and revere the Goddess. Instead, they feared an intransigent, jealous male god, Jahweh, whose power was sexual control through violence and coercion, just like that of their fathers and husbands:

'a man may strike his wife, pull her hair, her ear he may bruise or pierce. He commits no misdeed thereby.'[360]

Organised religion is the most efficient method of social control men have ever invented. It establishes a set of social values and hierarchies and failure to abide by its rules results in punishment, both before and even more horribly after, death. Fear, not love, became the force that governed society, and it still rules today.

In tandem with organised religion, men created hierarchical governance, and a mighty priest-King presided over both. Those at the top of the pyramid with him grew rich and powerful through their complete control over the rest of the population. They decided and wrote the laws and the punishments for breaking them. They built mighty armies and walled fortress cities to guard their wealth. Never satisfied, the powerful few used war to amass greater fortunes and increase their power, plundering and manipulating the land and its resources and dominating other men to the point of enslaving them, all ostensibly in the name of and for the greater glory of their God.

The 'great' religious codes, venerated by billions of men and women, have shaped cultures that attempt to define both the planet

---

359 *The Code of the Assura.*
360 *Ibid.*

and people as property, to be violently possessed by men.

All the Abrahamic monotheisms are based on a simple principle: God is a super-male who gave the men who worship him the Earth to do with as they will.

It is easy to recognise the patriarchy at work when Boko Haram kidnaps schoolgirls and later announces they are all 'married', a euphemism which equates to their having been sold as sex slaves. It is easy to see the patriarchy at work when the Taliban shoots Malala Yousafzai in the head for wanting to go to school or when another 'honour killing' hits the news or when we see women covered to the extent that their entire identity is removed. It is easy to see the patriarchy at work when Warren Jeffs rules the FLDS[361] as a paedophilic tyrant with sixty wives, 'reassigns' women from one man to another to punish the men for less-than-absolute obedience, and casts out young males who might eventually challenge his authority – all with the help of a few male acolytes and a police force to enforce his 'laws'.[362]

The patriarchy elsewhere may be more sophisticated and more careful to hide itself, but it is just as virulent. We can discern it in the coalitions of influential men, wielding 'sacred' texts, who cause politicians to pass laws that limit women's access to contraception and abortion, thus putting control of women's fertility back into the hands of men. We see it in the derisory sentences handed down to rapists. We see it in the routine mockery, abuse and even murder of LGBT people and in the attempts, backed by religious groups, to coerce African governments to introduce laws that would imprison them for life or worse, just for who they love. We see it when laws are passed that allow the richest donors and the largest corporations to decisively influence the US government and others through campaign donations and intensive lobbying. We see it in laws that punish the poor for being poor while the most egregious crimes against the public, such as those committed by the banking industry, go unpunished.

When neo-liberals insist that the names of those who hold gov-

---

361 Fundamentalist Church of Jesus Christ of Latter-Day Saints. Often referred to as 'the Mormons' although it is an extremist branch, not recognised by most Mormons.

362 Brower, S. & Krakauer, J. *Prophet's Prey: My Seven-Year Investigation into Warren Jeffs and the Fundamentalist Church of Latter-Day Saints.* Bloomsbury USA. 2011.

ernment bonds, the imaginary 'debts' that enslave whole nations and their people must never be revealed, or when governments agree treaties which allow corporations to sue sovereign populations for exercising their democratic rights, we are looking at the patriarchy. When climate change deniers in public office cancel environmental protections, citing pseudoscience bought and paid for by the very corporations that are causing the problem, we are hearing its voice.

Former US president Jimmy Carter addresses the recent rise of inequity in both rich and poor countries. He says:

> 'There is a similar system of discrimination, extending far beyond a small geographical region to the entire globe; it touches every nation, perpetuating and expanding the trafficking in human slaves, body mutilation, and even legitimized murder on a massive scale. This system is based on the presumption that men and boys are superior to women and girls, and it is supported by some male religious leaders who distort the Holy Bible, the Koran, and other sacred texts to perpetuate their claim that females are, in some basic ways, inferior to them, unqualified to serve God on equal terms. Many men disagree but remain quiet in order to enjoy the benefits of their dominant status. This false premise provides a justification for sexual discrimination in almost every realm of secular and religious life.'[363]

Rome took its patriarchy and spread it across Europe, inventing a religion, Christianity, to support and perpetuate it. European colonialism spread this religion across much of the globe, along with the basic premise of Roman Imperialism: we have the right to take everyone else's land and to treat the planet as our sole possession, because we are permitted to by the god we invented. Elsewhere, Islam, another patriarchal cult which comes from the same Abrahamic root and has at its core the same implacable misogyny, has subjugated immense populations through violence and fear.

---

363 Carter, Jimmy. *A Call To Action: Women, Religion, Violence and Power.* Simon & Schuster. 2014.

In the last century, in the West, some apparent improvement has been observed. People are not burned at the stake, and women have recovered some of their rights. In large measure this has only happened because the most recent economic system of the patriarchy, consumer capitalism, requires women to be pawns in the same exploitative game as men. The patriarchy is run by powerful men but not all men are part of the patriarchy. Men are frequently its victims too.

On the other hand, the oppression of women by the patriarchy is unending. The world is seeing a rape epidemic. In the US, 83,425 rapes were reported in 2011, meaning that a woman was raped every 6.2 minutes. In India, 24,206 rapes were reported in the same year. And these are only reported ones; studies have shown that 70% or more of rapes are never reported by the victims.[364] All across the world, these figures hold true.

In addition, using primarily the Internet, the latest standard-bearers for the patriarchy, so-called 'Male Rights Activists' (MRAs) put up a smokescreen of obfuscation, attempting to minimise the horror and take the blame away from men and put it onto women themselves. Women are held responsible for causing their own rapes and are counselled in what to wear and how to behave in order to minimise the risk, while trivial sentences for rapists are condoned. Amazingly, this blatant campaign of rape apologism is given credence.

Fewer than 3% of rapists are ever convicted. Most suffer no penalty. Why should the patriarchy punish its rapists? They are frontline troops in its battle to maintain its stranglehold on women. Rape is one of the most severe abuses against women; only more severe when accompanied, as is often the case, by murder. It is extreme, and it is violent, and most men do not do it. However, it is just the tip of a huge iceberg. Much more prevalent are the lesser abuses, the ones that most men are guilty of: the sexual innuendoes; the preferential treatment of males; the dismissal of women's ideas; the routine acceptance of the fact that women are under-paid and under-represented in governments, at high levels in business and industry, and

---

364 Brown, J, Horvath, M, *et al. Has anything changed? Results of a comparative study (1977–2010) on opinions on rape.* Government Equalities Office (UK). 2010.

even in the professions. These are abuses that most men have, either knowingly or not, contributed to, and all women suffer from them.

In a chilling parallel, as well as raping and abusing women, the patriarchy is doing the same thing to the planet Earth, the Goddess herself. There is no longer any doubt that human-induced climate change is happening, and the consequences may be disastrous. Rather than accept this and stop the rape, the patriarchy, through corporations, a sycophantic media and complicit governments, is doing everything it can to prevent any reduction of this abuse. Just as MRAs condone the raping of women, climate-change deniers condone the rape of the planet.

These are two sides of the same coin, the micro-rape and the macro-rape. Men rape women; the patriarchy rapes the Goddess by destroying the planet.

The patriarchy is the society we live in. It is a culture wherein men, without even thinking about it, expect and assume privilege over women and reinforce that through a framework of law and by patriarchal religions, political organisations, the academy, business, and the media, where powerful men have established domination and control.

The patriarchy is not a religion or an economic system, or individual men. It just uses these to get its way. The patriarchy is the expectation that men have rights over women's bodies and minds and the most brutal expression of that is rape. At its very core, the patriarchy is rape culture.

In the light of the evidence we have seen and the narrative we have traced, answering the question posed by the title of this book is simple. Men invented God because they wanted moral authority to assume total control over both women and the planet.

# SECTION THIRTEEN:

# Tomorrow and the Day After

Western culture is not new. It is the product of thousands of years of development and it evolved to suit the differing circumstances in which we found ourselves. Our cultural thread in the tapestry of human evolution changed when we moved into the temperate zone and experienced seasons. It changed when we discovered agriculture and settled life, when we built our first cities, when we developed warrior culture and yet again in the era of industrialisation and depredation.

It passed through curious byways, from Sumer to Akkadia, Assyria and Babylon, and via another branch through Egypt. It came together again in a desperately poor and harsh but strategically important part of the Levant, Judah in southern Canaan, where it evolved. Then, in reaction to the harshness of that evolution, it transformed, recovering a core that had been suppressed. It spread through the Hellenised Eastern Mediterranean and to Rome, where it eventually became the official culture of that great Empire. From there it was exported throughout Europe and ultimately across the world.

But it is only one cultural thread. It may have evolved to suit the strongest, but this thread is stiff and fraying, and it is no longer appropriate in today's world. Many species have evolved to be strong, and then gone extinct; excessive armour is a precursor to extinction. Knowledge about how we came to be the way we are is vital. We need to know and understand.

Knowledge is not power; knowledge plus action is power. Humanity's success has been due to our adaptability. We are not particularly strong, not particularly fast, not particularly big. Nonetheless, time and again, we have risen to the challenges that our environment presented, adapted and moved forward. The evolutionary prize – survival – goes to the most adaptive, not the strongest. It is time for us to adapt again; to spin a new cultural thread.

# It Was Always About Sex

Along with survival, the genetic imperative to procreate is the strongest instinct of all living things. Because it is so important to the continuance of species, sex is connected with the pleasure centres in the brain. It is hard to imagine a stronger method of mass subjugation than taking over control of this primary instinct.

In the patriarchal monotheisms, sex, that natural agent for emotional bonding, for building trust, generosity, comfort and security, became something to be ashamed of. Sex was not to be indulged in for pleasure but only for the mechanical production of children. Women's role was to ensure patriliny, and through it the patriarchy. They became property, with all aspects of their lives strictly controlled.

As the patriarchy developed, the domination, objectification, commodification, exploitation and degradation of women that began in the first cities of Sumer continued, and mutated. The virgin/whore duality emerged. Any deviation from the chaste, obedient, 'honourable' category immediately cast a woman into the opposite category. The 'honour' applied to the man who 'owned' her and she could be punished brutally for any harm that befell her.

The modern patriarchy continues to treat women as objects. Where one version of oppression hides women away and makes them feel invisible, another version strips them bare and makes them feel unworthy. Pornography, freely available to anyone with an Internet connection, along with mainstream advertising, music videos and other media, reinforce stereotypical, unrealistic and often unattainable ideals of what the patriarchy thinks women's bodies should look like and how women should behave. Young women and young men, growing up surrounded by such images, come to accept these perceptions as normal. The innate, real Goddess is obscured, and the manufactured doll becomes the ideal, for both women and men. This plays perfectly into the patriarchal consumer model.

The patriarchy is a system. It is not equivalent to 'men'. Many modern men understand that the system is deeply flawed and that they too are oppressed by it. Sex is natural and has no intrinsic moral parameter, yet men's sexual desire, sexuality and sexual pleasure have been perverted by the patriarchy into sins to be guilty and ashamed of. Their normal sexual interest, blocked from healthy expression, has devolved into prurience and aggression.

The patriarchy reinforces its oppression of women not only through pay differentials, 'glass ceilings' and limited access to power, but equally through light sentences for rape and spousal abuse, and through shaming and harassment via social media. In many parts of the 'civilised' West, women cannot go for a walk after dark because both girls and boys have been raised to understand that if a woman does so and is attacked it is 'her own fault'.

Within this system, only the patriarchal organisations such as church or state may sanction sex, through marriage. The patriarchy has strict rules about how and with whom we are permitted to have sex, and enforces these. It deems sex with partners of the same gender, sex outside of marriage or sex with people who do not conform to its norms, 'unacceptable'. It does this in order to cause feelings of guilt and shame, to invoke condemnation of the individuals concerned and, ultimately, to enforce control over them. This applies most visibly to the captains of politics and industry, who are acting within a culture controlled by the patriarchy and are expected to uphold its rules, but it affects everyone. Throughout society, sexual behaviour is judged either acceptable, and condoned, or unacceptable, and punished and the standard of judgement is the patriarchy's arbitrary codes.

Controlling all aspects of sexuality is a principal tool of the patriarchy. Lesbian, bisexual, gay and trans people fundamentally challenge the patriarchy by expressing sexualities and gender identities that do not conform to its rigidly-enforced binary model. The patriarchy's instinctive reaction to these has traditionally been violent punishment. Under the rule of Sharia, Islam's legal code, homosexual men are routinely judicially murdered. The non-Islamic world is equally culpable. In Africa today, nations including Uganda, Kenya and Nigeria are enacting draconian legislation that would make homosexual behaviour punishable by life imprisonment or even death. In Russia, laws punishing homosexuals are harshly enforced, and even where the legal codes are less definitive, beatings and killings of LBGT people continue apace. Transpeople are brutally murdered or driven to suicide by a vicious, intolerant mindset that insists that it is necessary to kill or repress anyone who varies from its arbitrary norms of gender expression. Others are forced to live lives of misery and fear, just for being who they are. Behind these abuses of basic human rights we see the familiar faces of patriarchal religion and state.

In the end, none of this is about Heaven and eternal glory, but about money, power and plunder here on Earth. It is about the will of men to rule over others. If political power were not their end, then why would it be necessary for clerics to condemn and kill those with whom they disagree about something as entirely personal as sex? Why would they need to put pressure on governing bodies to enact their judgements and punishments? If they know the Truth and others do not, then surely they serve no end by hurting those who do not follow their arbitrary rules. Their followers will be rewarded in their Heaven and the rest of us will not. If their end were not temporal power, then they would leave it at that, smug in their self-righteousness. But temporal power is the end; control over others is the purpose; exploitation of the planet, and everyone who lives on it, is the goal.

## Marriage Beyond the Patriarchy

Human pair-bonding can be one of the most satisfying and awe-inspiring experiences available to us. The feelings of love, closeness and complicity, strengthened by sexual desire and reward, combine the best of what it is to be human. Together, in the context of the shared adventure of life's journey, these emotions are even more deeply satisfying. In a good pair-bonded relationship, the couple are not only best friends but also lovers, enjoying the most satisfying fruits of both.

These powerful emotions combine to make a level of intimacy between two people possible that is spiritual in intensity and can indeed last for the lifetime of the partners.

Formalised marriage can be a wonderful thing. As long as the rights of both individuals are equal and protected, a commitment made between the partners, enacted in a formal ritual that incorporates symbolism plus intent and is witnessed by their community sends a powerful message. The individuals feel it at a profound level, and the community is more likely to help through difficult times.

It is the commitment that matters, and there is no need whatever for a patriarchal version of that ritual. The pair bond comes first and is always the most important factor; so if the couple, for whatever reason, falls out of love, then the marriage can end so that they may move on without excessive cost or social opprobrium.

The pair-bonding mechanism is much more complex than is often realised. In the first place, there is no need for the parties to be of different sex or even gender. In fact there is as much scope for variety in successful pair-bonding as there is in any other facet of human life. In addition, humans can develop sexualised pair-bonds that are lasting and profound, but not necessarily exclusive; we saw this amongst the Zo'é and it occurs in polyamorous cultures all over the world. Thus it is quite possible for both women and men to have profound, deep pair-bonds with several others at once, of any sex or gender. Over a lifetime this becomes even more complicated.

Same-sex, same gender and multiple, concurrent sexualised bonding models are all completely viable and all, as seen where they continue to exist, provide for the birth and raising of children, and the successful management of society. In many cultures such models have endured for hundreds or even thousands of years and are probably as old as humanity.

Even marriages that are arranged for the benefit of both parties may be successful, as long as the rights and freedoms of both parties are equal and both are willing to accept the arrangement without coercion or cultural pressure.

By usurping something so fundamentally human, so profoundly beautiful and so powerful, the patriarchy has, for millennia, used the human pair bond to enforce its control over society. It has prescribed not only with whom we are allowed to fall in love, but also how we are permitted to express that love. It has made certain acts of intimacy taboo or illegal – and in some cases, even proscribed such minor expressions of affection as public kissing or holding hands. Essentially, it has done the same to human pair-bonding as it has done to our sense of wonder at the natural world. It has appropriated positive emotions and perverted them to its ends.

Now that we have seen how this came to be, we can change it. We can create new rituals for the expression of voluntary unions between equals; unions which exist out of the mutual love of the parties, and we can move beyond the constraints imposed by the patriarchy over who those parties may be.

This is a significant step. The basis of the patriarchy's power is in its control over reproduction and sexual behaviour, principally of women but also of men. Denying the patriarchy this control and honouring people as individuals free to choose who and how they love may not destroy it, but does go a long way towards clipping its wings. Like the financial and social empowerment of women and their political enfranchisement, the removal of authority over consensual loving relationships undermines the foundation of the patriarchy and may contribute to its eventual, and long overdue, demise.

# A New World Order

The Earth is indeed our Mother; we are made of the stuff of her, the atoms and molecules of her body. Life first appeared in the water that is her amniotic fluid. Without the good fortune that she sits in exactly the sweet zone in space, just far enough from the sun for water to be liquid; that the Van Allen Belt is there to protect her surface and her children from being snuffed out by solar radiation; that she is just the right size to have a gravity that keeps an atmosphere clinging to her body; without countless other things, all qualities of the Earth, we would not be here to observe how lucky we are to exist, or to delude ourselves that it was all created just for us.

The Earth and we who live here are literally stardust, and that stardust is everywhere. Life is the product of chemical processes that might exist wherever the conditions are right, and there is now a science of astrobiology dedicated to the study of life on other planets. Today that science estimates that there may be more than 100 billion potentially life-bearing planets in our galaxy alone, and there are about 500 billion other galaxies in the universe.[365] It is not mere anthropocentricity to imagine that we are the only sentient beings within all of that; it is a conceit of delusional proportions!

But we are adapted to live on this one. Even if we could reach another planet there is no assurance we could thrive, or even survive there.

Never, since Toba, has there been such a clear and present menace to humanity. While Toba was a natural cataclysm that even now we could not prevent, the threat we face today is of our own making. It is the product of 6000 years of patriarchy, its cults and economic systems. It is time for our culture to evolve again, to find a new spirituality based in reality and scientific understanding. The biosphere of the Earth is our true progenitor and changes in it will affect us. If we are to consider anything sacred, it should be that.

We are not hanged by the rope of 'original sin' or 'prehistoric savagery'. We now know that those concepts are patriarchal constructs and have no validity outside of that system. We are not bound by ancient socio-political codes invented to justify rape and destruction or by the nefarious cabals of patriarchal businessmen and politicians today. Even our rigid notions of 'nuclear' family, 'sexually normative behaviour' and gender expression, turn out not to be intrinsic to us, but amongst the techniques the patriarchy uses to enslave us.

We did not succeed as a species by being brutal murderers, but by being friendly and cooperative, and by building a culture that was centred on women and children. We are perfectly capable of devising ethical codes that lead to a good, moral and decent society without any 'divine intervention' or fear of divine judgement. Civilisation, which has given us so much, is not the product of military killing systems. Instead, the patriarchy, the animator of those systems, is an

---

365   http://mnras.oxfordjournals.org/content/early/2013/03/26/mnras.stt318   retrieved 01/02/2015

opportunistic parasite that bleeds all that is good and worthy out of our innate humanity.

So we can have our cake and eat it; we can have all the benefits that civilisation brings, and none of the horrors such as the inequalities, the constant rape of women, the routine slaughter of the innocents, the stockpiling of weaponry that could kill every human tens of times over, and the enslavement of the world's population to vast and exponentially increasing, but completely imaginary debts. All we have to do is to emasculate the patriarchy, and put governance where it should be – with those who care about the whole community, not just the powerful.

The casting-down of the patriarchy and its replacement with a modern matriarchy might just be enough to save us. It is a far more practical solution than pipedreams of terraforming other planets or emigrating to live on space stations. We could do it now, while there is still a chance we might make deep enough changes to survive. We have the power to make this transition, and the prelates, politicians and corporate pirates cannot, in the end, stop us if our will is set.

Science and technology, which have allowed us to go so far in engineering our own demise, also have the power to save us. We could change the course of an approaching asteroid or comet and cause it to pass us by, plunging harmlessly into space. We could even, although there would unquestionably be great loss of life, survive tectonic earthquakes and super-volcanic eruptions that will happen; after all, we survived Toba with no knowledge of science. Surviving another Ice Age is within our competence. Most importantly, we could, even now, halt the ongoing destruction of the environment that sustains us.

The question is, will we? Will we put the future of our children before our personal and corporate greed and profligacy? Will we put our shoulders to the task of mitigating the harm we have already done by our unthinking exploitation of the planet we share?

We must change or the Earth, not through anger or malice but simply through a natural response to our depredations, will destroy us.

# Intentional Earthlings

We are humans. Uniquely amongst the species we know of, we can change ourselves. We can predict events and plan responses. We have always been Earthlings but now, with science and, possibly more importantly, with the knowledge of our human history, we can be *intentional* Earthlings.

Everyone can do this. All you have to do is go out into the world and wonder at the incredible beauty of the Earth, and determine to do whatever you can to protect it

When the *Voyager 1* space probe showed us the Earth from six billion kilometres away, we saw how tiny and isolated it is in the vastness of space. In that moment, we realised that our very existence is something that should inspire spiritual feelings of awe and wonder.

Pantheism expresses this. Unlike the organised religions of the patriarchy, it is a worldview for individuals. No priestly class is required to interpret for people or to intercede on their behalf. Instead, each person responds directly to the revelations of science and the needs of the planet, and takes her or his own path to celebrate *this* life, *this* world.

Of course, Pantheism will not be a perfect fit for everyone. For those who prefer a purely secular worldview that does not have any connotation of religion, science provides enough reason to protect the earth. Rationalism provides enough reason to allow all people to be educated, and logic and ethics provide enough reason to make the world safe for everyone, particularly the women and children.

Contrary to the expectations of the Enlightenment, organised religions have refused to die. For those who prefer their more traditional structure, another alternative is possible. All of today's patriarchal religions and cults, even the most misogynistic, warlike and cruel, originated in the balance of the matriarchy and the worship of the Goddess. In this book, we have detailed this progression and shown how men perverted religion. Perhaps, knowing how their faiths have been warped into instruments for the suppression of women, mass control and the justification of the patriarchy's violence, believers might change them from the inside. If informed members begin to move their attendance and their financial contributions to religions that embrace the ideals of: caring for 'creation'; equality for women and men; social justice; women's full control over their own bodies; celebration of the love between free and equal consenting adults, regardless of the form it takes, and the condemnation of violence, in any form, against anyone, religions will have to change. After all, religions rely on numbers, on membership.

The Earth movement is something that can be embraced by individuals from any spiritual orientation, but for it to be successful we need to sway political will so that actions can be taken on a grand scale. The key ingredient is education – education based on reality and evidence, not wishful thinking and dogma. When individuals are educated, they can make informed choices. When enough educated people adjust their spending habits, speak out in rallies and protests, in books and in the media, and participate in elections, the political will cannot help but change.

Fortunately, science has given us two new tools: the Internet and social media. The tribe of Earthlings has found new ways to communicate.

The 2011 *Occupy Wall Street* protest in New York gave rise to the Occupy movement against social and economic inequality worldwide. These were individuals communicating in personal, collective, creative ways not bound by the vested interests of corporate capitalism.[366]

On September 21, 2014, over 400,000 individuals converged on New York City for a climate march, most of them drawn there via social media. The self-serving deals between governments and corporations, and the damage caused by dirty coal, mountain top removal mining, fracking, oil spills and the tar sands can no longer be hidden from the population at large or masked with propaganda.

There are many kinds of education. In earlier cultures, it was the job of the priestly class to understand and instruct and the job of the people to believe and obey. The people did not dare to express disbelief. People fought and died for things they had been conditioned to

---

366 Which is but one face of the modern patriarchy that holds profit as its god.

believe in, even if they did not understand them. Who benefits from that kind of belief? Only the controlling systems; not the people. In our modern world, this 'priestly' job of instructing is largely done by marketing, and the 'religion' with the biggest advertising budget wins. But we can be subversive. We have the tools. Where our education systems prove insufficient or constrained, we can now educate ourselves and one another.

Understanding the history and evolution of belief is vital in today's world. Seeing the Big Picture arms us with insight, and enables us to see through the propaganda. It provides us with a frame of reference from which to mount our resistance. It lets us know that things have not always been the way they are, and need not continue to be this way.

Our planet is facing a disaster of truly 'Biblical' proportions, and all the Bronze-Age texts in the world cannot help us avoid it. Thanks to science, we now understand the truth about how we came to be here. We know, too, why we need to treat the Earth as precious and sacred. There is no imaginary sky-god who can pardon us for causing the planet's eco-sphere to reject us. There is no saviour in a fantastical and invented heaven. There is only life on Earth and what we make of it. Millennia of living under the patriarchal delusions that the Earth is ours to plunder and that an invented deity will save us from the consequences of our greed have brought us perilously close to causing our own destruction. Revering the Earth and taking care of this tiny, fragile home of ours, may yet save us from ourselves.

Just like our Palaeolithic foremothers, if women can control their fertility so that all of their children will have enough to eat, they will do so. Our overpopulated world needs mothers to have this right. We need equal representation for women in government and business. We need women and men to be equal in politics, religion and culture. We need all women, everywhere, to be educated, so that they will educate their children, for when the people are educated, leaders are held to a higher standard. Men will not be oppressed by this; instead they will contribute as equals to the survival of the Earth's human family.

The matriarchy was never as the patriarchs, terrified of its power, paint it. It was never a culture where men were oppressed as the patriarchy oppresses women. Rather it was a culture in which women and men were equal, each with their own vital roles to play in the single most important function of human society: ensuring the survival of the children.

Over the last 5,000 years, the patriarchy has become so pervasive that it has made itself invisible. It denies any alternative and, instead, tries to make us believe that it is the only natural way for humans to live. Yet we have shown that there is another way.

Through exploration of the myths and religions that shaped our world, we have come to understand why men made God. Whether or not we still require deities in our lives is a matter for individuals to decide. Regardless of that choice, we hope we have persuaded you that the Balance is what matters. Today, the futures of our children depend on taking definitive, coordinated action to protect their home, the planet Earth. Women and men must be equal partners in this.

It is time for us to evolve again. It is time for us to spin a new cultural thread – intentionally.

# AFTERWORD

*Homo sapiens*, our fascinating species, has many qualities. Perhaps the finest is our optimism. We always believe that around the corner, the road will become easier and things will get better. This is what keeps us going, our faith in the future.

The tale of this book is hard to read. We have enslaved, abused, maligned, suppressed and disenfranchised over half the human population. The biggest group by far is women. On the other hand we have promoted and elevated an elite group of men to rule through violence and fear.

This has resulted in an ecological catastrophe that threatens to destroy human culture. Let us be in no doubt; if we do not change, we will die. Some of us may be left to pick over the remains of the glory that once was, but we would not be the same. And this will happen despite the slick and glib lies of climate-change deniers and other apologists for the patriarchy, who use rhetoric and failed philosophies to try to suppress the truth that science reveals. Science, unlike religion, requires comprehension, not belief. It is true whether you believe it or not.

Could we, now, avert the catastrophe? Some, like James Lovelock, are dismissive of the idea. For many others, it is already too late; the tipping-point has passed and our culture is doomed. Just as our immune systems would change to combat a hostile threat, so the planet is changing in response to our depredations, eventually making it impossible for us to live here. The Earth will persist, but *Homo sapiens'* brief moment will pass.

When future aliens, having heard our radio signals, do visit us, will they find only the ruins of what we once were, like archaeologists discovering ruins in the jungles of Central America?

Perhaps they will, as we certainly would, spend many years trying to piece together what happened, how it came to pass that such a dominant species engineered its own destruction. Or perhaps they will have already seen similar cases and file us along with other species throughout the galaxies that took the wrong turn, holding on to the platitudes and lies of the demagogues and apologists until it was too late, and were overtaken by their planet's reaction.

We refuse to be sanguine about this. We do not intend to 'go gently into that good night', the oblivion not just of personal death, but the death of an entire culture and possibly even species. To the question, 'Are we worth saving?' our answer is yes, yes, and yes. Our children are worth saving and our loved ones are worth dying for.

Yes, yes and yes!

We have outlined the tortuous path our culture has followed. The first certain evidence we have of the establishment of the patriarchy comes from Sumer in the third millennium BCE. Over the next four thousand years it spread and dominated human culture. It brought its pantheons of male gods to supplant our original Goddess, and founded a culture of war and killing based on male violence and the suppression of women.

Then, some 600 years ago, something unexpected happened; a patriarchal culture in Europe mutated. This moment we call the Renaissance. From the Renaissance sprang a new outlook that questioned. Artists looked again at the human body and nature and became fascinated with depicting not the ideal but the reality that they saw. At the same time, scientists and philosophers began to think outside the envelope that religion had imposed.

The Enlightenment and all that it brought, our notions of freedom of speech and democracy also spring directly from the Renaissance. Modern medicine and our systems of education would not exist without it. We still live in Renaissance culture.

Our world is one that only a short while ago would have been undreamed-of. We have the potential to cure all our ills. We have already eradicated Smallpox, drastically reduced other diseases and we could easily feed all the humans on the planet. Today, more renewable energy sources are coming on line than non-renewable and replacements for conventional motor fuels have already arrived. It is reasonable for us to look around, observe all this progress and say, 'We can do this!'

The patriarchy is a social cancer. It survives by giving all men privilege over women and children, and that privilege is enforced by rape and violence. Yet the men it privileges it also consumes, through its wars and economic enslavement. Only the tiniest minority of men reap the benefit of the patriarchy and all others suffer under it. So the question we must ask ourselves is this: 'How do we stop sacrificing all that we are, everything that we have, and our grandchildren's lives so that a group of excessively wealthy men in positions of power in politics and business can get even richer and more powerful at our expense?'

Let us look again at Caral. A great city, prosperous, successful, that lasted over a thousand years with no trace of war or systemic violence. It was a beautiful city and, while we do not know much of the day-to-day life there yet, we may imagine that it was a good place to live. Or Çatal Hoyuk; again, no trace of war or violence, but instead a peaceful, pleasant place to live. Consider the Mosuo, today, who have no words for 'rape' or 'war' and who are famed for their contentment and relaxed attitudes. What makes them so different from us? Can we not live without war, violence, and coercion?

Yes, we can. Just as the people of Caral lived in peace, so can we. We can have all the benefits that our remarkable culture brings, our vision into the furthest reaches of the universe, our understanding of how life really came about. We can have our Internet that puts knowledge at our fingertips and our precious mobile phones that enable us to keep in close contact with the people we love most dearly but who are so distant.

The patriarchy is an invention and a recent one at that. We can live without it, as we did for tens of thousands of years. The benefits of city life are not dependent upon the patriarchy, as Caral, Çatal Hoyuk and other cultures attest. We can choose to do without the patriarchy.

Imagine for a moment what our world might be like without male violence, rape and war. Imagine if corporations were not allowed to destroy our environment for short-term gain. Imagine if, instead of rewarding greed and avarice, we punished it. Imagine if we rewarded contribution and cooperation. Imagine if our culture were focussed on ensuring the best possible world for our children's children. Imagine if we were all completely devoted to the Earth, our Goddess-Mother.

If we want that – and surely only the ignorant or disingenuous could claim to desire otherwise – how do we get there?

The answer is clear, because there are only two available models. To abolish the patriarchy, we must implement a matriarchy. Within a democracy this should be simple; we can do it with the way we vote, and the causes we support. We just have to ensure that women have representation commensurate with their percentage of the population. In other words, 53% of all seats in all legislatures must be reserved for women. At the head of our polities, instead of one man, let us have two Consuls – a woman and a man, and let us appoint Tribunes of the Children, with the power to veto any proposition that might damage future generations. In corporations we must put in place the same structures, so that the boards, management and workforces of all corporations are 53% women, and install audit systems to enforce this.

Lest it be imagined that this cannot be done, let us consider the example of Iceland. In 1975 Icelandic women went on strike and brought the country to its knees. Men were obliged to accept that women would be equally empowered with men. Half of all representatives in Iceland's Parliament, the Althing, are women. The result has been a complete success and forty years later, it continues. Iceland has taken the lead in rejecting the patriarchal economic arrangements that resulted in the 2008 banking crash and in 2015 began jailing the bankers who were responsible.

What Icelandic women did, all women can do. Women have the power to stop the world. All they need to do is strike. Say 'No'. Refuse to do anything, anything at all, until the matter is resolved. Across the planet, patriarchies would fold in days.

And it would not just be women. There are many men, today, who will stand up and be counted, for fairness, equality, justice and an end to rape and violence. Men who will stand up for the rights of their children and their children's children. Men who will embrace the LGBT community and insist on an end to discrimination in all its forms. Yet these men cannot impose a matriarchy; in the end, women must demand it.

*IV*

Empowering women will emasculate the patriarchy and end its thrall. We can then use the systems that we have already developed for the benefit of everyone, rather than the greed of a few.

Why is it that very few of us talk of Iceland and the example it might set for all of us? Because patriarchal control of the media determines what we are allowed to know and whose opinions we are allowed to hear. It is important for all of us to know this and pay attention to the subtext.

While everyone is entitled to an opinion, not all opinions are equal. Those of the ill-informed should not carry the same weight as those of the informed. This is a distinction we utilise in our personal lives every day. One does not consider the views of a plumber to be of equal weight to those of a neurosurgeon when discussing cerebral cancer. On the other hand, it is a rare householder who would regard the advice of the neurosurgeon as being as useful as that of the plumber, should the drains back up or air conditioning fail. They have different expertise, and we recognise that.

Scientific consensus, while admittedly fluid, is our most factual, evidence-based source of information about the universe and the world we live in. When consensus amongst scientists is overwhelming, the rest of us should recognise the expert view and accept it.

Today, 97% of climate scientists support the thesis that global warming is being caused by human intervention. Unfortunately, the media's obsession with 'the other point of view' has led to a situation where their scientific conclusions are presented as being of similar weight to those of the 3% who disagree. This is an atrocious distortion.

A skeptical observer would conclude that arriving at the truth is not the goal, and she would be right! The efforts of the patriarchy to obfuscate, deny and conceal the truth all too often go unchallenged or are presented as having real value when in fact they are a smokescreen of spin and untruth designed to protect the profits of a powerful few.

The Internet continues to play a role in challenging this hegemony. It gives those who cannot afford to buy a news outlet or pay for massive advertising campaigns the power to have a voice. All of us, as individuals, should be informing ourselves and speaking the truth to whomever will listen. When enough people understand, then action can be taken. Individuals will vote effectively and consume strategically. Civil disobedience, like the women of Iceland going on strike, or the Occupy protestors taking over large public spaces, or environmental activists confronting large corporations may also have a role to play. The stakes are that high.

Women and men are different. This is reflected in almost every parameter, both physical and psychological. But different is not better; the differences are complementary.

*Homo sapiens* evolved to maximise the benefits that accrue from these complementary differences, and this has been, in no small measure, a factor in our success. Modern studies show that humanity has evolved to cooperate rather than compete. The principal demonstration of that cooperation is between women and men, working together to provide a stable and safe environment in which to raise children. That is what the matriarchy is.

We know how life came into being. We understand evolution, both of species and of cultures. The Here and Now is all we have and the planet Earth is our only home. Dreams of colonising distant solar systems or even the other planets in our own are just that, dreams. We have to repair our planet, change our systems, or accept our impending demise. It really is that simple.

When we look at existing matriarchies, we see happy, relaxed, well-fed, contented men living full and productive lives, just as the women in these cultures do. The matriarchy is not the patriarchy inverted but something completely different, a social model that values everyone equally and exists for the benefit of all.

We have seen how, in matriarchies, sex is stripped of the absurd and false moralities imposed upon it by the patriarchy in order to further its control over individuals. Sex becomes, instead, an expression only of love and pleasure, a force that binds the society together.

The patriarchy is a vicious, corrupt and cruel social model that does not benefit most men, yet oppresses women and sacrifices children. It is leading us directly to planetary disaster and the toll of human suffering under its ghastly heel is limitless.

*VI*

We need to be rid of it. Doing so might not be enough to stave off the impending ecological catastrophe, but it will ensure that we deal with it in the best and most humane way possible.

We are the optimistic ape. We are constrained by our natures to believe that it is not too late, that we can do better. We can fix this.

The question is, 'What are we waiting for?'

# Bibliography and References

Scally *et al. Insights into hominid evolution from the gorilla genome sequence.* Nature 483,169–175. March 2012.

Oppenheimer, Stephen. *Out of Eden: The Peopling of the World.* Robinson. 2004.

Wrangham, Richard. *Catching Fire: How Cooking Made Us Human.* Profile Books, 2009.

Sievert, Lynnette Leidy. *Menopause A Biocultural Perspective.* Rutgers University Press, 2006.

Sloan, Cecil. *Nonpuerperal lactation in grandmothers.* The Journal of Pediatrics, 1956.

Jetha, C & Ryan, C. *Sex at Dawn: The Prehistoric Origins of Modern Sexuality.* HarperTorch. 2010.

Kuhn S. & Stiner, M. *What's a Mother to Do?* Current Anthropology Volume 47 No 6. December 2006.

Lovgren, S. *Sex-Based Roles Gave Modern Humans an Edge, Study Says.* National Geographic News. December 2006.

Ortner, Sherry. *Making gender: the politics and erotics of gender.* Beacon Press. 1996.

Tedlock, Barbara. *The Woman in the Shaman's Body: Reclaiming the Feminine in Religion and Medicine.* New York: Bantam. 2005.

Castaneda, C. *The Teachings of Don Juan: A Yaqui Way of Knowledge.* Penguin. 1990.

Kuzawa, C. *et al. Metabolic costs and evolutionary implications of human brain development.* PNAS 2014 ; published ahead of print August 25, 2014.

Fleischman, D.S *et al. Testing the Affiliation Hypothesis of Homoerotic Motivation in Humans: The Effects of Progesterone and Priming.* Archive of Sexual

Behaviour. 2014.

Herdt, Gilbert, (Ed.) *Ritualized Homosexuality in Melanesia.* University of California Press, 1984.

Ogas, O and Gaddam, S. *A Billion Wicked Thoughts.* Penguin Group US. E-book. 2011.

Caramagno, Thomas, *Irreconcilable Differences? Intellectual Stalemate in the Gay Rights Debate.* Praeger. 2002.

Lee, Richard B. *The !Kung San: Men, Women and Work in a Foraging Society.* Cambridge University Press. 1979.

Hawkesworth, John. *An account of the voyages undertaken by the order of His present Majesty.* London. 1773.

Sanday, Peggy Reeves. *Matriarchal Values and World Peace: The Case of the Minangkabau.* Paper delivered to the 2nd World Congress on Matriarchal Studies, University of San Marcos, Texas 2005.

http://walrus.wr.usgs.gov/tsunami/NAlegends.html retrieved 26/07/2014

King, D.N & Goff, J.R. *Benefiting from differences in knowledge, practice and belief: Maori oral traditions and natural hazards science.* 2010. (http://www. nat-hazards-earth-syst-sci.net/10/1927/2010/nhess-10-1927-2010.pdf retrieved 26/07/2014

*Out of Africa: modern human origins special feature: isotopic evidence for the diets of European Neanderthals and early modern humans.* Proc. Natl. Acad. Sci. U.S.A. 106 (38): 16034–9. September 2009.

Das Wilhelm, Amara. Tritiya-Prakriti: *People of the Third Sex: Understanding Homosexuality, Transgender Identity and Intersex Conditions Through Hinduism.* Xlibris Corp. 2010.

Paglia, C. *Sexual Personae: Art and Decadence from Nefertiti to Emily Dickinson.*Vintage 1992.

Wallis, Faith. *Bede The Reckoning of Time; translated, with introduction and commentary.* Liverpool University Press. 1998.

Dawkins, R. *The Greatest Show on Earth: The Evidence for Evolution.* Black Swan. 2010.

Mithen, Steven. *After the ice: a global human history, 20,000-5000 BCE.* Harvard University Press. 2006.

Akkermans, Peter M. M & Schwartz, Glenn M. *The Archaeology of Syria: From Complex Hunter-Gatherers to Early Urban Societies (c.16,000-300 BCE).* Cambridge University Press. 2004.
Hodder, Ian. *A Journey to 9000 years ago.* (http://www.freerepublic.com/focus/news/1955427/posts Retrieved 23/06/2014)

Mellaart, James. *Çatal Huyuk: A Neolithic Town in Anatolia.* Thames and Hudson. 1967.

Hodder, Ian. *New finds and new interpretations at Çatalhöyük.* Çatalhöyük 2005 Archive Report. Çatalhoyuk Research Project, Institute of Archaeology. 2005.

Gimbutas, Marija. *The Gods and Goddesses of Old Europe University of California Press.* (2nd Revised edition.) 2007

http://www.philtar.ac.uk/encyclopedia/indon/toraj.html (retrieved 14/11/2014)

American Psychiatric Association. *Diagnostic and Statistical Manual of Mental Disorders, Fifth Edition (DSM-5).* American Psychiatric Publishing. 2013.

Bujatti, M. & Biederer, P.: *Serotonin, noradrenaline, dopamine metabolites in transcendental meditation-technique.* Springer Wien. Journal of Neural Transmission. 1976.

Frymer-Kensky, Tikva. *In the Wake of the Goddesses: Women, Culture and the Biblical Transformation of Pagan Myth.* Ballantine Books. 1993.

Wolkstein, D with Kramer, S.N. *Hymns to Inanna.* Harper Perennial. 1983.

Teppo, S. *Sacred Marriage and the Devotees of Istar.* Published in Nissinen, M & Uro, R. (Ed.) *Sacred Marriages.* Indiana. Eisenbrauns. 2008.

Vermaseren, Maarten J. *Cybele and Attis: the myth and the cult, translated by A. M. H. Lemmers.* London. Thames and Hudson. 1977.

Benigni, Helen. *The Goddess and the Bull: A Study in Minoan-Mycenaean Mythology.* University Press of America. 2007.

Iping-Petterson, M.A. *Human Sacrifice in Iron Age Northern Europe: The Culture of Bog People.* (Doctoral Thesis) University of Leiden. 2011.

Finkelstein, I & Silberman, N. *The Bible Unearthed: Archaeology's New Vision of Ancient Israel and the Origin of Its Sacred Texts.* Touchstone. 2002.

Wood, Michael. *Legacy.* Island World Presentation. Central Independent Television. 1991.
Ricketts, E.F. & Steinbeck, J. *Sea of Cortez: A Leisurely Journal of Travel and Research.* Penguin Books. 2009.

MacKenzie, Donald A. *Myths of Babylonia and Assyria.* Gresham. 1915.

Kramer, Samuel Noah. *History begins at Sumer.* University of Pennsylvania Press. 1981.

Dijk, J. Van. *The Birth of Wood and Reed.* Acta Orientalia 28. 1964.

Leick, Gwendolyn. *Sex and Eroticism in Sumerian Literature.* Routledge. 1994.

*Inana's Descent into the Nether World.* http://etcsl.orinst.ox.ac.uk/cgi-bin/etcsl.cgi?text=t.1.4.1#

Kramer, Samuel Noah. *The Sumerians: Their History, Culture and Character.* University of Chicago Press, 1963.

Patai, R. *The Hebrew Goddess.* Enlarged edition. Wayne State University Press. 1990.

Stuckey, J. *Inanna and the Huluppu Tree: One Way of Demoting a Great Goddess.* http://www.matrifocus.com/LAM05/spotlight.htm

Lerner, Gerda. *The Creation of Patriarchy, Volume 1.* Oxford University Press, 1986.

Booth, Martin. *Opium: A History. London.* Simon & Schuster, Ltd. 1996.

Latimer, D,& Goldberg, J. *Flowers in the Blood: The Story of Opium.* New York: Franklin Watts. 1981.

Stuckey, Johanna. *Inanna and the 'Sacred Marriage'.* http://www.matrifocus.com/IMB05/spotlight.htm retrieved 21/08/2014

Frayne, Douglas. *Notes on the Sacred Marriage Rite.* BiOr 42. 1985.

Jacobsen, Thorkild (Ed). *The Sumerian King List.* Oriental Institute of the University of Chicago. 1939.

Veronica Ions. *Egyptian Mythology.* Paul Hamlyn. 1968.

Campbell, Joseph. *The Mythic Image.* Princeton University Press, 1974.

Burkert, W. *The Orientalizing Revolution – Near Eastern Influence on Greek Culture in the Early Archaic Age.* Harvard University Press. 1998.

Cuthbertson, Gilbert. *Political Myth and Epic.* Michigan State University Press. 1975.

Pinhasi, Fort & Ammerman, *Tracing the Origin and Spread of Agriculture in Europe, Public Library of Science, 2005* (http://journals.plos.org/plosbiology/article?id=10.1371/journal.pbio.003041)

Green, Miranda. *Exploring the World of the Druids.* Thames & Hudson. 1997.

Strabo, *Geography.*

Oliver, Neil. *A History of Celtic Britain, Part One: Age of Warriors.* BBC Broadcast. 2011.

Pflugk-Harttung, Julius Von. *The Druids of Ireland.* Transactions of the Royal Historical Society (New Series), 7. 1893.

Anderson, Alan Orr. *Early Sources of Scottish History AD 500 to 1286, Volume One.* Reprinted, with corrections by Marjorie O. Anderson. Paul Watkins, 1990.

Green, Miranda. *Celtic Goddesses.* London, British Museum. 1997.

Caesar, Gaius Julius. *De Bello Gallico.*

Schwartz, Howard. *Lilith's Cave: Jewish tales of the supernatural.* Harper & Row. 1988.

Crossan, John Dominic. *A Revolutionary Biography.* HarperCollins. 1995.

Metzger B.M. & Coogan M.D. *The Oxford Companion to the Bible.* Oxford University Press. 1993.

Watson, Alaric. *Aurelian and the Third Century.* Routledge. 2003.

Stavrokopoulou, Dr. Francesca. *The Bible's Buried Secrets.* BBC Television Broadcast. 2011

Rizal, Dr José, tr Derbyshire, C. *The Social Cancer: A Complete English Ver-*

*sion of Noli Me Tangere.* Manila Philippine Education Company. 1909.

Skinner, Marilyn B. *Sexuality in Greek and Roman Culture.* Wiley-Blackwell. 2013.

Burton, Neel. *Hide and Seek: the psychology of self-deception.* Acheron Press. 2012

Fraser, Antonia. *Mary Queen of Scots.* Phoenix. 2009

Kurlansky, M. *1968* Random House. 2008.

Jong, Erica. *Fear of Flying.* Signet. 1971.

Gimbutas, M. *Interview with Kell Kearns.* The Marija Gimbutas Collection (Box 101) (Audio). OPUS Archives and Research Centre. 1990.

Spender, Dale. *Women of Ideas and What Men Have Done to Them.* Routledge. 1982.

Coyne, J.A. *The fairy tales of evolutionary psychology: Of vice and men.* The New Republic. 3 April, 2000.

Sapolsky, R M. & Share L J. *A Pacific Culture among Wild Baboons: Its Emergence and Transmission* PLOS Biology. April 2004.

Brower, S. & Krakauer, J. Prophet's Prey: My Seven-Year Investigation into Warren Jeffs and the Fundamentalist Church of Latter-Day Saints. Bloomsbury USA. 2011

Carter, Jimmy. *A Call To Action: Women, Religion, Violence and Power.* Simon & Schuster. 2014.

Brown, J, Horvath, M, *et al. Has anything changed? Results of a comparative study (1977–2010) on opinions on rape.* Government Equalities Office (UK). 2010.

CPSIA information can be obtained at www.ICGtesting.com
Printed in the USA
LVOW10s0119110815

449503LV00002B/10/P